I0826033

1. Spikelet, Magnified.
2. Flower.

FOWL MEADOW. See p. 44.

3. Germ.

A PRACTICAL TREATISE ON GRASSES AND FORAGE PLANTS:

COMPRISING

THEIR NATURAL HISTORY, COMPARATIVE NUTRITIVE VALUE, METHODS OF CULTIVATING, CUTTING AND CURING, AND THE MANAGEMENT OF GRASS LANDS.

BY CHARLES L. FLINT, A.M.,

SECRETARY OF THE MASSACHUSETTS STATE BOARD OF AGRICULTURE, MEMBER OF THE BOSTON SOCIETY OF NATURAL HISTORY, ETC. ETC.

NEW YORK:

G. P. PUTNAM & CO., 321 BROADWAY.

LONDON:

N. TRÜBNER & CO., 12 PATERNOSTER ROW.

1857.

WILLIAM WHITE, Printer,
4 Spring Lane, Boston.

PREFACE.

It has been my endeavor, in the following pages, to treat my subject in a plain, simple manner, so as to enable the farmer to distinguish between the different species of grass by means of the descriptions given, and to awaken an interest in the pursuit of the subject, treating cursorily of the natural history of the grasses, and indicating to the reader the vast field of study which lies open to him in this department.

The illustrations, which will be found to be very carefully and accurately drawn, will tend to render the understanding of the text more easy, and thus make interesting to all much that would be attractive only to the scientific student of botany if they were omitted.

In looking at the subject in its economical aspect, I have tried to give all that is known to be of value, and have presented the conclusions of practical men in regard to points about which the opinions of individuals actively engaged in agriculture differ. It has been my object, in a word, to give the work an eminently practical character, and not to make it merely a collection of doubtful theories and vague generalities. It must be left to the reader to determine how far I have accomplished this purpose.

The local names of many species of grass are so numerous that I can hardly hope to have given them all, in every case, though what are known to me I have given as synonyms. Should the work meet with such favor as to call for another edition, I shall attempt to make it less imperfect in this respect.

It may not be irrelevant to remark here that but little is known of the real economical value of some of the grasses which I have described, and it is by no means impossible that many of our wild grasses which we now look upon as almost worthless, may be found at some future time to possess valuable nutritive qualities, and thus be added to our list of grasses which may be profitably cultivated.

It seems to be altogether unnecessary to multiply authorities, either here or in the body of the work, to prove the importance of the subject. Perhaps the most forcible expression of opinion on this point may be found in the French writer who asserts that the term grass is only another name for beef, mutton, bread and clothing; and in the Belgian proverb—"No grass, no cattle; no cattle, no manure; no manure, no crops!" For myself I can only say that if my researches,—imperfect as they doubtless have been,—shall have the effect of creating a more general interest in the subject, and leading to more careful inquiry and more general and accurate investigation, I shall be amply rewarded for any labor I may have undergone in the preparation of these pages.

C. L. F.

Boston, Feb., 1857.

GRASSES AND FORAGE PLANTS.

I propose to speak of the grasses, a family of plants the most extensive and the most beautiful, as well as the most important to mankind. It embraces nearly a sixth part of the whole vegetable kingdom; it clothes the globe with perpetual verdure, or adorns it at fixed seasons with a thick matted carpet of green, none the less beautiful for its simplicity, and it nourishes and sustains by far the greater part of the animals that serve us and minister to our wants.

When we consider the character of our climate, and the necessity of stall feeding during five or six months of the year, for which we are dependent mainly on the grasses, we shall see that in an economical point of view, this subject is one of the most important that can occupy the farmer's attention.

The annual value of the grass crop to the country, for pasturage and hay together, is not less than $300,000,000.

I shall endeavor to give a brief account of the natural history or description of all the useful grasses found in our fields and pastures, partly because it is essential to a complete understanding of the subject, and partly because there is at present no popular treatise on the subject within the easy reach of our farmers, and something of the kind is needed for reference; but I shall confine myself mainly to a plain and practical treatment of the subject, making such suggestions as I think may be useful, on the cultivation, cutting and curing of the grasses for hay, the comparative value of the different varieties, and the general management of grass lands.

This subject, familiar to me from my earliest recollection, has occupied my attention almost exclusively, during the past year. Within this period I have been able to make an extensive collection, embracing nearly all the varieties of our New England grasses, for preservation in the Agricultural Museum connected with my office.

The grasses are variously divided, classified and arranged. They are sometimes designated as natural or artificial; the former comprising all the true grasses,—that is, plants with long, simple, narrow leaves, each leaf having many fine veins or lines running parallel with a central prominent vein or midrib, and a long sheath (Fig. 1.) divided to the base, which seems to clasp the stem, or through which the stem seems to pass, the stem being hollow, with very few exceptions, and closed at the nodes or joints; and the latter—the artificial—comprising those plants, mostly leguminous, which have been cultivated and used like the grasses, though they do not properly belong to that family, such as the clovers, sainfoin and medic. In common language the term is often used in a sense not strictly proper, being not unfrequently applied to any herbage which affords nourishment to herbaceous animals, including, of course, not only many leguminous plants like clovers, but some others which would more properly be called forage plants.

But in botanical language, and speaking more precisely, the grasses, *Gramineæ*, embrace most of the grains cultivated and used by man, as wheat, rye, Indian corn, barley and rice, all of which will be at once recognized as having leaves and stems very similar in shape and structure to most of the plants popularly called grasses.

As the general appearance of plants is often greatly modified by climate, soil and modes of cultivation, it is important to fix upon certain characteristics which are permanent and unaltered by circumstances, by means of which the particular genus and species may be identified with ease and certainty. It is evident that these characteristics could not be simply in the leaves, or the stems, or the size of the plant, because there will be a great difference between plants growing in a poor, thin, sandy soil, and others of the same species on a deep, rich loam. Botanists have, therefore, been compelled to resort to other peculiarities to distinguish between different species; and the terms used

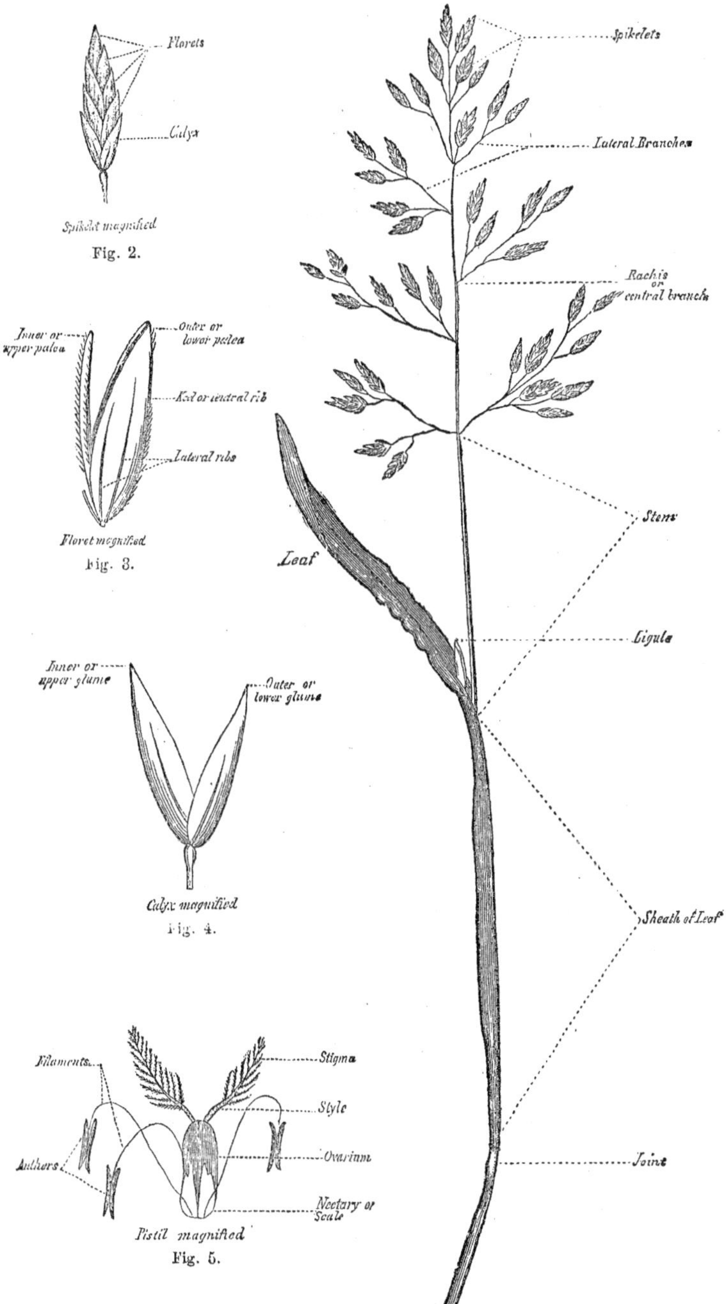

Spikelet magnified
Fig. 2.

Floret magnified
Fig. 3.

Calyx magnified
Fig. 4.

Pistil magnified
Fig. 5.

Fig. 1. Annual Spear Grass.

to express these, like the terms used in other departments of natural history, are technical; and hence, in detailing, the natural history of the grasses, the use of technical language to a greater or less extent, cannot be avoided. I shall endeavor, however, by the use of plates and synonyms to bring the description of species within the easy comprehension of every one who will carefully examine the subject.

The flowers of the grasses are arranged on the stem in spikes, as where they are set on a common stalk without small stalks or branches for each separate flower, as in Herds-grass, (*phleum pratense*,) or in panicles, or loose subdivided clusters, as in orchard grass, (*dactylis glomerata*.) A panicle is said to be loose or spreading, as in redtop, (*agrostis vulgaris*,) when the small branches on which the flowers are set, are open, or extended out freely in different directions; it is said to be dense, or crowded or compressed, when the branches are so short as to give it more or less of the spike form.

The spikelets (Fig. 2) have a calyx, (Fig. 4) containing one, two or more florets, (Fig. 3.) This whole arrangement will be seen in Fig. 1, which represents a stalk of the common annual spear grass, (*poa annua*,) a plant familiar to every one as often troublesome in gravel walks and on hard, dry soils. Here the joint, the stem or culm, clasped by the sheath of the leaf, the leaf itself, the ligule and the spikelets, all distinctly appear, and the reader will do well to make himself familiar with the few technical terms used by a study of this figure, in connection with Fig. 2, where the spikelet is so magnified as to show the florets and the calyx very distinctly, all of which are generally very easily seen with the naked eye, and Fig. 3, showing a floret still more magnified, with its two paleæ, the outer palea being the longer and generally keeled,—that is, having one, three or more longitudinal ribs, often having on the back, base or summit, an awn or beard of different lengths, as in the oat and brome grasses, the inner palea with two separate fringed ribs, each on a fold at the side. The calyx, bract or outer scale of the spikelet, is shown very much magnified in Fig. 4, composed of two glumes, the upper and lower, the upper glume being the larger. One or both of the glumes are sometimes wanting.

In Fig. 5, is shown the pistil magnified, consisting of the nectary, composed of one or two fleshy scales, (in some plants of this family both on one side, in some, entirely wanting,) and the germ, ovary, or seed bearing portion of the pistil. The stamens are also seen in the same figure, consisting each of a bag filled with a fine powder or pollen, supported upon a stalk or filament which is analagous to the stalk or stem of a leaf, while the bag which holds the pollen, called the anther, corresponds to the blade or body of the leaf. These are essential parts of the flower. At a particular stage of its growth, the anther, bursting, scatters its pollen, some of which, lighting upon the summit of the stigma, is said to fertilize it, when the new seed begins to enlarge, and a germ is formed capable of producing other plants.* This process is very apparent to the observation of the farmer in the case of Indian corn, on which the pollen is so abundant that it may be shaken off in clouds. It falls upon the stigmas or "silks," one of which is attached to each embryo seed or germ; and without this particle of pollen, the seed would not be capable of attaining maturity. The same is seen less palpably in the other grasses, as, for instance, in Herds-grass. The same arrangement occurs in this whole family of plants, though it is more evident in Indian corn, on account of its size, than in the smaller grasses. The anther, as will be seen, consists of two cells—very prominent and hanging, supported on the long, slender filaments, and forked or divided at the end. The two short and smooth styles rise from the summit of the ovary, and the stigmas are feathery or rough, sometimes branched or compound. Only one seed is contained in each ovary, and each seed is covered, when mature, with a thin husk or hull called the pericarp, which originally formed the germ or ovary; and the ripe seed or fruit is only the ovary arrived at maturity. The substance or albumen of the seed of all the grasses is mealy or farinaceous, as wheat, for instance, or rye, or Indian corn, which are most used as seeds, on account of their size and productiveness.

These are the prominent characteristics of this great and universally diffused order of plants, constituting, as it does, the chief support of animals as well as men. They belong, as has

* The germ is the first part of the seed that is distinctly formed, and hence, if Indian corn is plucked while "in the milk," or in a green state, fit for boiling, it will germinate the next year as well as if it were allowed to ripen.

been seen, to other plants than those commonly called grasses, the order gramineæ, as I have already stated, embracing the grains, as wheat, barley, rye, and many others, while it does not include the clovers, which properly belong to the order of leguminous plants.

These characteristics, or at least the most important of them, will be very easily kept in mind, as the long, narrow and lance shaped leaves, and the mealy nature of the seeds which makes nearly the whole family valuable and nutritious; but in studying the distinctive characteristics of the different species and varieties particularly valuable or interesting to an agriculturist as forage plants, it will be necessary to depend more upon the technical terms already referred to, though these will be avoided, or explained in the context as far as possible.

It will have been observed that considerable importance is given to the flowers and seeds as distinguishing characters of the grasses. It will often be found difficult from the mere external appearance of a variety of grass to determine to what species, or even to what genus it belongs, so great is the resemblance between the different species of this class of plants; but with the aid of a small magnifying glass there will very seldom be much difficulty in determining the species, especially if the plant is taken while in blossom. Indeed, it will often be possible to arrive at a conclusion from an inspection of a few of the more evident characters.

I shall limit myself mainly to a description of those species which it may be for the interest of the farmer to cultivate, or at least to encourage in his pastures, with such others as should be known to be avoided.

In the arrangement of species I shall follow mainly the natural order adopted by Professor Gray, to whom, as well as to many others, I am indebted for no small assistance, in studying the specific characteristics of many of the specimens collected and presented in the following pages.

The reader will find that a frequent reference to figures 1, 2, 3, 4 and 5 will greatly aid him in becoming familiar with the technical terms applied to the organs or parts of the flower which it is desirable to understand, and by means of which he will soon learn to distinguish the different species more readily.

In giving the scientific names, the first word that occurs in parenthesis is the name of the genus; the second, that of the species; as for instance, in Herds-grass, (*phleum pratense*,) phleum is the generic name, pratense the specific. A genus often contains many species.

The grasses which are described more or less minutely in the following pages, are named in

TABLE I. *List of Grasses and Forage Plants.*

Common Name.	Botanical Name.	Time of Blossoming.	Wild or Cultv'd.	Place of growth.
Rice Grass, . . .	Leersia oryzoides, .	August,	wild,	Low wet places.
White Grass, . . .	Leersia Virginica, .	August,	"	Damp woods.
Indian Rice, . . .	Zizania aquatica, .	August,	"	Borders of streams.
Meadow Foxtail, . .	Alopecurus pratensis, .	May, . .	cultiv'd,	Fields and pastures.
Floating Foxtail, . .	Alopecurus geniculatus,	July, Aug. .	wild,	Wet meadows, ditches
Slender Foxtail, . .	Alopecurus agrestis, .	July, . .	"	Fields and pastures.
Wild Water Foxtail, .	Alopecurus aristulatus,	June to Aug.	"	In wet meadows.
Timothy, or Herds-grass,	Phleum pratense, .	June, July, .	cultiv'd,	Fields and pastures.
Rush Grass, . . .	Vilfa aspera, . . .	September, .	wild,	Dry sandy soils.
Late Drop-seed, . .	Sporobolus serotinus, .	September, .	"	Wet sands.
Redtop, ...	Agrostis vulgaris, . .	July, . .	cultiv'd,	Fields and pastures.
English Bent, . .	Agrostis alba, . .	July, . .	"	Fields and pastures.
Fiorin, ...	Agrostis stolonifera, .	July, . .	"	Moist meadows.
Brown Bent, . . .	Agrostis canina, . .	June, July, .	- -	Fields and pastures.
Tickle Grass, . . .	Agrostis scabra, . .	June, July, .	wild,	Old fields.
Southern Bent, . .	Agrostis dispar, . .	July, . .	cultiv'd,	Fields, pastures.
Annual Beard Grass, .	Polypogon monspeliensis	June, July, .	wild,	Near the coast.
Wood-reed Grass, . .	Cinna arundinacea, .	July, August,	"	Shady swamps.
Nimble Will, . . .	Muhlenbergia diffusa, .	August, Sept.	"	Dry hills, woods.
Mexican Muhlenbergia, .	Muhlenbergia Mexicana,	August, .	"	Low grounds.
Sylvan Muhlenbergia, .	Muhlenbergia sylvatica,	August, Sept.	" .	Rocky woods.
Awnless Muhlenbergia, .	Muhlenbergia sobolifera,	August, Sept.	"	Open rocky woods.
Willdenow's Muhlenbergia, ...	Muhlenbergia Willdenovii	August, Sept.	"	Open rocky woods.
Awned Brachyelytrum, .	Brachyelytrum aristatum	June, . .	"	Rocky woods.
Blue Joint Grass, . .	Calamagrostis Canadensis	July, . .	"	Wet grounds.
Glaucous Small Reed, .	Calamagrostis coarctata,	August, .	"	Wet grounds.
Beach Grass, Sea Reed, .	Ammophila arundinacea,	August, .	wild and cultiv'd,	Drifting sands.
Upright Sea Lyme Grass,	Elymus arenarius, .	July, . .	cultiv'd,	Drifting sands.
Mountain Rice, . .	Oryzopsis melanocarpa,	August, .	wild,	Rocky woods.

TABLE I.—*Continued.*

Common Name.	Botanical Name.	Time of Blossoming.	Wild or cultv'd.	Place of growth.
Feather Grass,	Stipa avenacea,	July,	wild,	Dry sandy woods.
Poverty Grass,	Aristida dichotoma,	September,	"	Sandy fields, pine barrens.
Fresh Water Cord Grass,	Spartina cynosuroides,	August,	"	Banks of streams.
Salt Reed Grass,	Spartina polystachya,	Auguet,	"	Brackish marshes.
Rush Salt Grass,	Spartina juncea,	August,	"	Salt marches, beaches
Salt Marsh Grass,	Spartina stricta,	August,	"	Sea coast.
Sand Grass,	Tricuspis purpurea,	August, Sept.	"	Dry sands on the coast.
Orchard Grass,	Dactylis glomerata,	June,	cultiv'd,	Fields and pastures.
Pennsylvanian Eatonia,	Eatonia Pennsylvanica,	June,	wild,	Moist woods.
Rattlesnake Grass,	Glyceria Canadensis,	July,	"	Wet bogs.
Obtuse Spear Grass,	Glyceria obtusa,	August,	"	Borders of ponds.
Long Panicled Manna Grass,	Glyceria elongata,	June, July,	"	Woods and swamps.
Meadow Spear Grass,	Glyceria nervata,	June, July,	wild and cultiv'd,	Moist and wet meadows.
Pale Manna Grass,	Glyceria pallida,	July,	wild,	Shallow water.
Spike Grass,	Brizopyrum spicatum,	August,	"	Salt marshes.
June Grass,	Poa pratensis,	June, July,	cultiv'd,	Fields and pastures.
Blue Grass,	Poa compressa,	July, August,	"	Dry road sides and pastures.
Annual Spear Grass,	Poa annua,	April to Oct.	wild,	Fields and pastures.
Rough Stalked Meadow,	Poa trivialis,	July,	cultiv'd,	Fields and pastures.
Wood Meadow Grass,	Poa nemoralis,	June,	wild,	Fields and pastures.
Sea Spear Grass,	Poa maritima,	July,	"	By the sea side.
Common Manna Grass,	Poa fluitans,	June,	"	Moist and muddy ditches.
Wavy Meadow Grass,	Poa laxa,	July,	"	High rocky hills.
Water Spear Grass,	Poa aquatica,	August,	"	In wet soils.
Fowl Meadow,	Poa serotina	July & Aug.	cultiv'd,	In wet soils.
Creeping Meadow,	Eragrostis reptans,	July & Aug.	wild,	Sandy river banks.
Strong-scented Meadow,	Eragrostis poæoides,	Aug. & Sept.	"	Sandy fields, road sides.
Slender Meadow,	Eragrostis pilosa,	August,	"	Sandy and gravelly places.
Quaking Grass,	Briza media,	June,	"	Pastures.
Small Fescue Grass,	Festuca tenella,	July,	"	Dry sterile soils.
Sheep's Fescue,	Festuca ovina,	June,	cultiv'd,	High pastures and hills.
Meadow Fescue,	Festuca pratensis,	June,	"	Fields and pastures.
Tall Fescue Grass,	Festuca elatior,	June, July,	"	Fields and pastures.
Hard Fescue Grass,	Festuca duriuscula,	June,	"	Fields and pastures.
Red Fescue Grass,	Festuca rubra,	– –	wild,	Sandy places by the sea.
Slender Fescue,	Festuca loliacea,	– –	cultiv'd,	Moist meadows, pastures.

TABLE I.—*Continued.*

Common Name.	Botanical Name.	Time of Blossoming.	Wild or cultv'd.	Place of growth.
Nodding Fescue, . .	Festuca nutans, . .	July, . .	wild,	Rocky woods.
Crested Dog's Tail, . .	Cynosurus cristatus, .	July, . .	cultiv'd,	Fields and pastures.
Willard's Bromus, . .	Bromus secalinus, .	June, July, .	"	Fields, and in grain crops.
Smooth Brome Grass, .	Bromus racemosus, .	June, . .	wild,	Grain fields.
Soft Chess, ...	Bromus mollis, . .	June, . .	"	Fields and pastures.
Wild Chess, . . .	Bromus Kalmii, . .	June, July, .	"	Dry open woods.
Fringed Brome Grass, .	Bromus ciliatus, . .	July, Aug. .	"	Rocky hills, woods.
Meadow Brome, . .	Bromus pratensis, . .	July, . .	"	Dry arid pastures.
Common Reed Grass, .	Phragmites communis, .	September, .	"	Swamps and edges of ponds.
Perennial Rye Grass, .	Lolium perenne, . .	June, . .	cultiv'd,	Fields and pastures.
Italian Rye Grass, . .	Lolium Italicum, . .	June, . .	"	Fields and pastures.
Bearded Darnel, . .	Lolium temulentum, .	July, . .	– –	Grain fields.
Many-flowered Darnel, .	Lolium multiflorum, .	June, July, .	cultiv'd,	Fields and pastures.
Couch, or Twitch Grass,	Triticum repens, . .	June, July, .	wild,	Fields and pastures.
Squirrel-tail Grass, .	Hordeum jubatum, .	June, . .	"	Salt marshes.
Lyme Grass, . . .	Elymus Virginicus, .	July & Aug.	"	Banks of rivers.
Canadian Lyme Grass, .	Elymus Canadensis, .	August, .	"	River banks.
Slender Hairy Lyme, .	Elymus striatus, . .	July, . .	"	River banks.
Bottle-brush Grass, .	Gymnostichum Hystrix,	July, . .	"	Moist rocky woods.
Wood Hair Grass, . .	Aira flexuosa, . .	June, . .	"	Dry rocky hills.
Hassock Grass, . .	Aira cæspitosa, . .	June, July, .	"	Marshy wet bottoms.
Wild Oat Grass, . .	Danthonia spicata. .	June, . .	"	Dry pastures.
Downy Persoon, . .	Trisetum mollis, . .	July, . .	"	Rocky river banks.
Downy Oat Grass, . .	Trisetum pubescens, .	July, . .	"	Poor dry pastures.
Meadow Oat Grass, .	Avena pratensis, . .	July, . .	"	Pastures.
Yellow Oat Grass, . .	Avena flavescens, . .	July, . .	cultiv'd,	Fields and pastures.
Tall Meadow Oat Grass, .	Arrhenatherum avenaceum, . . .	May, June, .	"	Fields and pastures.
Meadow Soft Grass, .	Holcus lanatus, . .	June, . .	"	Fields and pastures.
Creeping Soft Grass, .	Holcus mollis, . .	July, Aug. .	wild,	Fields and pastures.
Seneca Grass, . . .	Hierochloa borealis, .	May, . .	"	Wet meadows.
Sweet-scented Vernal, .	Anthoxanthum odoratum	May, June, .	"	Fields and pastures.
Reed Canary Grass, .	Phalaris arundinacea, .	July, . .	"	By running streams.
Common Canary Grass, .	Phalaris Canariensis, .	July, August,	cultiv'd,	Gardens.
Millet Grass, . . .	Millium effusum, . .	June, . .	wild,	Damp cold woods.
Hairy Slender Paspalum,	Paspalum setaceum, .	August, .	"	Sandy fields by the sea.
Slender Crab Grass, .	Panicum filiforme, .	August, .	"	Dry sands on the coast.

TABLE I.—*Continued.*

Common Name.	Botanical Name.	Time of Blossoming.	Wild or cultv'd.	Place of growth.
Smooth Crab Grass,	Panicum glabrum,	August, Sept.	wild,	Fields and waste places.
Finger Grass,	Panicum sanguinale,	Aug. to Oct.	"	Neglected fields and gardens.
Agrostis-like Panic,	Panicum agrostoides,	July, August,	"	Wet meadows and river banks.
Prolific Panic Grass,	Panicum proliferum,	July, August,	"	Brackish marshes.
Hair Stalked Panic,	Panicum capillare,	August, Sept.	"	Dry sandy fields.
Tall Smooth Panic,	Panicum virgatum,	August,	"	Moist sandy soils.
Broad-leaved Panic,	Panicum latifolium,	June, July,	"	Damp thickets.
Barn Grass,	Panicum crus-galli,	August, Sept.	"	Rich cultivated grounds.
Bristly Foxtail,	Setaria verticillata,	July, Aug.	"	About farm-houses.
Bottle Grass,	Setaria glauca,	July,	"	Fields & barn-yards.
Green Foxtail,	Setaria viridis,	July, Aug.	"	Cultivated fields.
Bengal Grass,	Setaria Italica,	July, Aug.	cultiv'd,	Fields and ditches.
Bur Grass,	Cenchrus tribuloides,	August,	wild,	Sands near the coast.
Gama Grass,	Tripsacum dactyloides,	August,	"	Moist places on the coast.
Finger-spiked Wood,	Andropogon furcatus,	September,	"	Sterile, rocky hills.
Purple-wood Grass,	Andropogon scoparius,	July to Sept.	"	Sterile, sandy plains.
Indian Grass,	Sorghum nutans,	August,	"	Dry soils.
Indian Millet,	Sorghum vulgare,	July,	cultiv'd,	Cultivated fields.
Hungarian Millet,	Panicum germanicum,	– –	"	Cultivated grounds.
Chinese Sugar Cane,	Sorghum saccharatum,	July,	"	Fields and gardens.
Red Clover,	Trifolium pratense,	June, July,	"	Fields and pastures.
White Clover,	Trifolium repens,	May to Sept.	"	Fields and pastures.
Lucern,	Medicago sativa,	June, July,	"	Fields and pastures.
Sainfoin,	Hedysarum onobrychis,	June, July,	"	Cultivated fields.

RICE GRASS, CUT GRASS, FALSE RICE, (*Leersia oryzoides,*) grows very common in wet swampy places. Stems from two to three feet high, panicle erect, spreading with rough, slender branches, leaves narrow or long, sheaths exceedingly rough and sharp to the hand, drawn from the end backward. Florets oval and white, spikelets flat. Flowers in August. Native of the Levant. Name from Leers, a German botanist.

It is a beautiful grass, said to be useful at the South, where it is cultivated to some extent, and may be cut several times in a season. It is said there to make a valuable hay. Here it is regarded as a weed, and thorough draining will destroy it. The fine specimens of this grass in the State cabinet, were obtained at Westborough.

White Grass, Virginian Cut Grass, (*Leersia virginica,*) is rather smoother than the preceding; panicle oblong, spiked, flowers considerably smaller—white; found in damp woods. Flowers in August. Native of North America.

Indian Rice, or Water Oats, (*zizania aquatica,*) is also found in swampy borders of streams, in shallow water, and on the borders of ponds, and is common. It grows from three to nine feet in height, with flat, long, lanceolate leaves. Flowers in August, and drops its seed, when ripe, at the slightest touch. This furnishes food for water fowls, and was also used by the aborigines for food. Native of North America.

Meadow Foxtail, (*alopecurus pratensis.*) Generic characteristics: Spikelets, one flowered, glumes compressed and keeled, united at the base, lower palea awned on the back, upper palea wanting, stamens three, styles generally united, stigmas long, panicle compressed into a cylindrical spike like the tail of a fox, from which it derives its name. Native of Great Britain.

The specific characters are, an erect, smooth stem, two or three feet high, with swelling sheaths, spikes cylindrical, obtuse, equalling the sharp cone-like glumes, awn twisted and twice the length of the blossom. The spike not so long as that of Timothy. Flowers in May, in fields and pastures. Perennial—introduced. Fig. 6 shows the root, stem or culm, and spike of this grass, and Fig. 7 the blossom somewhat magnified.

The meadow foxtail closely resembles Herds-grass, but may be distinguished from it as having one palea only. The spike or head of meadow foxtail is soft, while that of Timothy or Herds-grass is rough. It flowers earlier than Timothy, and thrives on all soils except the dryest sands and gravels. It is common in some sections of this State, as the western part of Worcester County, where it is disliked by many farmers as a field grass, being very light in proportion to its bulk.

It is a valuable grass for pastures, on account of its early and rapid growth, and of its being greatly relished by stock of all kinds. The stems and leaves are too few and light to make it so desirable as a field crop. It thrives best on a rich, moist, strong soil, and the quantity of its nutritive matter when

Fig. 7.

Fig. 6. Meadow Foxtail.

raised on such soils is considerably greater than on sandy soils. As a pasture grass, its luxuriant aftermath, being in value nearly one-fourth greater than its first spring growth, recommends it still more highly. In this respect it is superior to Timothy, the aftermath of which is generally but slight. For lands designed to be laid down to permanent pasture it will make a prominent part of the seed. Where it occurs in fields, it loses largely its nutritive value if cut in the blossom. It is regarded in England as one of the most valuable of the native pasture grasses, forming there a very considerable portion of the sward, vegetating with great luxuriance, and starting up vigorously when eaten off by stock, producing seed in abundance, and enduring any amount of forcing and irrigation. It does not acquire its full perfection and hold of the soil until three or four years after being sown. The aftermath exceeds the flowering crop in quantity as well as in nutritive matter. The grass loses seventy per cent. of its weight in drying, and the hay contains about sixty-seven hundredths per cent. of nitrogen.

The seed of meadow foxtail is covered with the husks of the flower, soft and woolly, while the larger valve is furnished with an awn. There are five pounds of seed in a bushel, and 76,000 seeds in an ounce. An insect attacks the seed while it is forming, and it is also subject to blight, and hence the seed is somewhat difficult to procure and is held at a high price. We have many grasses superior to it for cultivation, but for permanent pastures it is superior to Timothy, which is not a suitable pasture grass.

Slender Foxtail, (*alopecurus agrestis.*) (Fig. 8.) This grass is rarely found here, never, indeed, except when intro-

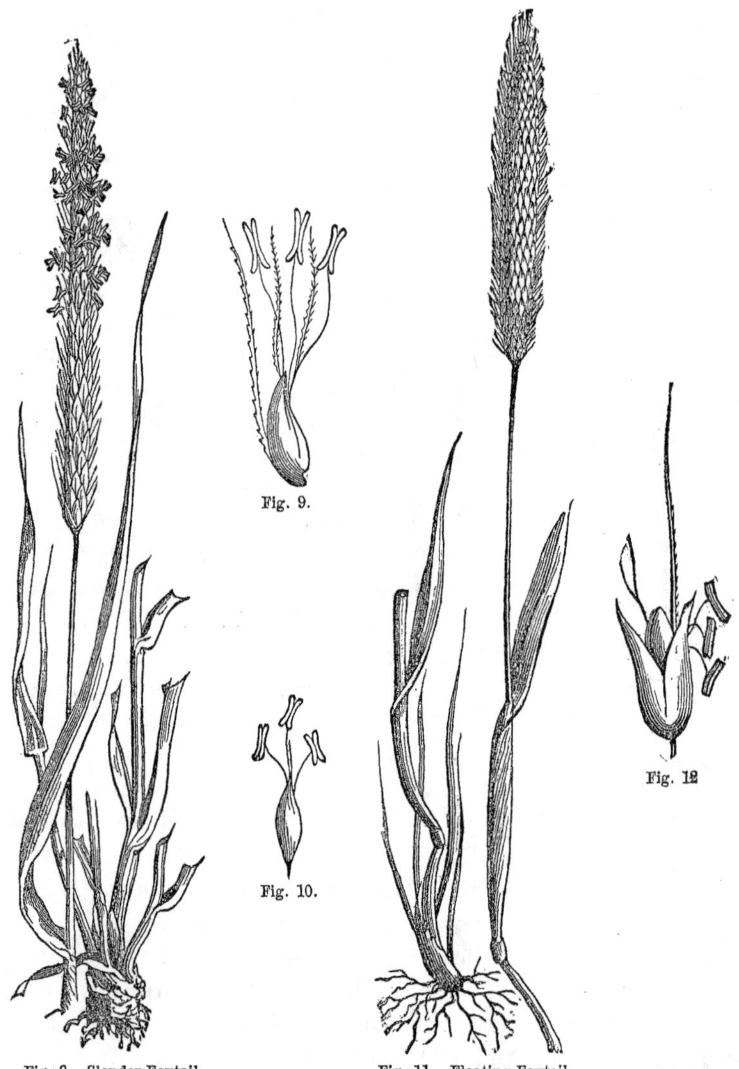

Fig. 9.

Fig. 10.

Fig. 12

Fig. 8. Slender Foxtail.

Fig. 11. Floating Foxtail.

duced in foreign seed, and therefore, scarcely deserves a detailed description. It is recognized by its long, slender panicle, tapering at each end, and the long awn which projects far beyond the palea, (Figs. 9 and 10.) It is distinguished from the common meadow foxtail by its slender panicle, its larger spikelets, its larger ligule and the roughness of the stem and leaves. It possesses no particular agricultural value. Flowers in July. Annual. Native of Great Britain.

FLOATING FOXTAIL, (*alopecurus geniculatus.*) Stem ascending, bent and forming knees at the lower joints, as shown in Fig. 11; awn projecting beyond the palea, (Fig. 12,) which is rather shorter than the obtuse glumes; anthers linear, upper leaf as long as its sheath; root perennial, fibrous, joints smooth, long and narrow, of a purple tinge; leaves flat, sharp, roughish on both sides, serrated on the edge. Inflorescence simple panicled; spikelets numerous, compressed, erect, with a one awned floret as large as the calyx. Floret of one palea, awn slender. Found in moist meadows, ditches, ponds and slow streams, floating on the water. It is distinguished from meadow foxtail in having the upper sheath about the length of its leaf, and by the projecting awn, while in the meadow foxtail the upper sheath is more than twice the length of its leaf. Flowers in July and August.

It is a grass not much relished by stock of any kind, while it yields but a small amount of herbage.

The WILD WATER FOXTAIL, (*alopocurus aristulatus,*) also grows in wet meadows, but is of no special agricultural value. Native of Great Britain.

TIMOTHY, or HERDS-GRASS, (*phleum pratense.*) Generic characters: Panicle spiked, spikelets compressed, palea shorter than the awned glumes, the lower one truncate, usually awnless; styles distinct, filaments hairy, spike dense, rough, or harsh. So called from an ancient Greek term signifying cat's tail, the name by which it is still most frequently known in Great Britain.

Specific characteristics: Spikes cylindrical or elongated; glumes hairy on the back, tipped with a bristle less than half their length leaves long, flat, rough, with long sheaths; root fibrous, often bulbous—perennial. Grows best on moist, peaty soils. (Fig. 13.) In Fig. 14 is seen a flower somewhat magnified. This grass—universally known and highly valued among the farmers of New England—is said to have received its name more than a century and a half ago from one Herd, of Piscataqua, who is said to have found it growing in a swamp there.

The name of Timothy, by which it is more generally known over the country and abroad, was obtained from Timothy Hanson, who cultivated it extensively, and according to some accounts, introduced it into England, from whence it is supposed to have been originally brought to this country. It forms a large proportion of what is called English hay. In point of nutritive matter, Sinclair says, the ripe crop greatly exceeds the crop at the time of flowering. If this is so, it is owing in part to the size and quantity of its mealy seeds. As many as thirty bushels, of forty-six pounds to the bushel, have been obtained to the acre.

Fig. 14.

Fig. 13. Timothy, or Herds-grass.

The results obtained by Prof. Way will be found on a subsequent page in the discussion upon the nutritive values of the various grasses. It may be remarked, in passing, that there are many considerations to determine the time of cutting and curing grass, besides its nutritive value at different stages of its growth, as its palatability at the time of blossoming, and the greater growth of aftermath which is lost by allowing the grass to ripen. This subject will form the topic of a subsequent section.

As a crop to cut for hay it is probably unsurpassed by any other grass now cultivated. Though somewhat coarse and hard,—especially if allowed to ripen its seed, yet if cut in the blossom, or directly after, it is greatly relished by all kinds of stock, and especially so by horses, while it possesses a large percentage of nutritive matter in comparison with other agricultural grasses. It is often sown with clover, but the best practical farmers are beginning to discontinue this practice, on account of the different times of blossoming of the two crops. Timothy being invaribly later than clover, the former must be cut too green, before blossoming, when the loss is great by shrinkage, and when the nutritive matter is considerably less than at a little later period, or the clover must stand too long, when there is an equally serious loss of nutritious matter in that. It thrives best on moist, peaty or loamy soils of medium tenacity, and is not suited to sandy or light gravelly lands; for though on such soils, by great care it can be made to grow and produce fair crops, some other grasses are better suited to them and more profitable. It grows very readily and yields very large crops on favorable soils. I have known instances where its yield was four tons to the acre of the best quality of hay, the Timothy constituting the bulk of the grass. It is cultivated with ease, and yields a large quantity of seed to the acre, varying from ten to thirty bushels on rich soils.

In one respect, perhaps, it must be admitted that this grass is inferior to meadow foxtail, and that is in the quantity of its aftermath; for while that of the latter is very great, the aftergrowth of Timothy is but slight, and if allowed to stand too long and then mown in a dry time, it starts so slowly as to leave the ground exposed to the scorching rays of the sun, unless indeed there happens to be a rapid growth of clover to protect it. The comparative value of this grass will be referred to hereafter. It is proper to say in this connection that it is frequently attacked by an insect apparently just before the time of blossoming, which causes the stalk to die. The ravages of this insect seem to have increased within the last few years. My attention has been repeatedly called, by observing and practical farmers, during the last few months, to the very large number of dead Herds-grass stalks.

Rush Grass, or Rough Leaved Vilfa, (*vilfa aspera,*) and Hidden Flowered Vilfa, (*vilfa vaginæflora,*) are sometimes found here; the former, rarely on dry hills and sandy fields, or pine plains; the latter, somewhat more frequently on similar soils and situations, both flowering in September, and neither considered of any value for cultivation. The Late

Flowering Vilfa, (*vilfa serotina,*) is somewhat common in sandy swamps. It is a very delicate grass, flowering at the same time with the preceding.

Late Drop Seed, (*sporobolus serotinus,*) is sometimes found in low, swampy places, with smooth, slender, flatish stems, leaves few and slender, panicle spreading, with hairy branches, glumes ovate, obtuse and half the length of the palea. Flowers in September. It is a delicate grass of no special agricultural value.

Redtop, Finetop, Burden's Grass, Dew Grass, Herds-Grass of Pennsylvania and Southern States, (*agrostis vulgaris,*) Fig. 15. Plants of this genus have one flowered spikelets in a loose open panicle; glumes nearly equal, the lower longer than the paleæ, which are thin and naked; stamens three—perennial.

The specific characters are, stems erect, slender, round, smooth and polished; roots creeping, panicle oblong, leaves linear, ligule very short, lower palea mostly awnless and three nerved. Flowers in July. Pastures and moist meadows very common—introduced. The term agrostis was the ancient Greek word for field, and was applied to all varieties of grass that grew there.

This valuable grass, so common in all our cultivated fields, has been an inhabitant of our soils for more than a century. It was called simply English grass by Eliot, Deane and other early writers, and by the English, Fine Bent. Indeed, the whole genus *agrostis* is commonly known in England as "Bent Grass." This grass is often sown with Timothy and clover, in which case, the clover, of course, soon disappears, being biennial, when Timothy follows, after which redtop usually takes its place, and with some wild grasses forms a close sward. In Pennsylvania and States further south, it is universally known as Herds-grass—a name applied in New England and New York to *phleum pratense* alone. It is of somewhat slow growth, but of good or medium quality. It is suited to moist soils, though common to all. This grass is probably rather overrated by us. It makes a profitable crop for spending, though not so large a crop is obtained as from Herds-grass. It is a good permanent grass, and consequently well suited to our pastures, standing our climate as well as any other grass. It should be fed close in pastures, for if allowed to grow up to

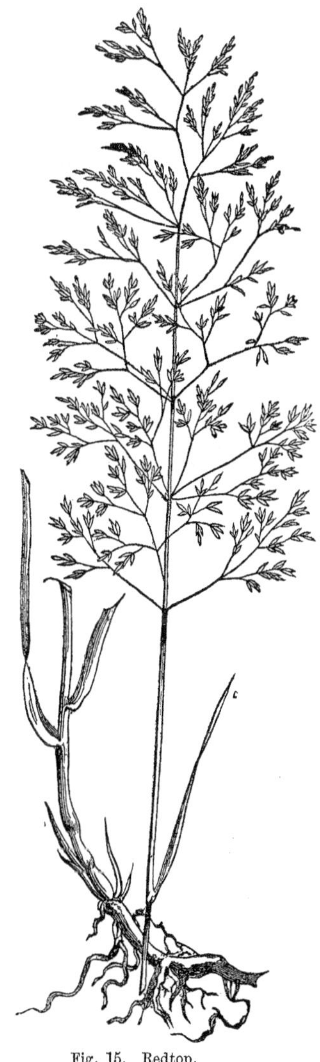

Fig. 15. Redtop.

seed the cattle refuse it; and this fact seems to show that it is not so much relished by stock as some of the other pasture grasses. The fact that cattle eat any grass greedily in the spring, is no proof of its excellence or nutritious qualities; since, then, all grasses are tender and full of juice, and many varieties of both grasses and shrubs are readily eaten, which at a more advanced stage of growth are refused. It is to be regretted that Prof. Way, in his valuable investigations into the nutritive value of the grasses, did not include this in the list analyzed by him. At present we have no accurate and reliable means of comparison of this with other species of grass. The flower of the true redtop is seen magnified in Fig. 16.

This grass goes by various names, and is greatly modified by soil and cultivation. On a moist, rich soil it grows larger than on a poor, thin soil, and not only larger but has a darker, purplish color, with a stem varying from eighteen inches to two feet or two and a half feet high; while on thin, poor, gravelly soils, it seldom grows over twelve inches, and often not over five or six inches high, while it has a lighter color. In the latter situations it goes by the name of Finetop, and is universally seen in old, dry pastures. In some sections of the State, as in Bristol County, it goes by the name of Burden's or Borden's grass, or Rhode Island Bent, and is highly esteemed.

Fig. 16.

Finetop may be regarded as a variety of redtop, produced by the character of the soil.

Dew Grass, White Top, White Bent, English Bent, Bonnet Grass, (*agrostis alba.*) Generic characters same as those of redtop.

Specific characters: Stem erect, round, smooth, polished, having four or five leaves with *roughish* sheaths, striated, upper sheath longer than its leaf, crowned with a long, acute, ragged ligule; joints smooth, branches numerous, recumbent, rooting at the lower joints where they come in contact with the ground, as in Fig. 17; panicle somewhat narrower than in redtop, lightish green, or with a slight tinge of purple; lower or inner palea one-half the length of the upper, and shorter than the glumes; five nerved, awnless—perennial. Native of Europe.

White top may be known from redtop by the sheaths being rough to the touch from above downwards, and the ligule being long and acute, and the keel of the large glume of the calyx toothed nearly to the base. In *agrostis vulgaris* the sheaths are smooth, ligule short and obtuse, and the keel of the large glume toothed only on the upper part.

It may be known from Brown Bent, (*agrostis canina,*) by having an inner palea in its floret, while in brown bent the inner palea is wanting. This grass is very common on the Connecticut River meadows where it appears to be indigenous, and is there called the English bent. Fiorin, (*agrostis stolonifera,*) is only a variety of the white top, or *agrostis alba*, which gained great notoriety some years ago in Ireland and England, volumes having been written in its praise, while it received the execrations of those who found it troublesome to eradicate on account of its creeping and stoloniferous roots. This grass belongs peculiarly to moist places which are occasionally overflowed. Fig. 17 represents it, and Fig. 18, a magnified flower. This grass is often used in the manufacture of bonnets. It is called Dew grass in some sections.

Brown Bent, or Dog's Bent Grass, (*agrostis canina,*) another variety of *agrostis*, has for its specific characters, a floret of one palea, sheaths smooth, ligule long, and grows from one to two feet high, awnless. The root is perennial and creeping. The stem is erect, slender, leaves flat and linear. The palea shorter than the glume and furnished with a long awn on the back, bent; spikelets at first greenish, afterwards brown or slightly purple. Meadows and pastures, and wet, peaty places—introduced. Flowers in June and July. It is of no special agricultural value.

HAIR GRASS, or FLY AWAY GRASS, TICKLE GRASS, (*agrostis scabra,*) is another species belonging to this genus, with a panicle very loose and spreading, *purplish*. Flowers in June and July. Mainly remarkable for the long hairy branches of its extremely loose panicle. Common in old fields and drained swamps. It is of no particular agricultural value. Very common at the West, in Ohio, Illinois, Michigan, and about Lake Superior. The large, loose panicles are exceedingly delicate and brittle when the plant is ripe and dry, and easily break away from the stalk when they are blown about by the wind, scattering their seeds far and wide; and hence it is frequently called "Fly Away Grass." This illustrates one of the admirable contrivances of nature for the distribution of the seeds of grasses and other plants; sometimes by means of birds, sometimes by a sort of wing attached to the light seed, and sometimes by the force of the wind alone, as in this case, when plants start up where no seed had been sown by the hand of man, and often to our astonishment.

Fig. 17. English Bent.

Fig. 18.

THIN GRASS, (*agrostis perennans,*) is still another variety of agrostis, with a panicle diffusely spreading, pale green; branches short, divided and flower-bearing from or below the middle; found in damp, shaded places. Flowers in June and July.

The ALPINE BROWN BENT, the UPRIGHT FLOWERED BENT, and many other species of agrostis might be mentioned. Of all the species of this genus, the redtop and white top are the most common as agricultural grasses among us.

The FIORIN, (*agrostis alba*, var. *stolonifera latifolia*,) or BROAD LEAVED CREEPING BENT, has been more highly commended in Europe than either of these. In the Woburn experiments which will be alluded to, this last was found to be inferior in nutritive value to orchard grass and meadow fescue, (*festuca pratensis*,) and superior to meadow foxtail (*alopecurus pratensis*.)

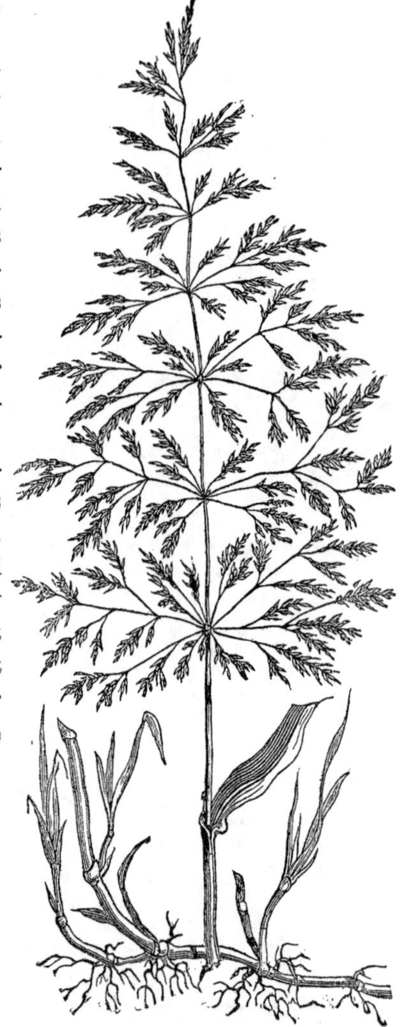

Fig. 20.

Fig. 19. Southern Bent.

The SOUTHERN BENT, (*agrostis dispar*,) (Fig. 19,) has been highly extolled in France. It is a native of the United States; was at one time highly commended in England, but was very soon discarded. It furnishes a hay of rather coarse quality, yields a large produce on good, deep sands and calcareous soils. It tillers very much, and when once rooted is very vigorous and lasting, and consequently makes a good pasture grass. It is very similar in appearance to some of the broad leaved varieties of *agrostis vulgaris*, and is said to yield a larger produce than that commonly known as redtop. It has stronger and more numerous creeping roots, broader leaves and more upright leafy stems. It is most frequently met with in the Southern States and in the south of France. Fig. 20 represents the flower of this grass magnified.

ANNUAL BEARD GRASS, (*polypogon monspeliensis*,) is a grass which is occasionally found near the coast. It may be known by having glumes with awns more than twice their length, growing from ten to fifteen inches high; stem erect, round, and a little rough; five or six leaves, flat, rather broad and acute; panicle dense, spikelets one flowered—introduced. It is easily distinguished from other grasses by the length of its awns or beards. Of no agricultural value.

WOOD REED GRASS, INDIAN REED, REEDY CINNA, (*cinna arundinacea*,) has spikelets, one flowered, feathered; glumes lanceolate, acute, strongly keeled, paleæ like the glumes, short awned—perennial; stems erect and reed-like, three or four feet high. The spikelets are green, or of a slight purplish tinge. Moist woods and swamps, common. Flowers in July and August. Panicle large, hairy, rather dense. A large, rank grass, differing from others in having but one stamen in each flower. Of no special agricultural value.

DROP SEED GRASS, (*Muhlenbergia diffusa*,) is a grass which derives its generic name from Dr. Henry Muhlenberg, a distinguished American botanist, pupil of the great Linnæus. It is commonly known in Kentucky and Tennessee by the name of "Nimble-will," and there forms a pasture grass of some value. Its stems are diffusely branched, from ten to eighteen inches high; panicles slender, contracted, glumes minute, awn nearly twice as long as the palea. It is sometimes found on dry hills and in woods. Flowers in August and September—perennial. Cattle eat it very readily. Not very common.

There is another species of this grass, the *Muhlenbergia glomerata*, from one to two feet high, much more common than the preceding, with stems upright, somewhat branched; panicle oblong, linear, contracted into an interrupted glomerate spike, with long peduncles or flower stalks and awned glumes—perennial. Flowers in August and September. Common in swamps and low grounds. Of no agricultural value.

The ERECT MUHLENBERGIA, or AWNED BRACHYELYTRUM, (*Muhlenbergia erecta*,) is often found in rocky woods, on the sides of Wachuset Mountain, and many other similar situations.

It is a simple, slender grass, two or three feet high; flowers few, root perennial, creeping, sheaths downy, leaves broad and flat, lanceolate, pointed. Flowers in June.

The MEXICAN MUHLENBERGIA, (*Muhlenbergia Mexicana,*) another species of this genus, has been mistaken by some for our fowl meadow. It has an erect stem, two to three feet high, much branched; panicles lateral and contracted, branches densely spiked and clustered, green or purplish; glumes pointed, awnless and unequal. It is perennial. Flowers in August. Frequently regarded as a troublesome weed in low grounds; somewhat common at the West and frequent here in low grounds, the borders of fields, and even in gardens, where its spreading roots are difficult to eradicate. Cattle eat it very readily, and as it blossoms late in the season, it is of some value.

The SYLVAN MUHLENBERGIA, (*Muhlenbergia sylvatica,*) is also rather common in low, rocky woods. Its stem is ascending, branched, spreading diffusely; panicles contracted, densely flowered; glumes nearly equal, bristle pointed, lower palea one awned, twice or three times the length of the spikelets. Flowers in August and September.

The AWNLESS MUHLENBERGIA, (*Muhlenbergia sobolifera,*) is sometimes found in open, rocky woods, from New England to Michigan, and farther south. It grows from one to two feet high, with a simple contracted panicle, very slender; glumes long, pointed, nearly equal, root perennial, creeping, woody, leaves pale green, sheaths open, ligule wanting. Flowers in August and September.

Still another species, sometimes called Hair Grass, (*Muhlenbergia capillaris,*) is sometimes, though not often found on sandy soils.

WILLDENOW'S MUHLENBERGIA, (*Muhlenbergia Willdenovii,*) is also not uncommon in rocky woods, growing about three feet high, with a slender, simple stem, contracted panicle, loosely flowered, glumes sharp pointed, half as long as the lower palea, which has an awn from three to four times the length of the spikelet.

None of the grasses of this American genus are of great value as agricultural grasses, except as they add considerably to the mass of living verdure which clothes our low lands in beauty to delight the eye and swell the heart of the lover of nature.

BLUE JOINT GRASS, (*calamagrostis canadensis.*) The generic characteristics are, one flowered spikelets, open panicle, contracted or spiked; glumes keeled, about equal to the paleæ, around which, at the base, is a thick tuft of white bristly hairs; lower palea generally with a slender awn on the back.

Specific description: Stems three to five feet high, greyish, leaves flat, panicle often purplish, the glumes acute, lanceolate, lower palea not longer than the very fine hairs bearing an extremely delicate awn below the middle, nearly equal to the hairs. Flowers in July. The blue joint grass is very common on low grounds. It is generally considered a valuable grass. It is eaten greedily by stock in the winter, and is thought by some to be as nutritious as Timothy.

The GLAUCOUS SMALL REED, (*calamagrostis coarctata,*) is also somewhat common in our wet meadows, open swamps and along low river banks. Its stems are from three to five feet high, seed hairy, crowned with a bearded tuft; lower palea shorter than the taper-pointed tips of the lanceolate glumes, almost twice the length of the hairs, with a rigid, short awn above the middle.

BEACH GRASS, SEA SAND REED, MAT GRASS, (*ammophila arundinacea,*) grows to a height of two or three feet, with a rigid culm, from stout roots running often to the distance of twenty or thirty feet; leaves wide, rather short, of a sea green color; panicle contracted into a close, dense spike, from six to twelve inches long, nearly white. It is found in the sands of the sea shore where its thick, strong, creeping, perennial roots, with many tubers the size of a pea, prevent the drifting of the sand from the action of the winds and waves, thus forming a barrier against the encroachments of the sea.

This grass is very generally diffused on sea coasts over the world, and is found inland on the shores of Lake Superior. It has also been cultivated by way of experiment, and with success, on the sands at Lowell, and still farther up on the banks of the Merrimack River. Though not cultivated for agricultural purposes, it is of great value in protecting sandy beaches. It is preserved in England and Scotland by act of parliament. Flowers in August.

In the year 1853, I was requested by the late T. W. Harris, to make this grass a special study in the course of my observations, and since that time I have tried in every way, by personal inquiries and by correspondence, to collect whatever there might be of interest in relation to it.

The town of Provincetown, once called Cape Cod, where the Pilgrims first landed, and its harbor, still called the harbor of Cape Cod,—one of the best and most important in the United States,—sufficient in depth for ships of the largest size, and in extent, to anchor three thousand vessels at once, owe their preservation to this grass. To an inhabitant of an inland country, it is difficult to conceive the extent and the violence with which the sands at the extremity of Cape Cod are thrown up from the depths of the sea, and left on the beach in thousands of tons by every driving storm. These sand hills when dried by the sun are hurled by the winds into the harbor and upon the town. A correspondent at Provincetown says: "Beach grass is said to have been cultivated here as early as 1812. Before that time, when the sand drifted down upon the dwelling-houses,—as it did whenever the beach was broken,—to save them from burial the only resort was to wheeling it off with barrows. Thus tons were removed every year from places that are now perfectly secure from the drifting of sand. Indeed, were it not for the window glass in some of the oldest houses in these localities, you would be ready to deny this statement, but the sand has been blown with such force, and so long against this glass as to make it *perfectly ground*. I know of some windows through which you cannot see an object, except to remind you of that passage where men were seen 'as trees walking.'

"Congress appropriated, between the years 1826 and 1839, about twenty-eight thousand dollars, which were expended in setting out beach grass back of the village, for the protection of the harbor. From the seed of this grass it is estimated that nearly as much ground has become planted with it as was covered by the general government. In 1854, five thousand dollars were expended most wisely by the general government in adding to the work so nobly begun; and the experience of former years was of great value to the efficiency of this latter effort. The work of fortification or protection is not yet complete. The eastern part of the harbor is much exposed to injury from the sand which now empties itself by the thousand tons every north wind, into the east harbor. Unless there is speedily another appropriation from congress, to be applied in the direction of East Harbor, it is easy to foretel the fearful consequences to it.

"It may be proper to state," says the same writer, "that this town does much in the way of '*beach grassing*' by its '*beach grass committee*,' whose duty it is to enter any man's enclosure, summer or winter, and set out grass, if the sand is uncovered and movable. By this means we are now rid of sand storms, which were once the terror of the place, being something like snow storms, for drifts which were to be removed. Our streets are now hardened with clay which has been imported, and instead of its being buried, as it would once have been in a few days, I notice that the surveyors have to resort to sprinkling it with sand in wet weather, so effectually has the culture of beach grass answered its end.

"The mode of culture is very simple. The grass is pulled up by hand and placed in a hole about a foot deep, and the sand pressed down about it. These holes are dug about one foot and a half apart. The spring is the usual time of planting, though many do this work in the fall or winter. The roots of the grass from which it soon covers the ground, are very long. I have noticed them ten feet, and I suppose upon high hills they extend down into wet sand."

Many years ago the beach which connects Truro and Provincetown was broken over, and a considerable body of it swept away. Beach grass was immediately planted, and the beach was thus raised to sufficient height, and in some places into hills. The operation of it is like that of brush or bushes, cut and laid upon the ground, in accumulating snow in a drifting wind. The sand is collected around the grass, and as the sand rises, the grass also rises to overtop it, and will continue to grow, no matter how high the sand hill may rise, and this process goes on over the whole surface of the plantation, and thus many acres have been raised far above their original level.

A committee of the legislature appointed in 1852, to inquire into the means of preserving Cape Cod Harbor, in speaking of the beach between the ocean on the north, and the channel of

East Harbor,—and which is all that prevents the sea from breaking over into Cape Cod Harbor,—say: "This tract consists of loose sand, driven about by every high wind, which throws it up in heaps like snow drifts. The wind, from any point from north-east to north-west, drives the sand directly from said beach into the channel of East Harbor, and is carried by a strong current into the north-east part of Cape Cod Harbor. The ocean on the north is wasting this narrow beach away in every storm, and the current in East Harbor channel undermining and destroying it on the south. The decay of said beach has been on the increase for several years; it has narrowed within seven or eight years, by the tide that runs through East Harbor channel, from eight to ten rods; where the mail stage travelled only one year since, is now the channel, with six feet of water at low tide, and from twelve to fourteen feet at high water."

The first effort made by the State for the preservation of this important harbor appears to have been in 1714. The town was incorporated in 1727, and was at that time a place of some extent, but the inhabitants soon began to leave, and in less than twenty years it was reduced to two or three families. After the Revolution the place revived, and is now a thriving town.

The object of the law of 1714 was to arrest the destruction of the trees and shrubbery on the province lands, and on the preservation of which it was thought the harbor depended, as they prevented the drifting of the sand.

In 1824 commissioners were appointed by the State government to examine the subject and report what action was necessary to prevent the rapid destruction of the harbor. They recommended an act to prevent the destruction of beach grass, and reported that the sum of thirty-six hundred dollars would be necessary to set out that plant, make fences, &c. The legislature in 1826 applied to congress for that sum, and congress has, at different times, made appropriations to the amount of about thirty-eight thousand dollars, which seems to have failed in some measure to accomplish the object intended, and East Harbor is still rapidly filling up.

Many years ago it was as customary to warn the inhabitants of Truro and some other towns on the Cape every spring, to turn out to plant beach grass, as it was in the inland towns to turn out and mend the roads. This was required by law, with suitable penalties for its neglect, and took place in April.

A farmer of much practical knowledge of this subject, says: "Since the cattle have been kept from the beaches, by the act of the legislature of 1826, the grass and shrubs have sprung up of their own accord and have, in a great measure, in the westerly part of the Cape, accomplished what was intended to be done by planting grass. It is of no use to plant grass on the high parts of the beach. Plant on the lowest parts and they will raise, while the highest places, over which the grass will spread, are levelling by the wind. To preserve the beach it must be kept as level as possible.

"Beach grass is of but little value except to prevent our loose, sandy beaches from being drifted about by the wind. We have but one species, and this is fast spreading over our upland, making it useless for cultivation. Land that would produce from twenty to twenty-five bushels of Indian corn to the acre, without any manure, twenty-five or thirty years ago, is now overrun with beach grass and will produce nothing else. If the dead grass is burnt off in the spring, it will make a pretty good pasture for cattle and horses. It keeps green longer than any other grass we have. It can be cultivated from the seed or by transplanting. Our loose, sandy beaches are the most suitable for its growth."

Beach grass seems to require the assistance of some disturbing causes to enable it to attain its full perfection. The driving winds in some localities, are sufficient, while in other places, where it does not thrive so well, it is probable that an iron tooth harrow would greatly improve and aid its growth. It has been extensively cultivated or propagated from the seed on many parts of Cape Cod, on Nantucket, and in fact to considerable extent all along our coast. It comes in of itself along Nantasket beach from seed borne by the tides, probably, from the Cape. It has been extensively used, at times, in this country, for the manufacture of coarse paper, though if I am rightly informed, its manufacture has been discontinued in this State. In other countries it is manufactured into door mats and brushes, mats for pack-saddles, meal bags and hats, and into ropes for various purposes.

Mountain Rice, (*oryzopsis melanocarpa,*) is a grass common in rocky woods; the large white grained mountain rice, (*oryzopsis asperifolia,*) common on steep and rocky hill-sides and dry woods, and the Smallest Oryzopsis, (*oryzopsis canadensis,*) are sometimes found. These grasses are easily distinguished from each other. The first has an awn thrice the length of the blackish palea; the second, an awn two or three times the length of the whitish paléa; the third, an awn short, deciduous or wanting. The first grows from two to three feet high, the second from ten to eighteen inches.

Feather Grass, or Black Oat Grass, (*stipa avenacea,*) is sometimes met with in dry, sandy woods, and is collected for vases and ornaments, but is of no agricultural value. It rises from one to two feet; its panicle is open, leaves almost bristle form, palea blackish, nearly as long as the almost equal glumes, awn bent above, twisted below. Flowers in July.

Poverty Grass, or Three Awned Grass, (*aristida dichotoma,*) and Slender Three Awned Grass, (*aristida gracilis,*) are found in old, sandy fields, dry, sterile hill-sides and pine barrens, but are of no value for cultivation. One or two other species of three awned plants also occur on similar soils, as the *aristida purpurascens* and the *aristida tuberculosa.* None of these species are of importance in agriculture.

Fresh Water Cord Grass, (*spartina cynosuroides.*) This is found on the banks of streams and lakes, rising to the height of from two to four feet, with slender culm, narrow leaves two to four feet long, tapering to a point, and spikes of a straw color. Flowers in August.

The Salt Reed Grass, (*spartina polystachya,*) has a stout culm from four to nine feet high, broad leaves, roughish underneath and on the margins; spikes 20 to 50 in number, forming a dense, oblong, purplish cluster. It is found on the salt marshes.

Rush Salt Grass, (*spartina juncea,*) grows from one to two feet high, stems slender, leaves narrow, rush-like, and very smooth. It is common on salt marshes and sandy sea beaches, and flowers in August.

Salt Marsh Grass, (*spartina stricta,* var. *glabra,*) grows from two to four feet high, has from five to twelve spikes from two to three inches long; spikelets crowded and lapping over each other. It is common on the coast.

SAND GRASS, (*tricuspis purpurea,*) is also found on dry, sandy soils, along the coast; flowering in August and September. It is acid to the taste, grows from six inches to a foot high, and has numerous bearded joints.

ORCHARD GRASS, ROUGH COCKSFOOT, (*dactylis glomerata.*) The generic characters are, spikelets several flowered, crowded in clusters, one-sided, panicle dense at the top, branching,

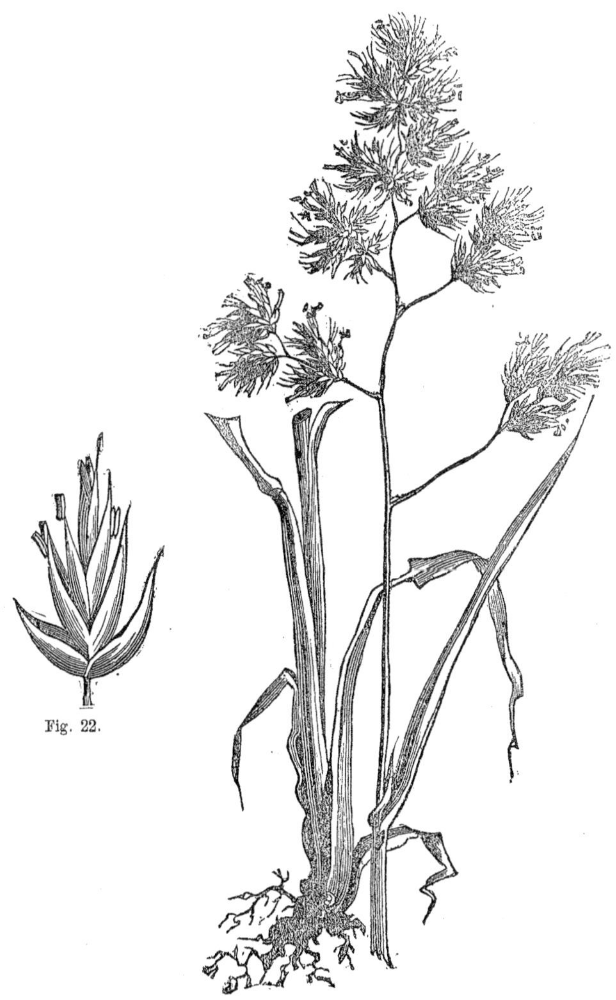

Fig. 22.

Fig. 21. Orchard Grass.

glumes two, herbaceous, keeled, long-pointed. Stamens three, seed oblong, acute, free. Named from *dactylus*, a finger.

Orchard grass flowers in dense tufts. Its stem is erect, about three feet high. I have found specimens in good soil, over five feet high. Leaves linear, flat, dark green, rough on both surfaces, which, with the fancied resemblance of its loose tufts to the foot of a barnyard fowl, have given it the common name in England of rough cocksfoot. Root perennial. Flowers in June and July. Not uncommon in fields and pastures. It is seen in Fig. 21. A magnified spikelet is shown in Fig. 22.

This is one of the most valuable and widely known of all the pasture grasses. It is common to every country in Europe, to the north of Africa, and to Asia as well as to America. Its culture was introduced into England from Virginia, where it had been cultivated some years previously, in 1764. It forms one of the most common grasses of English natural pastures, on rich, deep, moist soils. It became, soon after its introduction into England, an object of special agricultural interest among cattle feeders, having been found to be exceedingly palatable to stock of all kinds. Its rapidity of growth, the luxuriance of its aftermath and its power of enduring the cropping of cattle, commend it highly to the farmer's care, especially as a pasture grass. As it blossoms earlier than Timothy, and about the time of red clover, it makes an admirable mixture with that plant, to cut in the blossom and cure for hay. As a pasture grass it should be fed close, both to prevent its forming thick tufts and to prevent its running to seed, when it loses a large proportion of its nutritive matter, and becomes hard and wiry. All kinds of stock eat it greedily when green.

Judge Buel, distinguished as a man of taste, said of this grass: "I should prefer it to almost every other grass, and cows are very fond of it." Elsewhere he says: "The American Cocksfoot, or Orchard Grass, is one of the most abiding grasses we have. It is probably better adapted than any other grass to sow with clover and other seeds for permanent pasture or for hay, as it is fit to cut with clover and grows remarkably quick when cropped by cattle. Five or six days' growth in summer suffices to give a good bite. Its good properties consist in its early and rapid growth and its resistance of drouth; but all agree that it should be closely cropped. Sheep will pass over every other grass to feed upon it. If suffered to grow long without being cropped, it becomes coarse and harsh. Colonel Powell, (a late eminent farmer of Pennsylvania,) after growing it ten years, declares that it produces more pasturage than any other grass he has seen in America. On being fed very close, it has produced good pasture after remaining five days at rest. It is suited to all arable soils. Two bushels of seed are requisite for an acre when sown alone, or half this quantity when sown with clover. The seed is very light, weighing not more than twelve or fourteen pounds to the bushel. It should be cut early for hay."

Mr. Sanders, a well known practical farmer and cattle breeder, of Kentucky, says of it: "My observation and experience have induced me to rely mainly on orchard grass and red clover; indeed, I now sow no other sort of grass seed. These grasses mixed, make the best hay of all the grasses for this climate (Kentucky;) it is nutritious, and well adapted as food for stock. Orchard grass is ready for grazing in the spring ten or twelve days sooner than any other that affords a full bite. When grazed down and the stock turned off, it will be ready for regrazing in less than half the time required for Kentucky blue grass. It stands a severe drought better than any other grass, keeping green and growing when other sorts are dried up; in summer it will grow more in a day than blue grass will in a week. Orchard grass is naturally disposed to form and grow in tussocks. The best preventive is a good preparation of the ground, and a sufficiency of seed uniformly sown. The late Judge Peters of Pennsylvania,—who was at the head of agricultural improvement in that State for many years,—preferred it to all other grasses."

Orchard grass is less exhausting to the soil than rye grass or Timothy. It will endure considerable shade. In a porous subsoil its fibrous roots extend to a great depth. Its habit of growth unfits it for a lawn grass. Its seed weighs twelve pounds to the bushel, and to sow alone, about twenty-four pounds to the acre are required to make sure of a good crop. It should not be sown alone except for the sake of raising the seed. It is worthy of a much more extended cultivation among us.

Pennsylvanian Eatonia, (*Eatonia Pennsylvanica,*) is a grass common in moist woods. It has a loose panicle, grows two feet high, with short, flat leaves, of a pale green. Flowers in June.

RATTLESNAKE GRASS, (*glyceria canadensis.*) The generic characteristics of glyceria are, many flowered spikes, mostly flattish; glumes two pointed, nearly equal, awnless, the lower one obtuse, seven nerved; roots creeping—perennial. Wet places and standing water. The name of the genus is from a Greek word signifying sweet.

Rattlesnake grass has an oblong, pyramidal, spreading panicle, with beautifully drooping spikelets, six or eight flowered, and long, roughish leaves, which together make it an object of interest and search for bouquets and vases. It is very common in wet, boggy places, growing from two to three feet high, but possesses little or no agricultural value. Flowers in July.

The OBTUSE SPEAR GRASS, (*glyceria obtusa,*) has a dense, narrowly oblong panicle; spikelets six or seven flowered, erect, swelling; lower palea obtuse, leaves smooth, as long as the stem. This is an aquatic grass, found occasionally on the borders of ponds. Flowers in August. Of no agricultural value.

LONG PANICLED MANNA GRASS, (*glyceria elongata,*) is a very distinct species; stems one to three feet high, panicle branching, narrowly elongated, recurving, the branches appressed, spikelets pale, erect, three to four flowered, lower palea obtuse, rather longer than the upper; stamens two, stigmas compound, leaves very long and rough. Flourishes in wet woods and swamps. Flowers in June and July—perennial. Of no special agricultural value.

MEADOW SPEAR GRASS, NERVED MANNA GRASS, (*poa nervata,*) is the fowl meadow of some farmers, while the grass most commonly called fowl meadow, (*poa serotina,*) goes with them under the name of bastard fowl meadow. It has a broad, open panicle, six inches in length, with slender branches; spikelets small, ovate, oblong, green; leaves in two rows like a fan, a little rough; stem a little compressed, one to three feet high. It is a native American grass, flowering late in June. The nutritive value of this grass, according to Sinclair, is equal at the time of flowering and when the seed is ripe, while the nutritive matter of the lattermath is said to be greater than that of most other grasses. It is a hardy grass, grows best on wet or

Fig. 23. MEADOW SPEAR GRASS,

moist grounds, and is said also to succeed on light upland soils. It is somewhat coarse, and not particularly relished by cattle, though readily eaten in winter. It would be a valuable ingredient in a mixture for moist pastures. It is not very common. It is seen in Fig. 23, while in Fig. 23 (1) is seen a magnified spikelet, and the calyx in (2.) Native of North America.

The PALE MANNA GRASS, (*glyceria pallida*,) grows mostly in shallow water, and is very common. Panicle erect with hairy branches, spreading, rough; spikelets few, linear, oblong, five to nine flowered; lower palea oblong, minutely *five toothed;* leaves short, sharp pointed and pale green. Flowers in July. Culms one to three feet long, creeping at the base.

One or two other species are referred to this genus, glyceria, as the REFLEXED MEADOW GRASS, (*glyceria distans*,) found in salt marshes, along the coast, and closely allied to the SEA SPEAR GRASS, (*poa maritima*,) and the ACUTE FESCUE GRASS, (*glyceria acutiflora*,) rarely found in low, wet places. Of no value in agriculture.

SPIKE GRASS, (*brizopyrum spicatum*,) is a salt marsh grass, with culms or stems in tufts from creeping root-stalks, from ten to eighteen inches high. Flowers in August.

GREEN MEADOW GRASS, JUNE GRASS, COMMON SPEAR GRASS, KENTUCKY BLUE GRASS, &c., (*poa pratensis*.) The characteristics of the genus poa, are, ovate spikelets, compressed, flowers two to ten in an open panicle, glumes shorter than the flowers, lower palea compressed, keeled, pointless, five nerved, stamens two or three, seed oblong, free, stems tufted, leaves smooth, flat and soft.

Specific characters: Lower florets connected at the base by a web of long, silky filaments, holding the calyx; outer palea, five ribbed, marginal ribs hairy, upper sheath longer than its leaf; height from ten to fifteen inches, root perennial, *creeping*, stem erect, smooth and round, leaves linear, flat, acute, roughish on the edges and inner surface; panicle diffuse, spreading, erect. The plant is of a light green color, the spikelets frequently variegated with brownish purple. Introduced. Flowers in June. Fig. 24 represents this grass, and Fig. 25, a flower magnified.

This is an early grass, very common on the soils of New England in pastures and fields, constituting a considerable portion of the turf. It varies very much in size and appearance according to the soil on which it grows. In Kentucky it is universally known as Blue grass, and elsewhere frequently called Kentucky blue grass, and still more frequently, June grass. It has been called by some, without much reason, the most valuable of all the grasses in our pastures. It comes into the soil in some parts of the country when left to itself, and grows luxuriantly on soils best suited to it, and is relished by all cattle. Its creeping root is said by some to impoverish the soil. Wherever it is intended for hay it is cut at the time of flowering, as if the seed is allowed to ripen, more than a fourth part of the crop is lost. In its earliness, it is equalled by some of the other grasses, and in its nutritive constituents by several. After being cut in summer it starts up slowly. Low says: "It is inferior to the rough stalked meadow grass, and it may be questioned whether it deserves to be reckoned among the superior pasture grasses."

Fig. 25.

Fig. 24. June Grass.

It produces but one flowering stem in a year, while many of the other grasses continue to shoot up flower stalks, and run to seed through the season. On this account it is recommended highly for lawns, where uniformity is desired. The produce ordinarily is small, compared with other grasses, but the herbage is fine. It grows well in rather a dry soil, but will grow on a variety of soils, from the dryest knolls to a wet meadow. It does not withstand our severe droughts as well as some other grasses. Its reputation is far higher in this, than in its native country, where it is denied by most farmers even a place among the grasses to be recommended for cultivation. It endures the frosts of winter better, perhaps, than most other grasses; and in Kentucky, where it attains the highest perfection as a pasture grass, it sometimes continues luxuriant through their mild winters. It requires at least two or three years to become well set, and it does not arrive at its perfection as a pasture grass till the sward is older than that, and hence it is not suited to alternate husbandry, or where the land is to remain in grass only two or three years and then be ploughed up. In Kentucky, the best blue grass is found in partially shaded pastures. A well known farmer of that State, in a communication to the Ohio Farmer, says: "In our climate, and soil, it is not only the most beautiful of grasses, but the most valuable of crops. It is the first deciduous plant which puts forth its leaves here; ripens its seed about the tenth of June, and then remains green, if the summer is favorable in moisture, during the summer months, growing slowly till about the last of August, when it takes a second vigorous growth until the ground is frozen by winter's cold. If the summer is dry, it dries up utterly, and will burn if set on fire; but even then, if the spring growth has been left upon the ground, is very nutritious to all grazing stock, and especially to sheep and cattle, and all ruminating animals. When left to have all its fall growth, it makes fine winter pasture for all kinds of grazing animals. Cattle will not seek it through the snow, but sheep, mules and horses will paw off the snow and get plenty without any other food. When covered with snow, cattle require some other feeding; otherwise they do well all winter upon it.

"It makes also the best of hay. I have used it for that for twenty years. It should be cut just as the seeds *begin* to ripen, well spread, and protected from the dew at night by windrowing or cocking; the second evening stacked, with salt, or sheltered, with salt also. When properly cured, stock seem greatly to prefer it to all other hay. I would not recommend it for meadow, especially, however, because the yield is hardly equal to Timothy and clover, and because it is more difficult to cut and cure."

The same writer says: "Any time in the winter, when the snow is on the ground, sow broadcast from three to four quarts of clean seed to the acre. With the spring the seeds germinate and are very fine in the sprouts, and delicate. No stock should be allowed for the first year, nor until the grass seeds in June, for the first time in the second year. The best plan is to turn on your stock when the seed ripens in June. Graze off the grass, then allow the fall growth and graze all winter, taking care never to feed the grass closely at any time."

Another eminent cattle breeder speaking of this grass, says: "Perennial grasses are the true basis of agriculture, in the highest condition of that best employment for man. Grasses which are not perennial, are of immense value, especially as one of the shifts in the ordinary rotation of crops, suited to the agriculture of the great upper, or northerly portion of our continent, all of it above the *cotton* line. But it is the grasses which are perpetual, that I chiefly allude to, and among these, emphatically the blue grass, as it is called in the regions where it flourishes most. Whoever has limestone land, has blue grass; whoever has blue grass, has the basis of all agricultural prosperity; and that man, if he have not the finest horses, cattle and sheep, has no one to blame but himself. Others, in other circumstances, may do well; he can hardly avoid doing well, if he will try."

By reference to a table on a subsequent page, containing the results of the recent investigations of Prof. Way, the distinguished chemist of the Royal Agricultural Society of England, it will be seen how inferior this grass is when green, to Timothy, for instance, in all the nutritive, flesh-forming, and especially in the fat-forming principles which contribute so largely to the development and support of the whole animal system. The reader is referred to that table, and to another following it, containing analyses of these plants when dried and freed from water, and to the explanatory remarks on the nutritive principles of plants, which precede those tables.

BLUE GRASS, or WIRE GRASS, (*poa compressa.*) Stems ascending, flattened, the uppermost joint near the middle, leaves short, bluish green, panicle dense and contracted, expanding more at flowering; short branches often in pairs, covered with four to nine flowered, flat spikelets; flowers rather obtuse, linear, hairy below on the keel; ligule short and blunt; height about a foot. It is very common on dry, sandy, thin soils and banks, so hardy as to grow on the thin, hard soils covering the surface of rocks, along trodden walks, or gravelly knolls. It shoots its leaves early, but the amount of its foliage is not large, otherwise it would be one of our most valuable grasses, since it possesses a large per cent. of nutritive matter. Flowers in July. Most grazing animals eat it greedily, and it is especially relished by sheep. Its bluish green stems retain their color after the seed is ripe. It shrinks less in drying than most other grasses, and consequently makes a hay very heavy in proportion to its bulk. It is an exceedingly valuable pasture grass on dry, rocky knolls and should form a portion of a mixture for such soils. This should not be confounded with Kentucky blue grass alluded to above.

Annual Spear Grass, (*poa anuua*, see Fig. 1,) is, perhaps, the most common of all our grasses. Its stems are spreading, flattened, panicle often one sided, spikelets crowded, three to seven flowered, lower palea more or less hairy on the nerves below; leaves of a light green, sword-shaped, flat, often *crumpled at the margins*, as appears in Fig. 1, smooth on both surfaces, rough at the edges. *Florets not webbed*, and this distinguishes it from the June grass, (*poa pratensis*,) and its varieties. The outer or lower palea of this grass has no hairs on the lateral ribs as the *poa pratensis* has. This modest and beautiful grass flowers throughout the whole summer and forms a very large part of the sward of New England pastures, producing an early and sweet feed, exceedingly relished by cattle. It does not resist the drought very well, but becomes parched up in our pastures.

The Rough Stalked Meadow Grass, (*poa trivialis*,) though not so common as the June grass, (*poa pratensis*,) is still often met with, and is found to have webbed florets; outer palea five ribbed, marginal ribs not hairy, ligule long and pointed, stems two to three feet high. Distinguished from June grass by having rough sheaths, while in the latter the sheaths are smooth, the ligule obtuse and the marginal ribs of outer palea furnished with hairs. The rough stalked meadow grass has a fibrous root, that of the June grass is creeping. It flourishes in moist meadows where it flowers in July. Introduced. This grass is seen in Fig. 26, while Fig. 27 represents a flower somewhat magnified.

This is a valuable grass to cultivate in moist, sheltered soils, possessing very considerable nutritive qualities, coming to perfection at a desirable time, and being exceedingly relished by cattle, horses and sheep. For such soils it should form a portion of a mixture of seeds, producing, in mixture with other grasses which serve to shelter it, a large yield of hay, far above the average of grass usually grown on a similar soil. It should be cut when in seed and not in the flower. Seven pounds of seed to the acre will produce a good sward. The grass loses about seventy per cent. of its weight in drying. Its hay contains about one and sixty hundredths per cent. of azote, and the nutritive qualities of the lattermath exceed very considerably those of the crop cut in the flower or in the seed.

Fig. 27.

Fig. 26. Rough Stalk Meadow Grass.

Wood Meadow Grass, (*poa nemoralis*,) is met with in Hampshire and Berkshire counties. It grows from eighteen inches to two feet high, has a perennial, creeping root, an erect stem, slender, smooth, the upper sheath no longer than its leaf, with a very short ligule, the base of the floret having a silky web suspending the calyx, leaves, light green. It is common in moist, shady places, and appears as a tall, rank grass, with a long, finely arched panicle. It flowers in June and ripens its seed in July.

Though it has never to my knowledge been cultivated in this country, it appears to me worthy of attention for moist soils. It is certainly to be classed among the best of shaded pasture grasses, furnishing a fine, succulent and very nutritive herbage, which stock of all kinds are very fond of. Hay contains one and sixty-four one-hundredths per cent. of azote. The grass loses about fifty-five per cent. of its weight in drying. Fig. 28 represents this grass in blossom; Fig. 29 a magnified flower.

Fig. 28. Wood Meadow Grass. Fig. 29.

The Creeping Sea Meadow Grass, or Sea Spear Grass, (*poa maritima*,) referred by Gray to *glyceria*, is a beautiful grass which appears in and around salt marshes, growing from six to twelve inches high, and having a perennial, *creeping* root. Stem erect, round, smooth, leaves mostly folded and compressed, roughish on the inner surface, spikelets linear, with from six to ten florets *not* webbed, the outer palea of lower floret terminating in an acute point. Flowers in July. Grows naturally near the sea. It is seen in Fig. 30, and its flower magnified, in Fig 31.

6

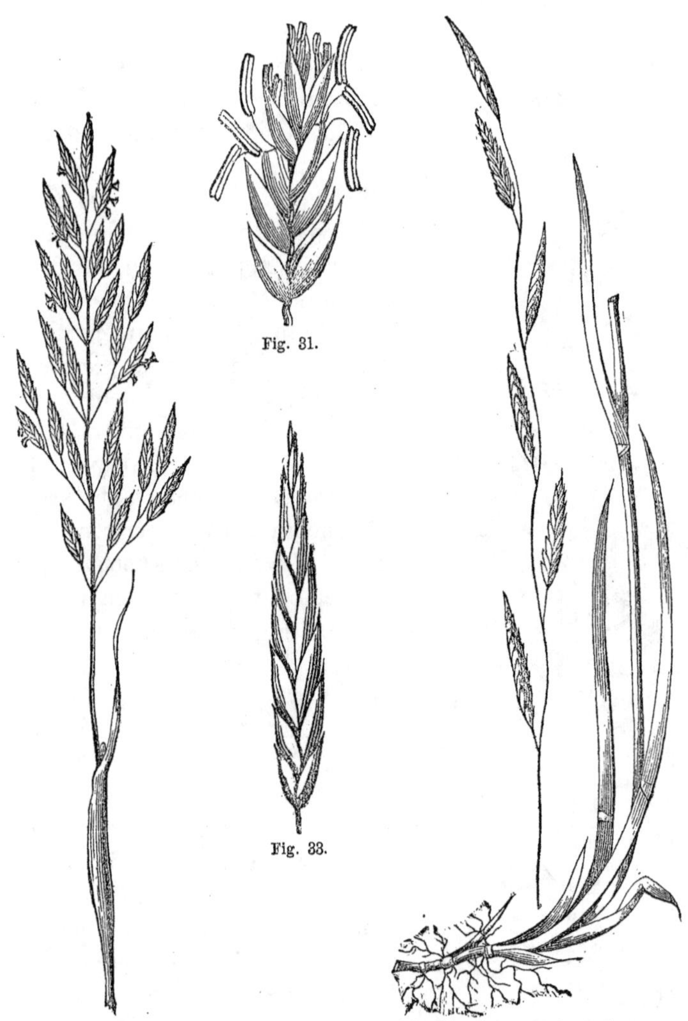

Fig. 31.

Fig. 33.

Fig. 30. Sea Spear Grass.

Fig. 32. Common Manna Grass.

The Floating Meadow Grass, or Common Manna Grass, (*poa fluitans*,) referred by Gray to *glyceria*, differs from the other species of the poa genus in the general appearance of its slender panicle and long, linear spikelets. It grows from fifteen inches to two feet high, with a perennial, creeping root, erect, round, smooth stem, leaves large, rather long, roughish on both sides, lower ones flat, upper ones generally folded; spikelets few, long and linear, as shown in Fig. 32, which represents the plant near the time of flowering. Fig. 33 shows a magnified spikelet of this grass, florets not webbed. Flowers late in June.

This grass grows naturally in very moist and muddy places, in ditches, on the margins of ponds and streams, and is very common. It is capable of cultivation as a permanent pasture grass, and its yield compares well with many of the other grasses. Its seeds are greedily sought by birds, and in some parts of Germany are said to be used as a delicacy in soups and gruels.

Fig. 34. Water Spear Grass.

Fig. 35.

The Wavy Meadow Grass, (*poa laxa,*) occurs rarely on high and rocky hills, but is not sufficiently common or valuable to need description.

The Water Spear Grass, or Reed Meadow Grass, (*poa aquatica,*) grows in wet soils, in Hampshire County; is a tall, reedy grass, four or five feet high with a panicle nearly a foot long, diffuse, with smooth, flexuous branches. From its large size and broad leaves it can hardly be mistaken for any of the other species of poa. Its root is perennial, creeping, stem erect, stout, smooth, joints seven, smooth, spikelets numerous, florets not webbed. Flowers in August. Seen in Fig. 34, and its spikelet in Fig. 35. This grass is referred by Gray and others, to *glyceria.* It is very common in wet meadows and will be easily recognized. More nutritive when in flower than when the seed is ripe. It contains a comparatively large per cent. of sugar. Makes a valuable fodder and cattle are very fond of it.

Several other species belonging to this genus, are frequently met with, as the BRANCHING SPEAR GRASS, on dry sandy soils, a very elegant species, with a large panicle of sea-green spikelets; the HAIR SPEAR GRASS, also an elegant grass growing on similar soils, with a hairy branching panicle over a foot long, leaves linear, nerved. But perhaps the most important of all is the FOWL MEADOW, or FALSE REDTOP, (*poa serotina.*) [See Frontispiece.]

The specific characteristics of this species are two to four, sometimes five, flowered spikelets, oval, spear shaped, ligules elongated, flowers acutish, green, often tinged with purple, roots slightly creeping; wet meadows and banks of streams, very common. Flowers in July and August. In long continued moist weather the lower joints send up flowering stems. The panicle is erect and spreading when in flower, but more contracted and drooping when ripe. It is perennial. Native of Germany.

It early commended itself to the attention of farmers, for Jared Eliot, writing in 1749, says of it: "There are two sorts of grass which are natives of the country, which I would recommend,—these are Herds-grass, (known in Pennsylvania by the name of Timothy-grass,) the other is Fowl Meadow, sometimes called Duck-grass, and sometimes *Swamp-wire Grass.* It is said that Herds-grass was first found in a swamp in Piscataqua, by one Herd, who propagated the same; that Fowl Meadow-grass was brought into a poor piece of meadow in Dedham, by ducks and other wild water-fowl, and therefore called by such an odd name. It is supposed to be brought into the meadows at Hartford by the annual floods, and called there Swamp-wire grass. Of these two sorts of natural grass, the fowl-grass is much the best; it grows tall and thick, makes a more soft and pliable hay than Herds-grass, and consequently will be more fit for pressing, in order to ship off with our horses; besides it is a good grass, not in abundance inferior to English grass. It yields a good burden, three loads to the acre. It must be sowed in low, moist land. This grass has another good quality, which renders it very valuable in a country where help is so much wanting; it will not spoil or suffer, although it stand beyond the common times for mowing. Clover will be lost, in a great measure, if it be not cut in the proper season. Spear-grass, commonly called English grass, if it stands too long, will be little better than rye straw; if this outstand the time, it is best to let it stand till there comes up a second growth, and then it will do tolerably well; but this fowl-grass may be mowed any time from July to October. * * * This I wondered at, but viewing some of it attentively, I think I have found the reason of it. When it is grown about three foot high it then falls down, but doth not rot like other grass when lodged; in a little time after it is thus fallen down, at every joint it puts forth a new branch; now to maintain this young brood of suckers there must be a plentiful course of sap conveyed up through the main stem or straw; by this means the grass is kept green and fit for mowing all this long period."

This grass grows abundantly in almost every part of New England, especially where it has been introduced and cultivated in suitable ground, such as the borders of rivers and intervals occasionally overflowed. It will not endure to be long covered with water, especially in warm weather. It is well to let a piece go to seed, save the seed and scatter it over low lands. It makes an excellent grass for oxen, cows and sheep, but is thought to be rather fine for horses. It never grows so coarse or hard but that the stalk is sweet and tender and eaten without waste. It is very easily made into hay, and is more nutritive, according to Sinclair, than either foxtail, orchard grass, or tall meadow oat grass. Owing to its constantly sending forth flowering stems, the grass of the lattermath contains more nutritive matter than the first crop at the time of flowering, hence the names *fertilis* and *serotina*, fertile and late flowering meadow grass. It thrives best when mixed with other grasses, and deserves a place in all mixtures for rich moist pastures.

The Creeping Meadow Grass, (*eragrostis reptans*,) is frequently found on the sandy banks of rivers, and is a beautiful and delicate grass. Flowering in July and August. Its leaves are short, nearly awl-shaped, spikelets smooth, long and lance shaped, flowers acute, sheaths loose, striate and a little hairy on the margin, panicles from one to two inches long. Not a cultivated grass.

The Strong-scented Meadow Grass, (*eragrostis poæoides*,) is sometimes found in sandy fields, roadsides, cultivated grounds and waste places. Its leaves are flat and smooth, lower sheaths hairy, spikelets containing from ten to twenty florets of a lead color. It flowers in August and September. Of no importance in agriculture.

A variety of this grass (the *megastachya*) is found more frequently on similar situations; flowering about the same time; emitting, when fresh, a sharp and disagreeable odor, by which it may be known.

The Slender Meadow Grass, (*eragrostis pilosa*,) the Hair-panicled Meadow Grass, (*eragrostis capillaris*,) the Hairy Meadow Grass, (*eragrostis pectinacea*,) are found in this State, but they are of no special importance for cultivation. They all occur on sandy, dry, waste places, the last only near the coast, and all flower in August and September.

Quaking Grass, (*briza media*,) is sometimes met with in the eastern part of the State, as in the pastures of Dorchester. Panicle erect, with very slender spreading branches, and large, purplish, tremulous spikelets from five to nine flowered, inner glume finely fringed, entire at the end. (Fig. 36.) In Fig. 37 is shown a magnified spikelet. It is a very beautiful, light, slender grass, about a foot high, perennial. Flowering in June and July. There is an annual, the Large Quaking Grass, (*briza maxima*,) with large many-flowered spikes, cultivated in gardens for ornament.

Small Fescue Grass, (*festuca tenella*.) The generic characters of this genus are oblong spikelets, somewhat compressed, from three to many flowered, two very unequal glumes, pointed, paleæ roundish on the back, from three to five nerved, awn pointed or bristle shaped, stamens three, flowers harsh, often purplish, panicle nearly erect, leaves narrow, rigid, of a grayish green.

The small fescue has a spike-like panicle, somewhat one-sided, from seven to nine flowered, awn of the awl-shaped palea, slender, leaves bristle-formed, stem slender, six to twelve inches high. It flourishes on dry and sterile soils, and is common. Flowers in July.

Fig. 36. Quaking Grass.

SHEEP'S FESCUE, (*festuca ovina,*) is known by its narrow panicle, short, tufted, bristle-shaped leaves, of a grayish color, somewhat tinged with red, its two to six flowered spikelets, awn, often nearly wanting. It grows from six to ten inches high in dense perennial rooted tufts. It forms an excellent pasturage for sheep. It flowers in June and July, in dry pastures. In Fig. 38 is seen the form of this grass, and in Fig. 39 is shown a magnified spikelet of it.

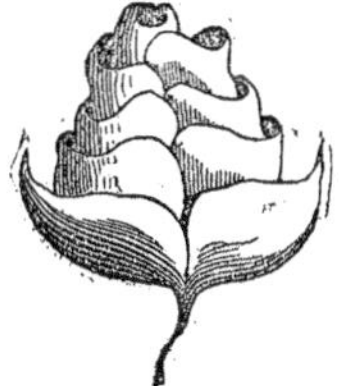
Fig. 37

MEADOW FESCUE, (*festuca pratensis,*) is one of the most common of the fescue grasses. It is said to be the Randall grass of Virginia. Its panicle is nearly erect, branched, close, somewhat inclined to one side; spikelets linear, with from five to ten cylindrical flowers; leaves linear, of a glossy green, pointed, striated, rough on the edges; stems round, smooth, from two to three feet high, roots, creeping, perennial. Its radical or root leaves are broader than those of the stem, while in most other species of fescue the radical leaf is generally narrower than those of the stem. Flowers in June and July, in moist pastures and near farm houses.

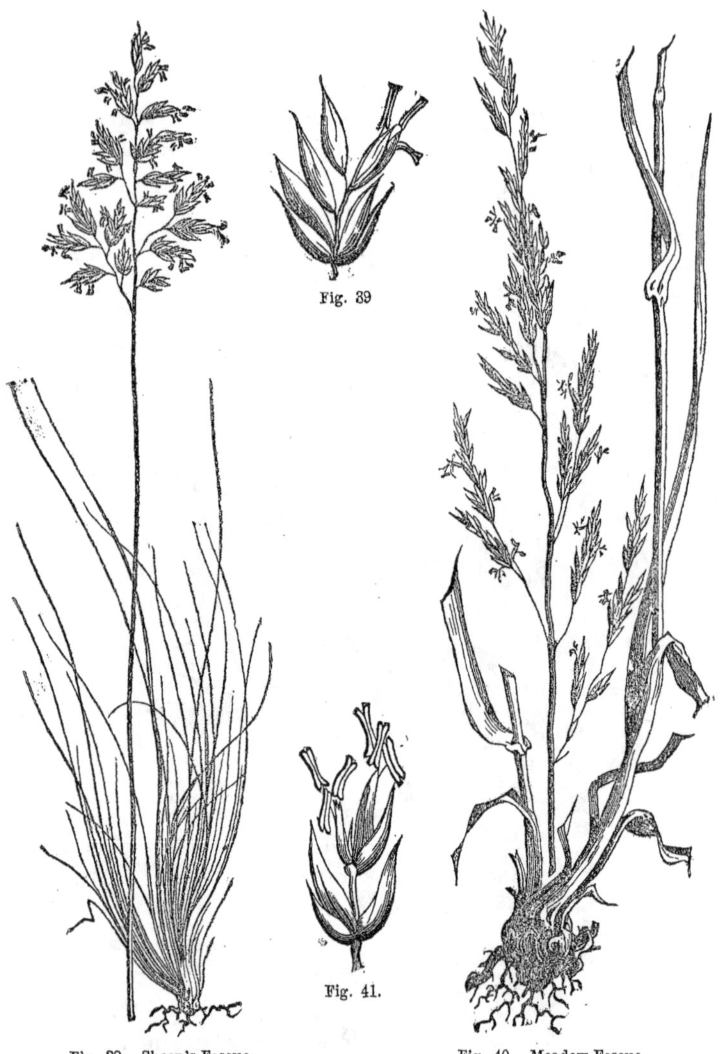

Fig. 39

Fig. 41.

Fig. 38. Sheep's Fescue.

Fig. 40. Meadow Fescue.

This is an excellent pasture grass, forming a very considerable portion of the turf of old pastures and fields, and is more extensively propagated and diffused by the fact that it ripens its seed before most other grasses are cut, and sheds them to spring up and cover the ground. Its long and tender leaves are much relished by cattle. It is never or rarely sown in this country, notwithstanding its great and acknowledged value as a pasture grass. If sown at all, it should be in mixture with other grasses, as orchard grass, rye grass, or common spear grass. It is of much greater value at the time of flowering than when

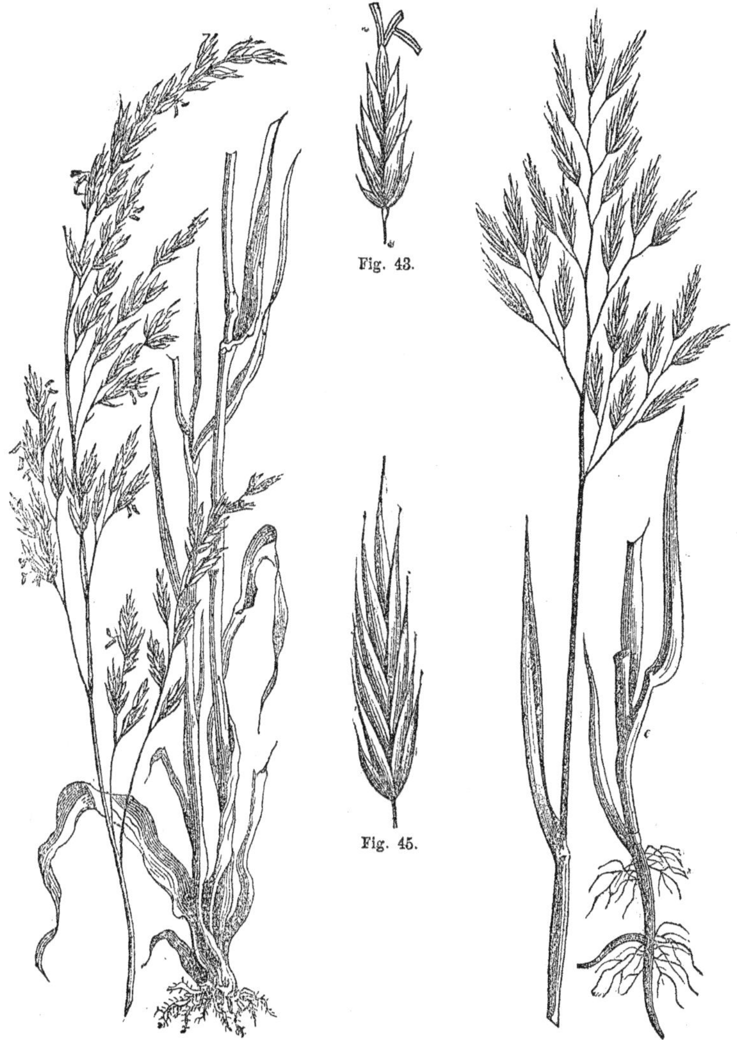

Fig. 43.

Fig. 45.

Fig. 42. Tall Fescue Grass.

Fig. 44. Red Fescue.

the seed is ripe. It is said to lose a little over fifty per cent. of its weight in drying for hay. It is shown in Fig. 40, and its magnified spikelet in Fig. 41.

The TALL FESCUE GRASS, (*festuca elatior*,) is also found pretty commonly in moist meadows and around farm houses. Its panicle is contracted, erect, or somewhat drooping, with short branches, spreading in all directions; spikelets crowded, with five to ten flowers, rather remote, oblong, lanceolate; leaves flatish, linear, acute; stems two to four feet high, root perennial, fibrous, somewhat creeping and forming large tufts. Fig. 42 shows this plant at the time of flowering, and Fig. 43 a magnified spikelet of the same. Flowers in June and July.

It is a nutritive and productive grass, growing naturally in shady woods and moist, stiff soils. Cattle are very fond of it. Said by some to be identical with the meadow fescue.

The Hard Fescue Grass, (*festuca duriuscula*,) is also found to some extent, though not so commonly as the meadow fescue. It is by some regarded as a variety of the sheep's fescue, taller and with a panicle more open, leaves flat, and spikelets four to eight flowered. It grows from one to two feet high. Flowers in June, in pastures and waste grounds.

The Red Fescue, (*festuca rubra*,) by some regarded as only a variety of the preceding, is one of the largest of the varieties of fescue. Its leaves are broadish, flat, root extensively creeping, and throwing out lateral shoots. Found in dry pastures near the sea shore, in sandy soils. It is a grass of better quality than some of the other varieties, but never cultivated here as an agricultural product. The color of its leaves is somewhat more grayish than the preceding and often tinged with red. It is shown in Fig. 44, while its spikelet is seen magnified in Fig. 45.

The Slender Spiked Fescue, (*festuca loliacea*,) is a species nearly allied to the tall fescue and possesses much the same qualities. It grows naturally in moist, rich meadows, forming a good permanent pasture grass, but as it is met with only very rarely, if ever, among American grasses, and is of no value for cultivation, it scarcely deserves a more extended notice. Fig. 46, a specimen of this plant in blossom. Fig. 47, a magnified flower of it.

The Nodding Fescue, (*festuca nutans*,) is also rarely met with in rocky woods, and needs only to be mentioned.

Crested Dog's Tail, (*cynosurus cristatus*.) (Fig. 48.) This grass is rarely found here, and scarcely needs description. Its spikes are simple, linear, spikelets awnless, stems one foot

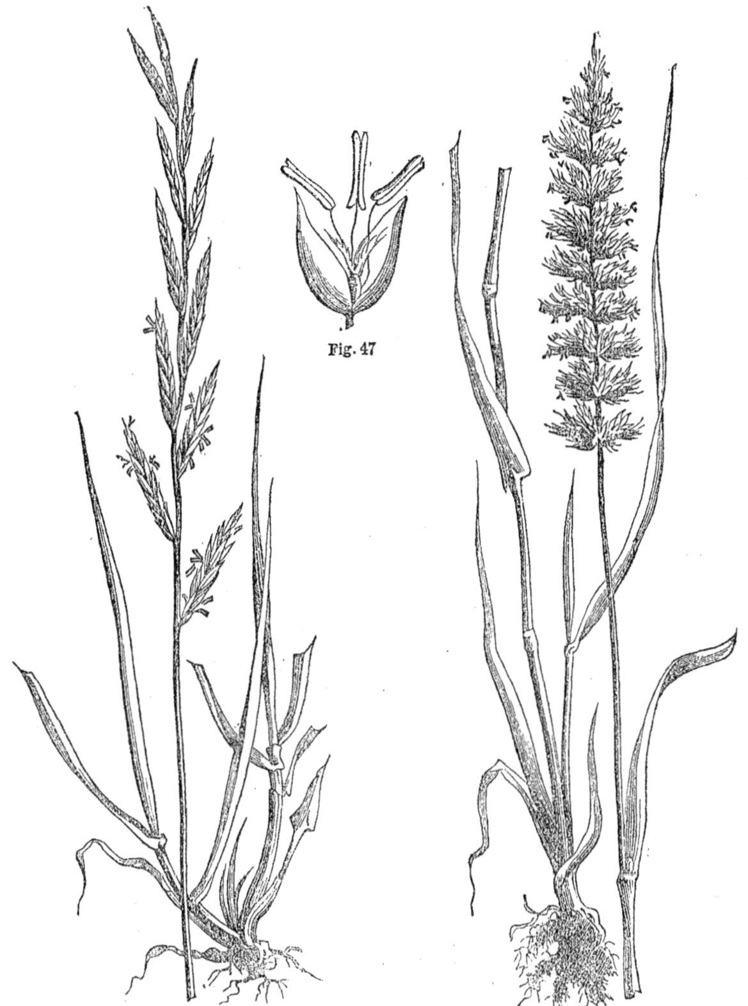

Fig. 47

Fig. 46. Slender Fescue.

Fig. 48. Crested Dog's Tail.

high, stiff, smooth, root perennial, fibrous and tufted. Flowers in July. It is said by some to be a valuable agricultural grass, but cattle seldom eat it, on account of its wiry stems; but on dry, hard soils and hills pastured with sheep, it is of value as a hardy, permanent grass. It is used in the manufacture of straw plait. Fig. 49 represents a magnified spikelet of the crested dog's tail.

WILLARD'S BROMUS, CHESS, CHEAT, (*bromus secalinus.*) The

characteristics of this genus (*bromus*) are, spikelets from five to many flowered, panicled, glumes not quite equal, shorter than the flowers, mostly keeled,—the lower, one to five, the upper, three to nine nerved,—paleæ herbaceous, lower one convex on the back, or compressed, keeled, five to nine nerved, awned or bristle pointed from below the tip, upper palea at length adhering to the groove of the oblong grain, fringed on the keel, stamens three, styles attached below the apex of the ovary. The grasses of this genus are coarse, with large spikelets, somewhat drooping generally when ripe.

The specific characteristics are, a spreading panicle slightly drooping, spikelets ovate, smooth, of a yellowish green tinge, showing the rachis when in seed, and holding from six to ten rather distinct flowers. In the spikelet exhibited in the cut, (Fig. 50,) seven can be distinctly counted, the eighth or ninth imperfectly developed can often be found; stems erect, smooth, round, from two to three feet high, bearing four or five leaves with striated sheaths; the upper sheath crowned with an obtuse, ragged ligule, the lower sheaths soft and hairy, the hairs pointing downwards; joints five, slightly hairy, leaves flat, soft, linear, more downy on the upper than on the under side, points and margin rough to the touch. *Summit of the large glume midway between its base and the summit of the second floret*, a constant mark of distinction from *bromus racemosus* and *bromus mollis*. (Fig. 50,) (b.) Fig. 51 shows the form of the spikelet a few days before coming to maturity. Flowers in June and July. It has no relation to Italian rye grass.

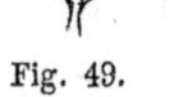
Fig. 49.

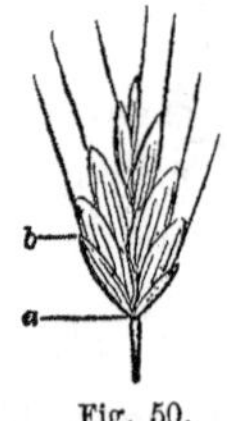

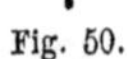
Fig. 50.

Fig. 51.

Distinguished from *bromus arvensis* in the spikelets having fewer florets, and the outer palea being rounded at the summit.

Nothing more clearly illustrates the want of accurate knowledge of subjects intimately connected with agriculture, and immediately affecting the farmers' interests, than the history of the introduction and propagation of this worthless pest to our grain fields. It has been heralded in the papers, in connection with the names of distinguished friends of agriculture, with the earnest hope that it might receive extended trials. Monstrous prices have been charged and paid by the unsuspecting farmer for its seed, in many cases four and five dollars a bushel, a pledge being exacted that it should not be allowed to go to seed, for a reason, probably, which will shortly appear. Committees of agricultural societies have been invited to examine and report upon it; and in a letter now lying before me, the disinterested propagator very kindly offers to put up ten barrels of bromus seed for $100, saying, that " of course the earliest applicants will be sure of obtaining till all is gone, which would scarcely give a barrel to a State. * * Years must elapse before the country can be supplied as it now is with Herds-grass and clover seed. My offer invites co-operation and participation in the profits and pleasures now available"—for taking advantage of the honest credulity of the public?

A quantity of bromus seed was sent to the State Farm for the purpose of experiment, with a letter with directions to sow with clover in the spring of 1855. The crop was cut while yet green, and before the grass had developed sufficiently to distinguish it with certainty. This present year (1856) directions were given to let it stand later in the season. While engaged in the collection and study of specimens in the course of the summer, I gathered samples of this grass when it was still immature, the spikelets having very much the appearance indicated in Fig. 51. Without giving it a very close examination at the time, I pronounced it the *bromus arvensis*, which at that stage of its growth it very much resembles. A few days after, I was astonished to see it develop into Chess (*bromus secalinus.*) This was the first ripe specimen of Willard's bromus I had seen. I examined it with care with a strong magnifying glass, and to avoid the possibility of mistake, I submitted specimens of it to Prof. Gray, of Cambridge, and to Prof. Dewey, of Rochester, New York, both of whom, after examination, pronounced it genuine chess.

But Mr. Willard having quoted from the report of a committee of an agricultural society in which it was said that if a "jury of cows should confirm the opinion of Mr. Willard as to the superiority of the grass, then will the agricultural community owe him a debt of gratitude for having introduced to notice here a species of grass which is highly beneficial on light sandy soils, much superior to any other species, and producing most abundantly on land of better quality," I very recently directed this grass to be submitted to such a jury, empanelled and kept under the charge of Mr. L. P. Chamberlain at the State Farm, which unhesitatingly pronounced a verdict in accordance with the facts, which were as follows:—

The grass which was first submitted for comparison with the bromus was the Reed Canary grass, (*phalaris arundinacea,*) a grass of very slight nutritive and palatable qualities, as will appear by reference on a subsequent page to the careful analysis made of it at my request by Prof. E. N. Horsford, of the Lawrence Scientific School, Cambridge. The English hay used was such as commonly goes by that name among farmers, made up of Timothy and Redtop mainly, of fair quality. The meadow or swale hay was taken from a wet meadow, made up of coarse swale grasses, such as are common in eastern Massachusetts, and pass under the term of "meadow hay." The bromus was carefully picked out from all other grasses. The two kinds given in each trial were put into the same crib, but separated by a partition.

First trial—Bromus and reed canary grass. There was no choice. Both were eaten alike till they were gone.

Second—Bromus and English hay; preferred English hay.
Third—Bromus and swale hay; " swale.
Fourth—Bromus and oat straw; " bromus.
Fifth—Canary grass and English hay; " English hay.
Sixth—Canary grass and swale; " swale at once.
Seventh—Canary grass and oat straw; " oat straw.
Eighth—Canary grass and cornstalks; " cornstalks.

Ninth—Bromus and cornstalks. Ate nearly alike of each till both were gone.

Tenth—Bromus and millet. Chose the millet and did not touch the bromus.

This is a true transcript of the verdict of that intelligent jury, and it is precisely what I should have anticipated from what I knew of the grasses. The trial by jury should be final.

It is unnecessary to say that "Cheat" is a troublesome weed

to the farmer, especially when it appears in his grain fields. It is an early grass, but the quantity of herbage, and especially its quality, make it unfit for cultivation. Indeed, the only species of any value, or at all fit for cultivation, belonging to this large genus of grasses, is the *bromus arvensis*, and even that has been discarded from modern agriculture.

I have been thus minute in speaking of this grass, because I have felt it my duty to disabuse the minds of farmers with regard to it, a duty in which I have recently, and since the above was written, been anticipated by my friend, Sanford Howard, Esq., author of a valuable paper on the Grasses, in the Transactions of the New York State Agricultural Society, for 1855.

I have but little acquaintance with, and no prejudice against, Mr. Willard, but regret exceedingly that he or any one else should make a mistake so serious to the community, and take so much pains to propagate " cheat." Fortunately the plant is annual. The fact of its having been cut before it was ripe, in 1855, accounts for its growing on the same piece in 1856.

SMOOTH BROME GRASS, or UPRIGHT CHESS, (*bromus racemosus*,) has a panicle erect, simple, rather narrow, contracted when in fruit. Flowers closer than in the preceding, lower palea exceeding the upper, bearing an awn of its own length. Stem erect, round, more slender than in chess, sheaths slightly hairy. In other respects it is very much like Willard's bromus, but may always be distinguished from it as well as from *bromus arvensis*, in the summit of the large glume being half-way between its base and the summit of the *third* floret, on the same side; whereas in Willard's bromus the summit of the large glume is half-way between its base and summit of the *second* floret. This character is constant, and offers the surest mark of distinction. It is common in grain fields. Flowers in June. It is worthless for cultivation.

SOFT CHESS, or SOFT BROME GRASS, (*bromus mollis*,) is sometimes found. I procured beautiful specimens of it at Nantucket, where it was growing in the turf with other grasses on a sandy soil near the shore. Its panicle is erect, closely contracted in fruit, spikelets conical, ovate, stems erect, more or less hairy, with the hairs pointing downwards from twelve to eighteen inches high, joints four or five, slightly hairy, leaves flat, striated, hairy on both sides, rough at the edges and points; summit of the large glume midway between its base and the apex of the third floret, by which it is always distinguished from Willard's bromus. Flowers in June. Birds are fond of the seed, which are large and ripen early. Of no value for cultivation.

The Wild Chess, (*bromus kalmii*,) is another species, found often in dry, open wood-lands. It has a small, simple panicle, with the spikelets drooping on hairy peduncles, seven to twelve flowered and silky; awn only one-third the length of the lance-shaped flower, stem slender, eighteen inches to three feet high, leaves and sheaths hairy. Flowers in June and July. Of no value for cultivation.

Fringed Brome Grass, (*bromus ciliatus*,) is often found in woods and on rocky hills and river banks. It has a compound panicle, very loose, nodding, spikelets seven to twelve flowered, flowers tipped with an awn half to three-fourths their length, stem three to four feet high, with large leaves. Flowers in July and August. Of no value for cultivation.

The Meadow Brome Grass, (*bromus pratensis*,) is a perennial weed in the corn fields of England, and is only recommended in any part of Europe for dry, arid soils, where nothing better will grow. Fig. 52 represents this grass, and Fig. 53 a magnified spikelet.

Not one of the brome grasses is worthy of a moment's attention as a cultivated agricultural grass, and the cleaner the farmer keeps his fields of them the better.

The Common Reed Grass, (*phragmites communis*,) is a very tall, broad-leaved grass, with the flower in a large terminal panicle. It looks at a little distance very much like broomcorn; stem five to twelve feet high. It grows on the borders of ponds and swamps. It is said to be the largest grass in the United States. It occurs in several localities in Franklin County, and it is not uncommon in the eastern part of the State. Flowers in September.

Perennial Rye Grass, common Darnel, (*lolium perenne.*) Generic characters—spikelets many flowered, solitary on each joint of the continuous rachis, placed edgewise. Specific characters—stem erect, smooth, fifteen inches to two feet high, root perennial, fibrous, joints four or five, smooth, often purplish, leaves dark green, lanceolate, acute, flat, smooth on the outer surface

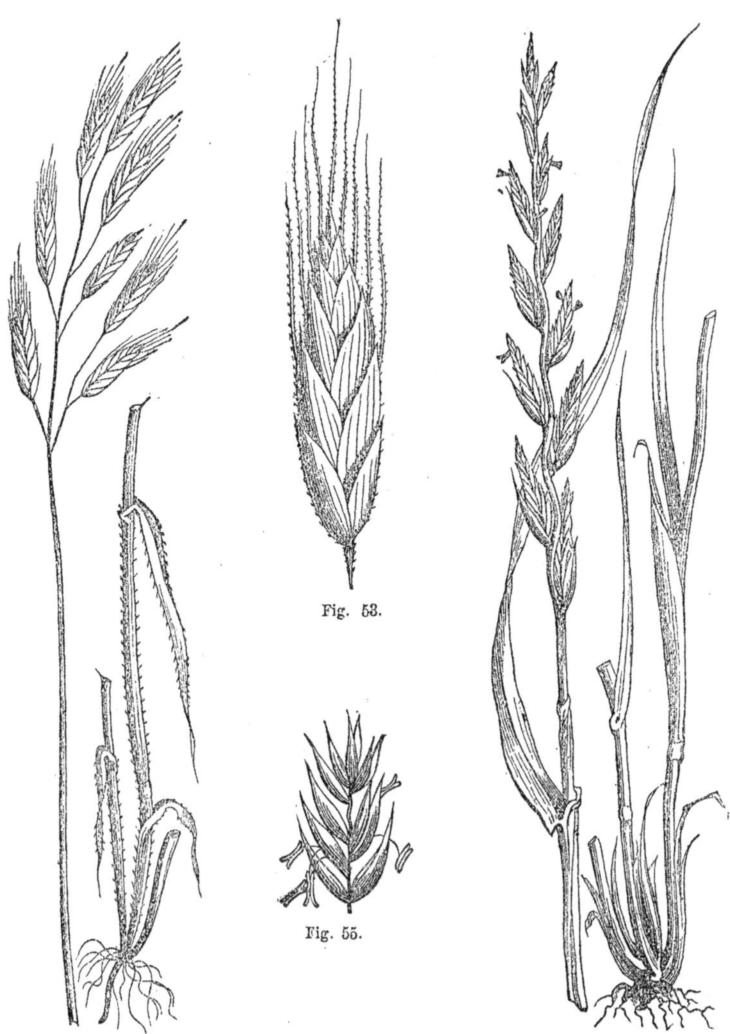
Fig. 53.

Fig. 55.

Fig. 52. Meadow Brome Grass.

Fig. 54. Rye Grass.

and roughish on the inner, glume much shorter than the spikelet, flowers six to nine, awnless. Flowers in June. Shown in Fig. 54. Fig. 55 represents a magnified spikelet of this plant.

This grass has had the reputation in Great Britain, for many years, of being one of the most important and valuable of the cultivated grasses. It is probably much better adapted to a wet and uncertain climate, than to one subject almost annually to droughts, which often continue many weeks, parching up every

8

green thing. There is, perhaps, no grass, the characteristics of which vary so much from the influences of soil, climate and culture as perennial rye grass. Certain it is that this grass has been cultivated in England since 1674, and in the south of France from time immemorial. It is admitted to be inferior in nutritive value to orchard grass, (*dactylis glomerata,*) when green.

Whenever it is cut for hay, it is necessary to take it in the blossom, or very soon after, since otherwise it becomes hard and wiry, and is not relished by stock of any kind; and it changes very rapidly after blossoming, from a state in which it contains the greatest amount of water, sugar, &c., and the least amount of woody fibre—into the state in which it possesses the least amount of water, sugar, &c., and the greatest amount of woody fibre and other insoluble solid matter. A specimen analyzed about the 20th of June, and found to contain 81¼ per cent. of water and 18¾ per cent. of solid matter, was found only three weeks later to contain only 69 per cent. water, and 31 per cent. solid matter. It is undoubtedly a valuable grass, and worthy of attention; but it is not to be compared, for the purposes of New England agriculture, to Timothy or to orchard grass. It produces abundance of seed, soon arrives at maturity, is relished by stock, likes a variety of soils, all of which it exhausts; lasts six or seven years, and then dies out.

Italian Rye Grass, (*lolium italicum,*) has been recently introduced into this State, and is now undergoing experiment which will assist in determining its value for us. It differs from perennial rye grass in the florets having long, slender awns, and from bearded darnel, (*lolium temulentum,*) in the glumes being shorter than the spikelets. This difference will be manifest on reference to Fig. 56, and Fig. 57, which represents a magnified spikelet. It turfs less than the perennial rye grass, its stems are higher, its leaves are larger and of a lighter green, it gives an early, quick and successive growth till late in the fall.

To say that it is, or would be, the best grass in our climate and on our soils, would be altogether premature; but it has the credit abroad of being equally suited to all the climates of Europe, giving more abundant crops, of a better quality, and better relished by animals than the perennial rye grass. It is one of the greatest gluttons of all the grasses either cultivated

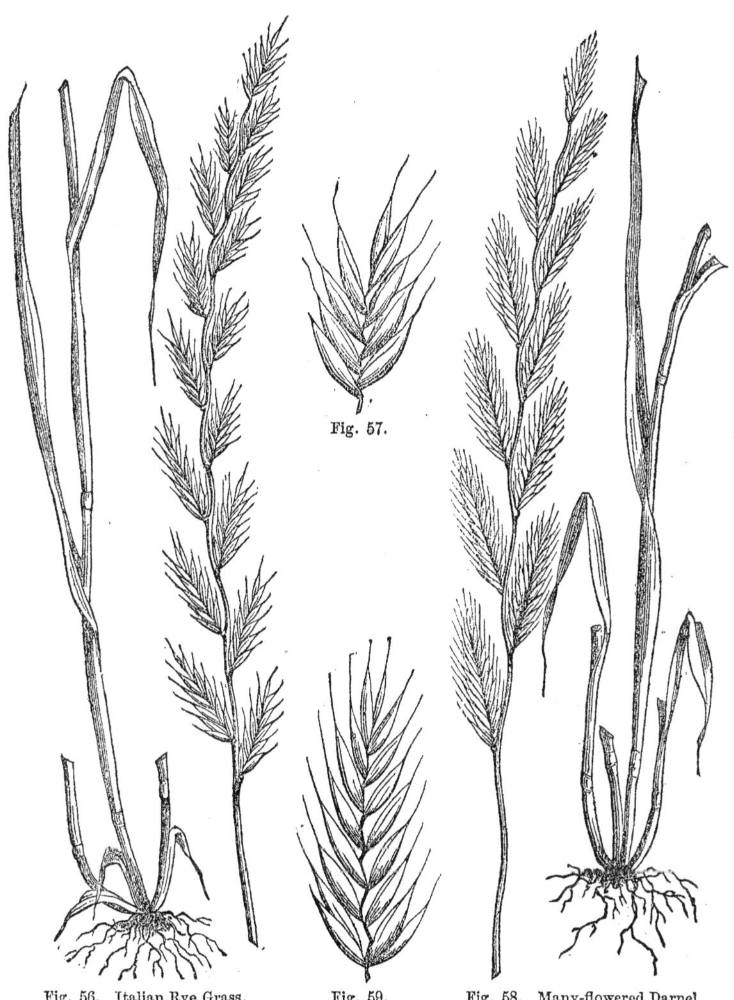
Fig. 57.

Fig. 56. Italian Rye Grass. Fig. 59. Fig. 58. Many-flowered Darnel.

or wild, and will endure any amount of forcing by irrigation or otherwise, while it is said to stand a drought remarkably well. The soils best adapted to it seem to be moist, fertile and tenacious, or of a medium consistency; and on such soils it is said to be one of the best grasses known to cut green for soiling, affording repeated luxuriant and nutritive crops. I have not seen enough of it to speak from personal observation or experience of the comparative profit of this grass and Timothy for cultivation here, but its comparative nutritive value is well known from the thorough and reliable analyses of Prof. Way. By these it appears that 100 parts of Timothy grass, as taken from the field, contain 57.21 per cent. of water, 4.86 per cent. of albuminous or flesh forming principles, 1.50 per cent. of fatty matters, 22.85 per cent. of heat producing principles, such as starch, gum, sugar, &c., 11.32 per cent. of woody fibre, and 2.26 of mineral matter or ash, while 100 parts of Italian rye grass taken from the same kind of soil and in the same condition, green, contained 75.61 per cent. of water, 2.45 of albuminous or flesh forming principles, .80 of fatty matters, 14.11 of heat producing principles, starch, gum and sugar, 4.82 of woody fibre, and 2.21 of mineral matter or ash. Of these, the flesh forming principles, fatty matters, and heat producing principles, are, of course, by far the most important; and in all these our favorite Timothy very far excels the Italian rye grass, showing a nutritive value nearly double. Nor has the Italian rye grass any advantage over Timothy or Herds-grass in the dried state, though the difference is by no means so marked, the former dried at 212° Fahrenheit containing 10.10 per cent. of flesh forming principles, the latter 11.36; the former containing 3.27 per cent. of fatty matter, the latter 3.55; the former containing 57.82 per cent. of heat forming principles, the latter 53.35.

There are 432,000 seeds in a pound of Italian rye grass and from thirteen to eighteen pounds in a bushel.

The Bearded Darnel, (*lolium temulentum*,) is sometimes found in our grain fields, with its glume equalling the five to seven flowered spikelets, and awn longer than the flower. Its grain is poisonous—almost the only instance known among the grasses.

The Many-Flowered Darnel, (*lolium multiflorum*,) is, perhaps, the most showy species of rye grass, cultivated. It is but very rarely, if ever, met with here, though it was introduced from France to England about thirty years ago, and is cultivated to some extent. Fig. 58 shows the appearance of this grass, and Fig. 59 a magnified spikelet. It is very nearly allied, if not identical with Italian rye grass.

Couch Grass, Quitch Grass, Twitch Grass, Dog Grass, Chandler Grass, &c., (*triticum repens*.) The chief generic marks of this grass are, three or several flowered spikelets, compressed, with the flat side towards the rachis; glumes nearly equal and opposite, nerved, lower palea like the glumes convex on the back, awned from the tip, upper flattened, stamens three; mostly annuals, but others are perennials, to which the couch grass belongs. The specific characters of couch grass are, roots creeping extensively, stem erect, round, smooth, from one to two or two and a half feet high, striated, having five or six flat leaves with smooth, striated sheaths; the joints are smooth, the two uppermost very remote, leaves dark green, acute, upper one broader than the lower ones, roughish, sometimes hairy on the inner surface, smooth on the lower half. Inflorescence in spikes. Flowers in June and July. Introduced from Europe. (Figs. 60 and 61.)

Fig. 60. Couch, or Twitch Grass.

Fig. 61.

This plant is generally regarded by farmers as a troublesome weed, and efforts are made to get rid of it. Its long, creeping roots, branching in every direction, take complete possession of the soil and impoverish it. When green, however, it is very much relished by cattle, and if cut in the blossom it makes a nutritious hay. Dogs eat the leaves of this grass and those of one other species for their medicinal qualities in exciting vomiting. I have seen acres of it on the Connecticut River meadows, where it had taken possession and grew luxuriantly, and is called wheat grass, from its resemblance to wheat. It goes in different parts of the State by a great variety of names, as Quake grass, Quack grass, Squitch grass. It is important to destroy it if possible, and the means of doing it will be alluded to on a subsequent page.

Squirrel-tail Grass, (*hordeum jubatum*,) is widely diffused over our salt marshes. Its specific characters are a slender stem, smooth, about two feet high, with rather short leaves, and low, lateral, abortive, neutral flowers on a short pedicel, short awned, the perfect flower bearing an extremely long awn about the length of the similar hairy glumes, all spreading. It is common on moist sands and marshes on the sea shore. Flowers in June.

The common two-rowed barley, (*hordeum distichum*,) belongs also to the same genus as well as the common four or six-rowed barley, (*hordeum vulgare*.)

Lyme Grass, Wild Rye, (*elymus virginicus*,) is frequent along the banks of rivers. Its generic characteristics are two to four spikelets at each joint of the rachis, all fertile, each one to seven flowered, glumes both on one side of the spikelet, paleæ two, lower one usually awned, mostly perennial, some species annual.

Specific description: Spike upright, dense and thick on a short peduncle usually included in the sheath; two or three spikelets together, two or three flowered, smooth; shortly awned, stamens three, stems stout, from two to three feet high, leaves broad and rough. Flowers in July and August. Of no special value as an agricultural grass.

Canadian Lyme Grass, (*elymus canadensis*.) Spike rather loose and curving at the extremity, spikelets mostly in pairs of three to five, long awned, rough, hairy flowers, the lance awl-shaped glumes, tipped with shorter awns, stem three to four feet high, root creeping, leaves broad, flat, linear, sheaths smooth and ligule short. Flowers in August. It is common on the banks of rivers.

Slender Hairy Lyme Grass, (*elymus striatus*,) is sometimes found in rocky woods and on the banks of streams, as the most slender and smallest flowered species of this genus. It flowers in July, and is so rare and of so little value as an agricultural grass, as not to need further description.

Upright Sea Lyme Grass, (*elymus arenarius*.) This grass, which much resembles beach grass, grows from two to five feet high, with a perennial long creeping root, stem erect, round, smooth, leaves long, narrow, hard, greyish, pointed, grooved, rolled in, smooth behind and rough on the inner surface. It flowers in July. Differs from the common beach grass in having a short obtuse ligule, and spikelets without footstalks, of three or four florets, while beach grass has a long and pointed ligule, and spikelets with footstalks, and of only one floret.

Sinclair calls this grass the sugar cane of Great Britain. It contains a large quantity of saccharine matter, and it is probable that mixed with beach grass, as it is in Holland, it would be valuable to cut up and mix with common hay for winter feed. It is used precisely as beach grass is here, to prevent the encroachments of the sea, and to arrest the drifting of sand. It is not found growing wild in this country as beach grass is. I have cultivated it, by way of a partial experiment, on Nahant Beach, and it has been sown in other parts of the country.

Bottle-brush Grass, (*gymnostichum hystrix,*) is found rather commonly in moist rocky woodlands, and along shaded banks of streams, and may be known by its loose upright spike and spreading spikelets, smooth sheaths and leaves, smoothish flowers tipped with an awn three times their length. Flowers in July.

Wood Hair Grass, or Common Hair Grass, (*aira flexuosa,*) is a common grass on our dry and rocky hills, and road sides, and high upon Wachuset Mountain. The generic name is the Greek *aira*, darnel, or tares, and its characteristics are, two flowered spikelets, in an open diffuse panicle; flowers both perfect, shorter than the glumes, hairy at the base, lower palea three to five nerved, awned on the back, grain oblong, smooth.

Specific characters: Stems slender, one to two feet high, nearly naked, leaves dark green, often curved, bristle-formed, branches of the panicle hairy, spreading, mostly in pairs, lower palea slightly toothed, awn starting near the base, bent in the middle, longer than the glumes, which are purplish—perennial. Flowers in June. This plant is sometimes found 3,500 feet above the level of the sea. Sheep eat it readily. Of no value for cultivation. Fig. 62 represents this grass in blossom, and Fig. 63 a magnified flower of it. It contains when dry but .63 per cent. of nitrogen.

Hassock Grass, (*aira cæspitosa,*) also belongs to this genus *aira.* Stems erect, round, roughish, in close tufts, leaves flat, linear, acute, with roughish striated sheaths, upper sheath longer than its leaf, panicle pyramidal or oblong, large, at first drooping, afterwards erect, with branches spreading in every direction; awn barely equalling the palea, outer palea of lower floret shorter than the glumes, membranous, jagged or four-toothed on the summit, hairy at the base, with slender awn rising from a little above the base, and extending scarcely above the palea. Distinguished from *aira flexuosa* in the awn of the lower floret not protruding beyond the glumes of the calyx. In *aira flexuosa* the awn of the lower floret protrudes more than one-third its length beyond the glumes.

It has an unsightly look in fields and pastures, on account of its growing in tufts or clusters or hassocks. Cattle seldom touch it. Prefers stiff or marshy bottoms, where the water stands. June.

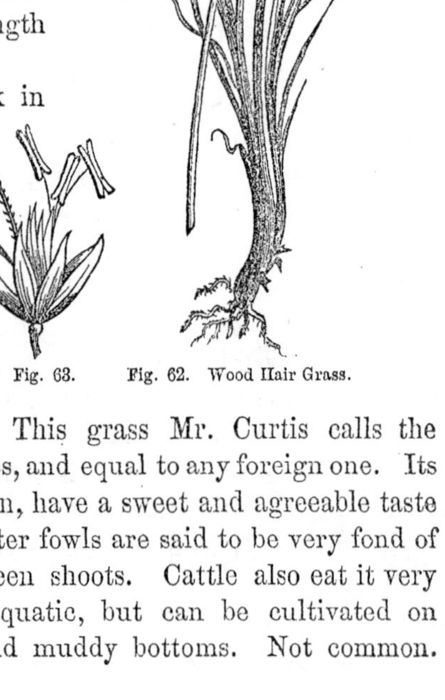

Fig. 63. Fig. 62. Wood Hair Grass.

WATER HAIR GRASS, (*aira aquatica.*) Fig. 64. This grass Mr. Curtis calls the sweetest of the British grasses, and equal to any foreign one. Its stems and leaves, when green, have a sweet and agreeable taste like that of liquorice. Water fowls are said to be very fond of the seeds and the fresh green shoots. Cattle also eat it very readily. It is strictly an aquatic, but can be cultivated on imperfectly drained bogs and muddy bottoms. Not common. It flowers in July.

Fig. 64. Water Hair Grass

Fig. 65. Downy Oat Grass.

WILD OAT GRASS, WHITE TOP, (*danthonia spicata*,) is common in dry, sunny pastures, with a stem one foot high, slender, with short leaves, narrow sheaths, bearded; panicle simple, spikelets seven flowered, lower palea broadly ovate, loosely hairy on the back, longer than its awl-shaped teeth—perennial. Flowers in June. It is called white top in some localities, but is not the grass most commonly known by that name—the agrostis alba.

Downy Persoon, (*trisetum mollis,*) is a grass with dense panicles, much contracted, oblong or linear, awn bent or diverging, lower palea compressed, keeled, leaves flat and short; found on rocky river banks and mountains, about one foot high. It flowers in July. Of no agricultural value.

The Downy Oat Grass, (*trisetum pubescens,*) is a very hardy perennial grass, naturalized on chalky soils, and on such soils its leaves are covered with a coating of downy hairs which it loses when cultivated on better lands. It is regarded as a good permanent pasture grass on account of its hardiness and its being but a slight impoverisher of the soil, and yielding a larger per cent. of bitter extractive than other grasses grown on poor, light soils. It is therefore recommended abroad as a prominent ingredient of mixtures for pastures. It flowers early in July. Fig. 65 represents this plant as it appears in blossom. Formerly classed as *avena pubescens.*

Meadow Oat Grass, (*avena pratensis,* Fig. 66,) is a perennial grass, native of the pastures of Great Britain, growing to the height of about eighteen inches. It furnishes a hay of medium quality. Flourishes best on dry soils. Flowers in July. Figs. 67 and 68 represent the flowers of this grass magnified.

The Yellow Oat Grass, (*avena flavescens,* now generally classified as *trisetum flavescens,*) can scarcely, perhaps, be regarded as naturalized here. It is a perennial plant of slow growth and medium quality, furnishing a hay containing about 1.79 per cent. of azote or nitrogen; suitable for dry meadows and pastures. It is sometimes regarded as a weed, growing about eighteen inches high. It fails if cultivated alone, but succeeds with other grasses, and is said to be the most useful for fodder, of the oat grasses. It grows best with the crested dog's tail and sweet scented vernal. It contains a larger proportion of bitter extractive than most other grasses, and for that reason is recommended by some English writers as a valuable pasture grass. It flowers in July. Fig. 69 represents this grass, and Fig. 70 a flower of it magnified.

Tall Meadow Oat Grass, or Tall Oat Grass, (*arrhenatherum avenaceum,*) is the avena elatior of Linnæus. Specific characters: Spikelets open panicled, two flowered, lower flower staminate, bearing a long bent awn below the middle of the back; leaves flat, acute, roughish on both sides, most on the

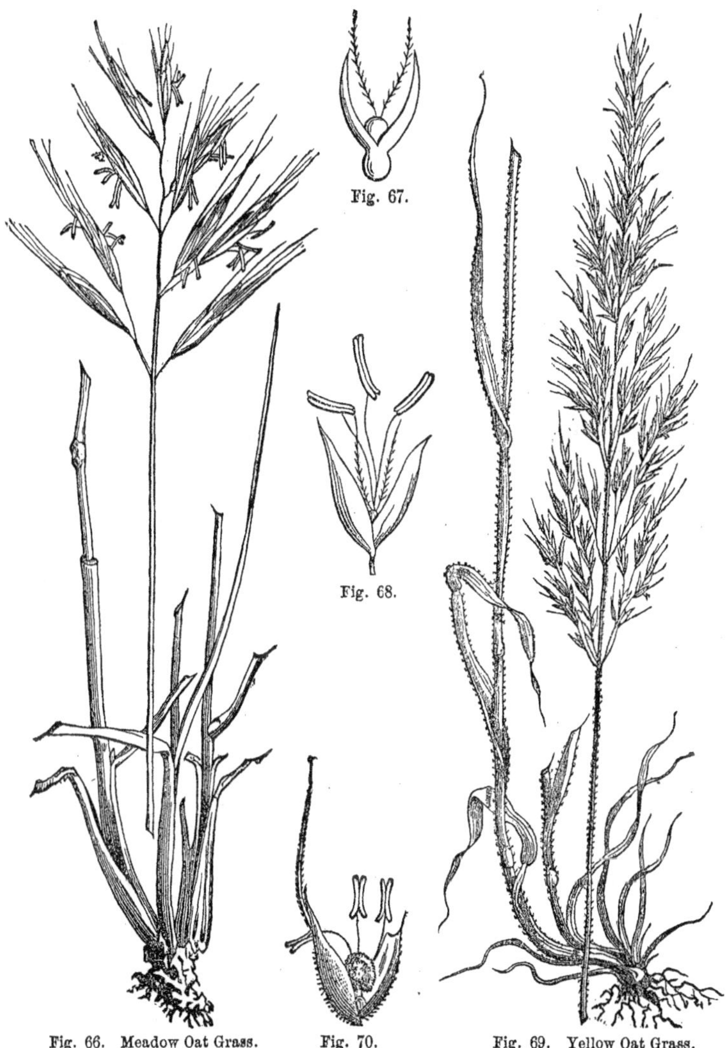

Fig. 66. Meadow Oat Grass. Fig. 70. Fig. 69. Yellow Oat Grass.

inner; panicle leaning slightly on one side, glumes very unequal; stems from two to three feet high, root perennial, fibrous, sometimes bulbous. It is readily distinguished from other grasses by its having two florets, the lower one having a long awn rising from a little above the base of the outer palea. Introduced. Flowers in June and July. Shown in Fig. 71. A magnified spikelet is seen in Fig. 72.

This is the Ray grass of France. It produces an abundant

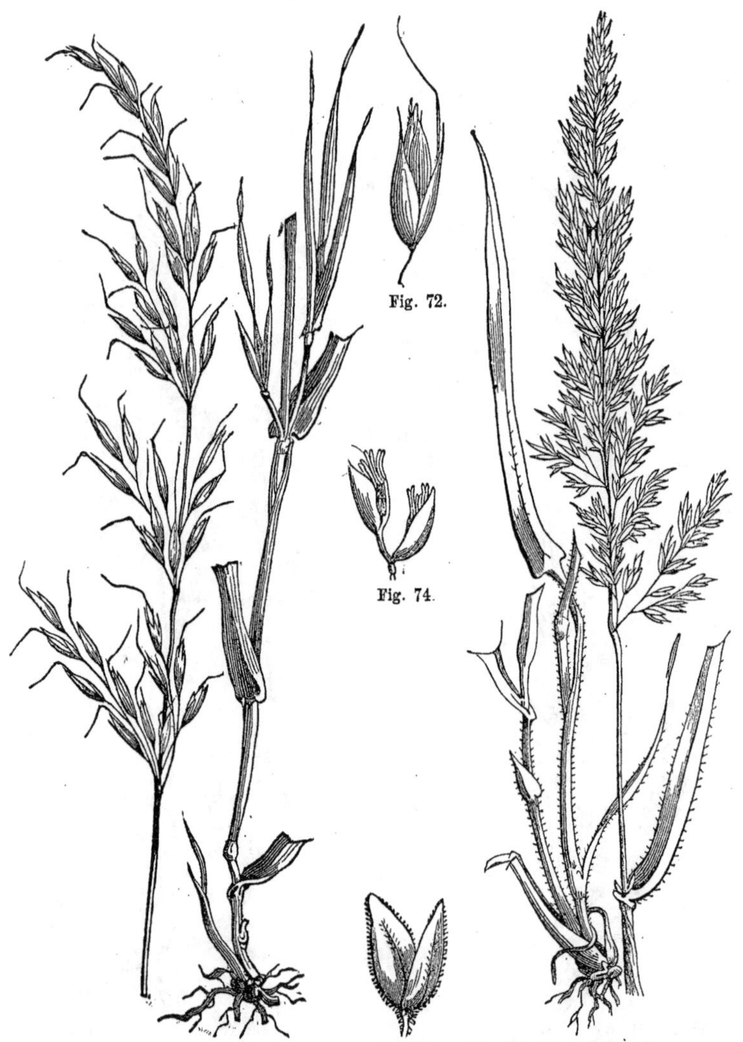

Fig. 71. Tall Meadow Oat Grass. Fig. 75. Fig. 73. Meadow Soft Grass.

supply of foliage, and is valuable either for hay or for pasture, and has been especially recommended for soiling purposes, on account of its early and luxuriant growth. It is often found on the borders of fields and hedges, woods and pastures, and sometimes very plenty in mowing lands. After being mown it shoots up a very thick aftermath, and on this account, partly, is regarded as nearly equal for excellence to the common foxtail, (*alopecurus pratensis.*)

It grows spontaneously on deep, sandy soils, when once naturalized. It has been cultivated to some extent in New England, and is esteemed by those who know it, mainly for its early, rapid and late growth, making it very well calculated as a permanent pasture grass. It will succeed on tenacious clover soils.

Meadow Soft Grass, Velvet Grass, (*holcus lanatus*,) has its spikelets crowded in a somewhat open panicle, and an awn with the lower part perfectly smooth. The generic characters are, two flowered spikelets jointed with the pedicels, glumes boat-shaped, membranaceous, inclosing and exceeding the flowers; lower flower perfect, its lower palea awnless and pointless, upper flower staminate only, bearing a stout bent awn below the apex. Stamens three; grain free, slightly grooved. This species grows from one to two feet high, stem erect, round, root perennial, fibrous, leaves four or five, with soft, downy sheaths, upper sheath much longer than its leaf, inflated, ligule obtuse, joints usually four, generally covered with soft, downy hairs the points of which are turned downwards; leaves pale green, flat, broad, acute, soft on both sides, covered with delicate slender hairs. Inflorescence compound panicled, of a greenish, reddish or pinkish tinge; hairy glumes, oblong, tipped with a minute bristle. Florets of two paleæ. Flowers in June. Introduced. In Fig. 73 is seen a drawing of this grass, and in Figs. 74 and 75, its flowers magnified.

This beautiful grass grows in moist fields and peaty soils, but I have found it on dry, sandy soils on Nantucket, and specimens have been sent me from Boxford and other places where it grew on upland fields, and was cultivated with other grasses. It is productive and easy of cultivation. It is of but little value either for pasture or hay, cattle not being fond of it. When once introduced it will readily spread from its light seeds which are easily dispersed by the wind. It does not merit cultivation except on poor, peaty lands, where better grasses will not succeed. This grass loses about .63 of its weight in drying, and the hay contains about 1.92 per cent. of nitrogen.

The Creeping Soft Grass, (*holcus mollis*, Fig. 76,) not yet naturalized here. It is of no value, and is regarded as a troublesome weed. Distinguished from the preceding by its

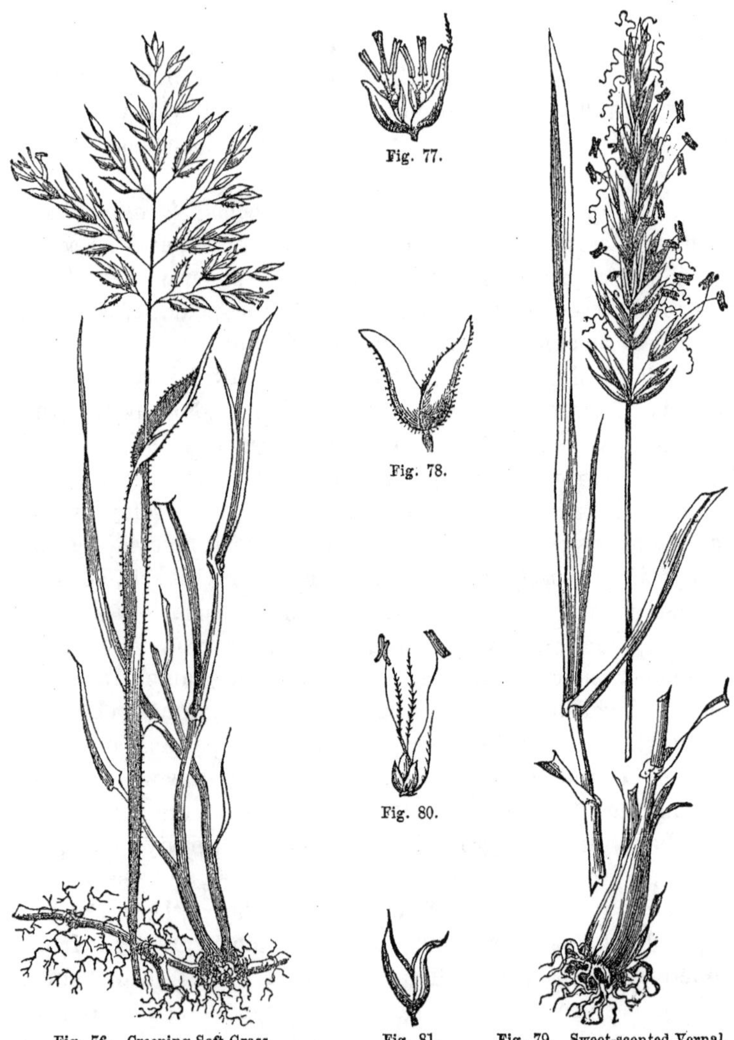

Fig. 77.

Fig. 78.

Fig. 80.

Fig. 76. Creeping Soft Grass.

Fig. 81.

Fig. 79. Sweet-scented Vernal.

awned floret and its creeping root. The flowers of this grass are seen magnified in Figs. 77 and 78.

SENECA GRASS, OR VANILLA GRASS, (*hierochloa borealis,*) has spikelets three flowered, flowers all with two paleæ, branches of the panicle smooth; grows from twelve to eighteen inches high. Stems erect, round, smooth, panicle somewhat spreading, rather one sided, leaves short, broad, lanceolate, rough on the inner side, smooth behind; spikelets rather large.

Grows in wet meadows. Flowers in May. Common and generally diffused, but of no value for cultivation, on account of its powerful, creeping roots and very slight spring foliage. It derived its generic name, *hierochloa*, holy grass, from two Greek words, signifying sacred grass,—from the fact that it was customary to strew it before the doors of the churches on festival and saint's days, in the north of Europe. In Sweden it is sold to be hung up over beds, where it is supposed to induce sleep.

SWEET SCENTED VERNAL GRASS, (*anthoxanthum odoratum.*) Specific characteristics: Spikelets spreading, three flowered, lateral flowers neutral, with one palea, hairy on the outside and awned on the back; glumes thin, acute, keeled, the upper twice as long as the lower; seed ovate, adhering to the palea which incloses it; root perennial. Flowers in May and June. Stems from one and a half to two feet high. Introduced from Europe. This grass is seen in Fig. 79.

This is one of the earliest spring grasses, as well as one of the latest in the autumn. It is almost the only grass that is fragrant. It possesses a property peculiar to this species, or possessed by only a few others, known as coumarin. It is said to be this which not only gives it its own aromatic odor, but imparts it to other grasses with which it is cured. The green leaves when bruised give out this perfume to the fingers, and the plant may thus be known. The grass has but little value of itself, its nutritive properties being slight; nor is it much relished by stock of any kind, but as a pasture grass on almost all soils, and with a large mixture of other grasses, it is very valuable for its early growth, and this gives it the character of a permanent pasture grass.

It is not uncommon in our pastures and road sides, growing as if it were indigenous. I have found fine specimens of it on dry soils at Nantucket and elsewhere.

The aftermath or fall growth of this beautiful grass is said to be richer in nutritive qualities than the growth of the spring. Though it is pretty generally diffused over the country, it is only on certain soils that it takes complete possession of the surface and forms the predominant grass in a permanent turf, as it is said to do in some sections around Philadelphia. The flavor of the spring butter sold in that city is ascribed by some to the prevalence of this grass. There seems to be nothing inconsistent in this supposition, since it is well known that disagreeable flavors are often imparted to the milk and the butter by the substances taken as food by the cow, as turnips, for instance, or cabbages, or cauliflowers; and if an objectionable flavor may be imparted by one substance, it is reasonable to suppose an opposite flavor may be given by another. Much, of course, depends on the manufacture; as poor butter is found in the Philadelphia market, as in any other, while as good could be, and is found, in the Boston market as any in the world. The best butter, I learn on inquiry, is as expensive in the former city as elsewhere, while it is true that a high price will command and obtain a good article wherever the art of butter making is at all understood.

I am informed by Dr. Emerson, of Philadelphia, to whom I am indebted for valuable specimens of this grass, that he has made experiments in flavoring other grasses with a slight addition of benzoic acid in the form of an essence, previous to feeding them out to milch cows, and that the flavor of the best Philadelphia spring butter was thus imparted to the butter made from them.

A curious and beautiful peculiarity is exhibited in the seeds of this grass, by which they are prevented from germinating in wet weather after approaching maturity, and thus becoming abortive. The husks of the blossom adhering to the seed when ripe, and the jointed awn by its spiral contortions, when affected by the alternate moisture and dryness of the atmosphere, act like levers to separate and lift it out from the calyx even before the grass is bent or lodged and while the spike is still erect. If the hand is moistened and the seeds placed in it, they will appear to move like insects, from the uncoiling of the spiral twist of the awns attached to them.

The flowers of the sweet scented vernal grass are seen in Figs. 80 and 81. There are 923,200 seeds in a pound, and eight pounds in a bushel. It cannot be said to belong to the grasses useful for general cultivation.

REED CANARY GRASS, (*phalaris arundinacea.*) Generic characteristics: Spikelets crowded in a dense or spiked panicle, perfect flower flattish with two neutral rudiments of flowers, one on each side at its base, awnless, two shining paleæ, closely inclosing the smooth, flattened grain; stamens three.

Specific description: panicle very slightly branched, clustered, somewhat spreading when old, but not so much generally, as appears in Fig. 82; glumes wingless, rudimentary florets hairy, stem round, smooth, erect, from two to seven feet high, leaves five or six in number, broad, lightish green, acute, harsh, flat, ribbed, central rib the most prominent, roughish on both surfaces, edges minutely toothed, smooth, striated sheaths. Flowers in July. Grows on wet grounds by the sides of rivers and standing pools, best suited to somewhat tenacious soils.

Fig. 82. Reed Canary Grass. Fig. 83.

A beautiful variety of this species is the RIBBON or STRIPED GRASS of the gardens, familiar to every one. The reed canary grass grows in the utmost luxuriance at the State Farm, at Westborough, and produces a large and early crop. It will bear cutting two or three times in a season, but if not cut early, the foliage is coarse. Cattle are not fond of it at any stage of its growth, but if cut early and well cured, they will eat it in the winter if they can get nothing better. For some experiments with this hay in comparison with others, see p. 61.

This grass is common in low, rich soils where the water is either standing or sluggish, and is not unfrequently produced by transplanting the roots of the striped grass into suitable soils. In one instance within my knowledge, it came in and produced an exceedingly heavy crop, simply from roots of ribbon grass which had been dug up from a garden and thrown into the brook to get them out of the way. Several other instances of a smilar nature have also come to my notice. One farmer has propagated it extensively in his wet meadows by forcing the ripe seed panicles into the mud with his feet. As the stripe of the ribbon grass is only accidental, dependent on location and soil, it constitutes only a variety of the reed canary grass and loses the stripe when transferred to a wet and muddy soil.

The cut, Fig. 82, was made from a specimen too far advanced to show this grass as it ordinarily appears; the panicle or head is too spreading and not sufficiently long. I have fine specimens with panicles three times as long as appears in the drawing, and more in the shape of a spike of Timothy.

To ascertain the exact nutritive qualities of this grass when cured as hay, a careful analysis has been made at my request, by Prof. E. N. Horsford, of Cambridge, with the following result: Of water, the specimen contained 10.42 per cent.; ash, 5.31 per cent.; nitrogen, .55 per cent.; nitrogenous ingredients, flesh forming principles, 3.53 per cent.; woody fibre, starch, gum, sugar, &c., 80.73 per cent.* It will be seen by

* The following are the details of this valuable analysis :—

1st. Of the Leaves stripped from the Culms or Stalks;
2d. Of the Stalks from which the Leaves and Joints were removed; and
3d. Of the Joints.

Weight of different portions of the Plant.

		Grammes.	Av. Gr's.
I.	Leaves of four Stalks, air-dried, weighed, ...	2.9239	2.8989
II.	" " " " "	2.8740	
I.	Four Stalks, without Joints, or Leaves, air-dried, weighed, . .	4.1167	3.6592
II.	" " " " " . . .	3.2018	
I.	Joints of four Stalks, air-dried, weighed, ...	.5161	.4624
II.	" " " "	.4088	
	Average Total, ...	7.0205 Grammes.	
	Average weight of Stalks with Leaves and Joints,	1.7551 Grammes.	

Water Determination.

I. Of the Leaves, .9234 grammes lost at a temperature of 212° Fah. .1014 grammes—equal to 10.98 per cent.
II. Of the Stalks, 1.9836 grammes lost at 212° Fah. .1902 grammes—equal to 9.58 per cent.
III. Of the Joints. 2.4529 grammes lost at 212° Fah. .2630 grammes—equal to 10.72 per cent.

Ash Determination.

I. Of the Leaves, air-dried, 2.9239 grammes gave .2590 grammes Ash—equal to 8.85 per cent.
II. Of the Stalks, air-dried, 4.1167 grammes gave .1475 grammes Ash—equal to 3.58 per cent.
III. Of the Joints, air-dried, .5161 grammes ga e .0181 grammes Ash—equal to 3.50 per cent.

reference to a subsequent page, containing analyses by Prof. Way, that this grass is very far inferior to many of the grasses examined by him. The panicles of this grass if allowed to stand after the time of flowering, become filled with ergot, or long, black spurs, issuing from between the glumes, and occu-

None of the above ashes effervesced with acid, indicating the absence of carbonates. They gave but the faintest reaction for lime. Indeed microscopic, as well as chemical examination, showed the Ash to be composed almost entirely of Silica.

Nitrogen Determination.

I. Of the Leaves, 1.4370 grammes, air-dried, gave .2600 grammes of Platino-Chloride of Ammonium—equal to 1.13 per cent. of Nitrogen, and 7.21 per cent. of Nitrogenous ingredients.
II. Of the Stalks, air-dried, 1.6009 grammes gave .0205 grammes Platino-Chloride of Ammonium—equal to .08 per cent. of Nitrogen, and .51 per cent. of Nitrogenous ingredients.
III. Of the Joints, air-dried, 2.4529 grammes gave .1789 grammes Platino-Chloride of Ammouium—equal to .45 per cent. of Nitrogen, and 2.87 per cent. of Nitrogenous ingredients.

The preceding results, in tabular form, appear as follows:—

Relative Weight of different portions.

	Average	of one	percentage.
Leaves of four Stalks, ...	2.8989 grammes.	.7247 grammes.	41.29
Four Stalks, ...	3.6592	.9148	52.12
Joints of four Stalks, ...	.4624	.1156	6.59
			100.00

Average weight of one plant without the roots, ... 1.7551 grammes.

Percentages.

	Water.	Ash.	Nitrogen.	Nitrogenous Ingredients.*	Woody Fibre, Starch, Sugar, &c.
Leaves, . .	10.98	8.85	1.13	7.21	72.96
Stalks, . .	9.58	3.58	.08	.51	86.33
Joints, . .	10.72	3.50	.45	2.87	82.91

For comparison as to the relative nutritive values, there follow some determinations made of hay from several localities by Henneberg and Thos. Way.

Hay analyzed gave		Nitrogen.	Nitrogenous Ingredients.
For Leaves, ...	1.13	5.71 per cent.†	3.53 per cent.
For Stalks, . . .	.08		
For Joints, ...	.45		
Clover, ...		1.57	10.01 "
Hay, No. 1, saline soil, . .		1.49	9.51 "
" No. 2, May, ...		1.39	8.87 "
" " June, ...		1.49	9.51 "
" " October, ...		1.70	10.85 "

It will be seen that some of the samples contain nearly three times as much of Nitrogenous Ingredients as the sample submitted for examination, and it will be inferred from this consideration that, other things being equal, the hay at the head of the list is decidedly inferior in nutritive value.

* Three parts of Nitrogen correspond with 19.16 parts of Nitrogenous Ingredients, as vegetable albumen, fibrin and casein.

† Estimated according to percentages of different parts.

pying the place of grain. This, if there were no other reason, would be sufficient to determine that it should be cut at or before the time of flowering. I have never seen rye worse affected than my specimens of this grass are. The effects of this mysterious disease are well known. The noxious power it exerts on the system of animals which receive even a small portion of it, is oftentimes dreadful, producing "most horrible gangrenes, rotting of the extremities, internal tortures and agonizing death; it has been known to slough and kill not a few human beings who have accidentally or inadvertently eaten grain or flour infected with it."

The flower of the reed canary grass is shown in Fig. 83. The variety called striped grass, (*colorata*,) is exceedingly hardy and may be propagated to any extent by dividing and transplanting the roots. In moist soil it spreads rapidly and forms a thick mass of fodder which might be repeatedly cut without injury, though it is of little value for feeding stock.

The COMMON CANARY GRASS, (*phalaris canariensis*,) is cultivated in gardens, and to some extent in fields and waste places for the sake of the seed for the canary bird. It has a spiked, oval panicle, glumes wing-keeled; rudimentary flowers smooth and half the length of the perfect one. Flowers in July and August.

MILLET GRASS, (*millium effusum*,) is found growing commonly in moist, shady woods, mountain meadows, and on the borders of streams. Panicle widely diffuse, compound, glumes ovate, very obtuse, leaves broad and flat, thin, root perennial, flower oblong. Flowers in June. Introduced. Of no value for cultivation, the foliage possessing but slight nutritive qualities. The seeds are sought by birds. It will thrive transplanted to open places.

HAIRY SLENDER PASPALUM, (*paspalum setaceum*,) has an erect or decumbent, slender culm, from one to two feet high, leaves and sheaths hairy, spikes slender, smooth, mostly solitary on a long peduncle, spikelets narrowly two rowed. Flowers in August. It is found on sandy fields and plains near the coast, and is rather common.

SLENDER CRAB GRASS, (*panicum filiforme*,) is another species of the subgenus digitaria, or finger grasses, and resembles the last somewhat, but the *upper glume equals the flower*, while the lower is nearly wanting, and the spikes are more erect. It flourishes on sandy, dry soils, especially near the coast. Flowers in August. Of no value for cultivation.

SMOOTH CRAB GRASS, (*panicum glabrum*,) resembles the last, with the spikes digitate, three to four, spreading, rachis flat and thin, spikelets ovoid. It is common in cultivated grounds, waste places, and on sandy fields. Flowers in August and September. A troublesome weed.

FINGER GRASS, COMMON CRAB GRASS, (*panicum sanguinale*.) The panic grasses are widely spread and common over the State. The generic characters are, two flowered panicled spikelets, flowers with or without awns, glumes two, lower one short or minute, the upper long as the fertile flower, upper flower perfect, closed, flattish, awnless, stamens three.

The stems of the finger grass are from one to two feet high, erect, spreading, leaves and sheaths hairy, spikes four to fifteen, digitate, upper glume half the length of the flower, lower one small. This grass grows on waste or neglected cultivated grounds and gardens, and yards, and is generally regarded as a troublesome weed. Introduced. Flowers from August to October.

AGROSTIS-LIKE PANIC GRASS, (*panicum agrostoides*,) differs from the preceding species in having the stems flattened, upright, two feet high, leaves long, sheaths smooth, spikelets on the spreading branches crowded and one sided, *ovate*, *oblong*, *acute*, purplish. It is common on wet meadows and borders of rivers. Flowers in July and August.

PROLIFIC PANIC GRASS, (*panicum proliferum*,) grows on brackish marshes and meadows, and is common along the coast. It sometimes appears on dry places. Cattle are fond of it. It differs from the preceding in having culms thickened, succulent, branched and bent, ascending from a procumbent base, and spikelets appressed, lance-oval, of a pale green color.

HAIR STALKED PANIC GRASS, (*panicum capillare*,) grows in sandy soils and cultivated fields every where. Its culm is upright, often branched at the base, and forming a tuft, sheaths flattened, very hairy, panicle pyramidal, hairy, compound and very loose, spikelets scattered on long pedicels, oblong, pointed. Flowers in August and September.

TALL SMOOTH PANIC GRASS, (*panicum virgatum*.) Stems

upright, three to five feet high, leaves very long, flat, panicle large, loose and compound, branches spreading when grown, and drooping, spikelets scattered, oval, pointed, glumes usually purplish. Grows pretty commonly in moist, sandy soils, and flowers in August.

BROAD-LEAVED PANIC GRASS, (*panicum latifolium.*) This is a grass with a perennial, fibrous root, and stem from one to two feet high, and leaves broad, long, taper-pointed, smooth or slightly downy, branches of panicle spreading, spikelets long, obovate, downy. Flowers in June and July. It is common in moist thickets and woods. Of no value for cultivation.

The HIDDEN-FLOWERED PANIC GRASS, (*panicum clandestinum,*) the YELLOW PANIC GRASS, (*panicum xanthophysum,*) the POLYMORPHUS PANIC GRASS, (*panicum dichotomum,*) the FEW-FLOWERED PANIC GRASS, (*panicum depauperatum,*) the WARTY-FLOWERED PANIC GRASS, (*panicum verrucosum,*) are sometimes found, the first, in low thickets and along the banks of rivers, not very common; the second, on dry and sandy soils, pine plains, rare; flowers in June; the third, in dry and low grounds, not very common, flowers in June and July; the fourth, on dry, sandy hill-sides, more common than the preceding; the fifth, in sandy swamps, near the coast. None of these are valuable for cultivation, nor are they troublesome as some of the preceding species of panic are, on account of their places of growth.

BARN GRASS, or BARNYARD GRASS, (*panicum crus-galli,*) is more common. Its spikes are alternate and in pairs, sheaths smooth, rachis bristly, stem from two to four feet high, stout, erect, or somewhat procumbent, leaves half an inch broad, panicle dense, pyramidal, glumes acute, awn variable in length and sometimes wanting, outer palea of the neutral flower, usually awned; one or two varieties have rough or bristly sheaths. It grows on moist, rich or manured soils and along the coast in ditches. Flowers in August, September and October.

Some experiments have been made to cultivate this common species in the place of millet, to cut for green fodder. It is relished by stock and is very succulent and nutritive.

HUNGARIAN MILLET, MOHA DE HONGRIE, (*panicum germanicum,*) has been cultivated to some extent in this State, from seed received through the Patent Office. It is an annual forage plant introduced into France in 1815, where its cultivation has become considerably extended. It germinates readily, withstands the drought remarkably, remaining green even when other vegetation is parched up, and if its development is arrested by dry weather, the least rain will restore it to vigor. It has numerous succulent leaves which furnish an abundance of green fodder, very much relished by all kinds of stock.

It flourishes in somewhat light and dry soils, though it attains its greatest luxuriance in soils of medium consistency and well manured. It may be sown broadcast and cultivated precisely like other varieties of millet. This millet is thought to contain a somewhat higher percentage of nutriment than the common millet, though I am not aware that it has been analyzed. A practical farmer of Worcester county says of it: "I have raised the "Moha de Hongrie," on a small scale only. In my garden it has grown *thick* and *fine*.

"As it is a leafy plant and remains green until its seeds mature, I think it may prove valuable for fodder, both green and dry. It grows and matures in about the same time as the common millet.

"I have now one bushel of seed, grown on six square rods. This quantity will enable me to test it practically, another season."

This plant is seen in Fig. 84, which gives a correct representation of it.

The Bristly Foxtail, (*setaria verticillata*,) is a grass sometimes, though rarely, found about farm houses. It has cylindrical spikes two or three inches long, pale green, somewhat interrupted with whorled, short clusters, bristles single or in pairs, roughened or barbed downwards, short. Not cultivated.

Bottle Grass, sometimes called Foxtail, (*setaria glauca*.) This is an annual with a stem from one to three feet high, leaves broad, hairy at the base, sheaths smooth, ligule bearded, spike two to three inches long, dense, cylindrical, bristles six to eleven in a cluster, rough upwards, perfect flower wrinkled. The spike is of a tawny or dull orange yellow when old. Flowers in July. It is common in cultivated grounds and barnyards. Introduced.

The Green Foxtail, sometimes also called Bottle Grass,

(*setaria viridis*,) has a spike cylindrical, more or less compound, green, bristles few in a cluster, longer than the spikelets, flower perfect, striate lengthwise and dotted. It is common in cultivated grounds.

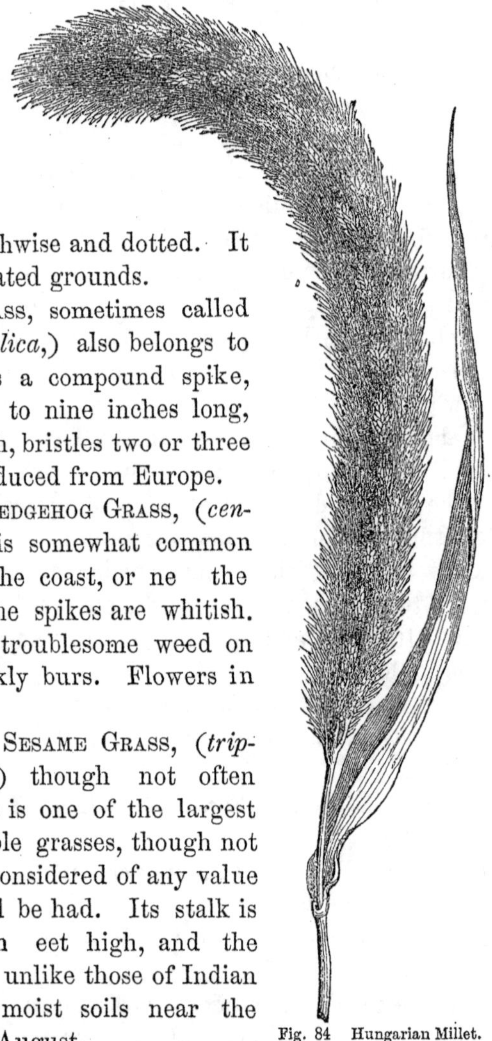

The BENGAL GRASS, sometimes called MILLET, (*setaria italica*,) also belongs to this genus. It has a compound spike, thick, nodding, six to nine inches long, yellowish or purplish, bristles two or three in a cluster. Introduced from Europe.

BUR GRASS, or HEDGEHOG GRASS, (*cenchrus tribuloides*,) is somewhat common on sandy soils on the coast, or ne the salt water, where the spikes are whitish. It is regarded as a troublesome weed on account of its prickly burs. Flowers in August.

GAMA GRASS, or SESAME GRASS, (*tripsacum dactyloides*,) though not often found in this State is one of the largest and most remarkable grasses, though not one that would be considered of any value where better could be had. Its stalk is from four to seven eet high, and the leaves look not very unlike those of Indian corn. Grows on moist soils near the coast. Flowers in August.

Fig. 84 Hungarian Millet.

FINGER-SPIKED WOOD GRASS, (*andropogon furcatus*.) Of this genus about sixty species are known to botanists. But few of these are indigenous to this country. Its generic characteristics are, a neuter or staminate lower flower, glumes and paleæ often wanting, upper flower perfect, glumes awnless, lower palea awned. Flowers in panicles and spikes.

Specific description: Stems four feet high, leaves nearly smooth, spikes digitate or generally by threes and fours, lower flower awnless; the spikelets are roughish, downy, awn bent. Flowers in September. This grass is common on sterile soils, rocky banks and hill-sides. Not cultivated.

PURPLE WOOD GRASS, or BROOM GRASS, (*andropogon scoparius*,) and the INDIAN GRASS, or WOOD GRASS, (*andropogon nutans*,) grow on sterile and dry, barren soils, and sandy plains, and are common, though of no value for cultivation. They flower from July to September.

The CHINESE SUGAR CANE, (*sorghum saccharatum?* not yet finally classified.) Panicle open or spreading, spikelets two or three, the lateral ones sterile, the middle or terminal one fertile, glumes tough and hard, sometimes awnless, stamens three.

Specific description: Stem from six to fifteen feet high, according to the soil on which it grows, erect, smooth, leaves linear, flexuous, gracefully curving down at the ends, resembling Indian corn in its early growth, and broomcorn, to which it is nearly allied, at maturity. Flowers in a panicle at the top, at first green, changing through the shades of violet to purple, when more advanced. See Fig. 85, taken from a plant somewhat over seven feet in height.

This plant has lately been introduced and used both for forage and the manufacture of sugar and molasses or sirup. In some instances it has been used for making vinegar, brandy and other liquors. As it is a true grass, and is at present exciting considerable interest throughout the country, it is proper to notice it in this connection.

The genus sorghum embraces over thirty species, most of which originated in Asia, where some of them have been cultivated time out of mind. Specimens of the sorghum saccharatum were introduced into France by means of the seed, about six or eight years ago, where they have been cultivated with considerable success. So far as we know, this species is the best and most valuable for cultivation for the various purposes alluded to. Most of the seeds first used in this country were obtained from France, through the efficient agency of the Patent Office, at Washington, having been first cultivated in the spring of 1855.

Any positive assertions with respect to the value of this plant, would, perhaps, be premature, but I have had very good opportunities of observation upon it, and have met many individuals from different latitudes who have cultivated it with great success, and numerous experiments upon it are still in progress, which will determine its relative value and its modes of cultivation. It is, undoubtedly, very rich in saccharine matter in all latitudes within the geographical range of Indian corn. It has been said that the percentage of sugar decreases somewhat in the higher latitudes; but this does not seem to have been established as a fact, and the opposite conclusion, will, very probably, be arrived at, even though the percentage of sugar found to be crystallizable should be greater in more tropical regions.

The plant grown in Massachusetts the past year contained about twenty-three per cent. of sugar, while that grown in the District of Columbia contained but fourteen per cent. And this accords with what we know of Indian corn, since it is pretty well established that the corn grown in high latitudes is richer in saccharine matter than that grown at the South. The meal of northern corn is also better, and will bring at all times a considerably higher price in the market.

Of the Chinese sugar cane about seven-eighths of the whole plant consist of juice, especially when grown in a southern latitude where the juice is somewhat more abundant, the cane being more succulent there; and we may readily credit the statement that vinegar has been made from this juice at the rate of fifteen hundred gallons to the acre.

When cut for sugar the most favorable time is just after it has passed the blossom, or when the seed is "in the milk," and if raised for this purpose the time of planting should be later than that of Indian corn. The leaves are stripped off and the stalk is crushed in any convenient mills or rollers, though more suitable mills will undoubtedly be constructed.

Should it be found on more careful trial to be equal to what is reported of it, it will make an entire revolution in the sugar growing interests of the country, and thus become a plant of great national importance. It is said that the crop of sugar raised in Louisiana has gradually decreased from nearly five hundred thousand hogsheads in 1853, to less than one hundred thousand, in 1856, while the price of sugar and molasses—a greater amount of which is consumed in this, than in any other

Fig. 85. Chinese Sugar Cane.

country on the globe, in proportion to the population—is loudly calling the attention of farmers and planters to its production; and the Chinese sugar cane is regarded by some as a substitute for the species of sugar cane most commonly cultivated there, the *saccharum officinarum.*

But I propose to speak of it in this connection mainly as a forage plant, though it may prove perfectly practicable and profitable to cultivate it for the purpose of making sugar and molasses. Some years ago the practice of sowing Indian corn in drills for the purpose of cutting up green for fodder, was recommended by a progressive agriculturist, and though at first ridiculed, it soon came to be planted in small patches of a few rods square, by practical farmers here and there, till now it is regarded as almost an indispensable crop, not only to carry a stock of cattle through a severe summer drought, when our pastures are short and dry, but to cut and cure in large quantities for winter use. The weight and value of an acre of fodder is very great. Of late years there has been an inclination to use sweet corn for this purpose, under the supposition that it possessed a larger quantity of saccharine matter in its stalks and leaves than the yellow varieties. When the use of sweet corn was first recommended, it was said that cattle were so much more fond of it than of yellow corn, that they would select its stalks if tied up in a bundle with the stalks of yellow corn. The same is now asserted of the Chinese sugar cane, and as it comes to me very well authenticated, I see no reason to doubt it.

Of the economy of the culture of corn to feed out green in the manner alluded to, there can be no question, and no thrifty and prudent farmer thinks of neglecting it; for if we suffer from drought, as we are liable to every season, he is sure to regret it. Now if a substitute of superior value can be found, of as easy and simple cultivation, every farmer will avail himself of it. Whether this substitute will be found in the Chinese sugar cane, remains, perhaps, to be proved; but so great has been its success thus far as to lead us to anticipate its adoption and extensive cultivation for that purpose. In one case authentically reported, nearly ten tons of fodder were raised on an acre, cut up and cured, and weighed three months after cutting. This is not at all surprising when we consider that even larger yields of Indian corn have been and are frequently obtained, when raised, cut and cured in the same manner.

When grown for fodder, two or three cuttings may be obtained from it, the first being made just before the time of blossoming, when the plant immediately starts up with a vigorous growth and renews its leaves, and sends up its flowering panicles with great rapidity. No less than five cuttings were obtained in Florida during the last year, but the seasons in more northern latitudes would not admit of so many. It is well known that Indian corn will shoot up the second time in the same manner, when once cut or eaten down while green.

This plant grows best in a dry soil and hot sun, in both of which it can be accommodated as far north as New England. It should be planted at or just after the time of Indian corn, and it will mature its fruit in about one hundred days from the seed. For the purposes of sugar making it is best cultivated on rather poor, warm soils, but for feeding out to fattening animals, it should be cultivated on richer ones. If raised for sugar it is better harvested somewhat late in the season, when the temperature ranges from 45° to 55°, when it is not so apt to suffer from the acetous fermentation to which it will be liable if cut earlier. But if raised mainly for the seed, it would be well to plant it somewhat earlier in the spring, in which case it might be cut earlier in the fall. Though the seed is now exceedingly dear on account of its scarcity and the extensive demand for it, yet it is estimated that it can be raised at the price of oats, fifty and sixty bushels to the acre having been obtained without any extraordinary care. The seed can be made into bread or into a beverage resembling chocolate, or fed to poultry and other farm stock.

The Chinese sugar cane, if sown with a view to obtaining its seed, or to attaining its full and perfect development, should be cultivated in hills after the manner of planting Indian corn, and hoed and cultivated in the same manner; but if sown for fodder, it will be found to yield a more luxuriant crop in drills, as we cultivate Indian corn for that purpose. In the former case, one quart of seed will suffice for an acre as it tillers very much, each seed sending up several shoots or seed bearing stems; in the latter case, a larger quantity would be required.

As a fodder plant it has been found not to increase the quantity of milk, milch cows fed upon it having fallen off very decidedly, while they rapidly increased in flesh, and the quality and richness of the milk was found to be improved. This may, therefore, be found to be an objection to its use with some, to whom the quantity is indispensable and the quality of no consequence; but even such may find it desirable to cure and feed it to cows in winter.

It was raised in Dorchester during the past year from seed raised there the year previous, which is conclusive proof that the seed can be ripened in this latitude so as to germinate, though for all practical purposes it is not material to us whether it will ripen here readily or not, if it is found to do so in the Middle States.

As already intimated, the results of experiments have been successful, and these experiments will be carefully repeated the coming season.

A farmer in the State of New York, whose communication appears in the volume of the Patent Office Report on Agriculture, for 1855, says: "The proper time for planting, I should say, would be the same as that of early corn, as I find it quite hardy, and stalks of it cut down the end of October made fresh shoots after two rather heavy frosts, and still were good for feed. From twenty-five plants I obtained half a bushel of ripe seed.

"The mode of cultivation I would recommend, would be to sow after the ground is well manured and deeply ploughed, in drills four feet apart, the plants two feet asunder in the drills, with not more than one plant in a place, as each sends up from four to six shoots. When the plants are well started, say a foot in height, turn over the earth on each side with a plough, after which keep them clear of weeds with the hoe.

"When well cultivated and in good soil, the plant attains from ten to fourteen feet in height and produces excellent fodder from the root to the top. I believe a heavier weight of nutritious feed for all kinds of cattle can be procured from it in a given space of ground, than from any other plant, and I think it will prove of great benefit to every section of the country where it is introduced, not only as a green feed during the hot months, but after being cut up and cured like the corn plant, its stalks may be steamed during the winter, and given to horses, oxen or cows, which will commence eating at one end and not leave them till entirely consumed. The seeds, also, I have no doubt, will prove valuable as a feed for poultry, as I find they eat them with avidity. I look upon this plant as of great value as a forage crop, and possibly, it may be profitably cultivated for sugar, as the juice contains nearly ten per cent. of saccharine matter as clear as crystal, and on a very small scale, beautiful clarified sugar was produced by my friend Dr. Ray."

Other statements are equally unqualified in the expression of confidence in the value of this plant. I subjoin the following practical suggestions on the cultivation of it, from a valuable little manual by Mr. Hyde, of Newton Centre, who has experimented with it. He says:—

"Select a warm and dry soil, such as you would select for Indian corn.

Prepare your ground precisely as you would for corn, either by spreading your manure, or putting in hills,—about the same distance between the hills, where the ground is rich.

In planting, which should be done early, put into each hill six or eight seeds. Cover lightly with well pulverized soil,—say, three-fourths to one inch deep; pull out all but four or five at second hoeing. If planted in drills, seed enough should be used so that after hoeing there may be a stalk to every four or five inches; from a pound and a half to two pounds of seed should be used.

Cultivate and hoe as with corn; care should be taken that the ignorant do not hoe up the young plants, taking them for barn-grass, which they very much resemble.

When the panicles appear they should be cut off of all that which is intended for sugar or sirup making.

When the plant has just passed into bloom, the stalk may be used for sirup, but will continue to grow better until the seed is in the milk-stage, or little later.

The stalks should be cut close to the ground, with a bill-hook or some such tool, and stripped of their leaves, and the green, succulent top cut off, when they are ready for the mill; the leaves and top may be fed green to cattle, or dried.

The stalks should be passed through the mill twice or more, until most or all of the juice is expressed.

The juice should not be allowed to stand long after being expressed, but boiled at once, if possible. A slow fire should be made under the kettle,—which should be of brass, or much better of copper,—and the juice should not be allowed to boil until the green scum has all been taken off. Lime-water may be used to aid in clarifying and to neutralize the acid; the exact quantity is not yet determined, but to every five gallons of juice, say from one to two teaspoonfuls of powdered lime, or the same dissolved in water, and strained, before being put into the juice.

When all the green scum has been removed, the fire may be increased, and the juice boiled down until nearly as thick as common molasses in hot weather, when, if intended for sirup, it should be removed from the fire, for this completes the process. If intended for sugar, it should be allowed to boil longer, and until it will 'string into threads,' or present an appearance of being sufficiently boiled to grain, when it should be thrown off into troughs, or coolers, at once. I am not able to give exact information in regard to the time it should be boiled to crystallize readily. Further experiments will determine.

If made into sugar, it should be removed from the coolers to casks with holes bored in them, so that the molasses may drain off and leave the sugar dry, as it should be. These casks are generally placed on timbers, with a cement cistern underneath to hold the drippings, or molasses. After remaining in the 'purgery' until sufficiently drained, it comes out fit for sale, or use.

If cultivated exclusively for fodder, it should be planted as early as the weather will allow, and quite as thick as stover-corn. When the panicles appear, or even before, it may be cut either for soiling or for drying, and the roots will at once throw up another crop.

If it is desired, the juice may be fermented, like the juice of apples, being put into casks at the mill, and treated like cider.

The begass, or waste, may be dried and used for fuel, or for making paper, or rotted down for manure.

If the storms should blow down the seed-cane, no fears need be entertained, as it will remain weeks in that condition without injury. I must here caution all persons who grow this cane against planting it in the vicinity of broomcorn, Dourah corn, or Guinea corn; for it readily mixes with these plants, and it would render the seed worthless for planting."

As already suggested, more accurate investigations are required to determine the relative importance of this plant for the various economical purposes alluded to. If it should be found, on chemical analysis, that the large percentage of saccharine matter in the plant consists of what is called glucose, a substance of comparatively little value, incapable of crystallization to any extent, instead of a saccharine substance capable of easy granulation, it would very materially affect the value of the plant for the purposes of sugar making, but could hardly affect its real value as a forage plant. This point will soon be determined.

If, as has been stated, it is found to be suitable for the manufacture of alcoholic liquors, it should, perhaps, be regarded by the philanthropist as an important addition to our cultivated crops. It is well known that enormous quantities of our best grains are now withdrawn from their legitimate use as food for man, for the manufacture of these articles. Many distilleries use upwards of two thousand bushels of Indian corn or other grains, on an average, every day, and the consumption of grain for these purposes throughout the country is incredibly large.

The Chinese sugar cane will probably be found to be an exhauster of land, requiring large quantities of the phosphates and silicates of the soil for the development of the hard coating of its stems. It has been estimated that nine tons of it to the acre would take from the soil fourteen hundred pounds of mineral substances. This would seem to indicate a dry, gravelly, or a sandy soil, as best suited to supply it wants.

Indian Grass, Wood Grass, (*sorghum nutans*,) is a grass sometimes found on our dry, sterile soils, with a panicle oblong, somewhat compressed, from six to ten inches long, stem from three to five feet high, leaves linear, grayish, sheaths smooth, spikelets light brown and glossy, drooping when mature, hairy at the base, awn twisted. It flowers in August.

Indian Millet, (*sorghum vulgare*,) is a cultivated species and has several well marked varieties, one of which is the Broom-

CORN. It is called Guinea corn in the West Indies, Dourah in Arabia, and Nagara in the north of China. It is sometimes used as a forage plant.

As already intimated, more than thirty species supposed to belong to this genus are known to have been introduced into France, though it is very probable that a more accurate classification will distribute many of them among the other genera.

The tall cereal which has long been cultivated in the south of Europe and in Barbary, under the general name of sorghum, resembles Indian corn in quality, and is often called *small maize*. Its stems contain a pretty large per cent. of saccharine matter, and it is useful to cut green as a forage plant.

Indian millet, when raised on good soil and under favorable circumstances, is said to yield a larger quantity of seed to the acre than any other cereal grass known, not excepting even Indian corn. Its nutritive quality is nearly equal to that of wheat. The common millet is the *panicum miliaceum*.

INDIAN CORN, MAIZE, (*zea mais*,) is a well known plant of American origin, a true grass, and one of the most beautiful and useful of this great family. Its value as a forage plant has already been alluded to in speaking of the Chinese sugar cane, and need not be dwelt upon here. Subject as we are, to the severest droughts, which parch up and essentially injure our pastures, this plant has been found to be of the utmost importance to cut up green, affording an abundant and nutritious fodder, exceedingly succulent and greatly relished by cattle of all kinds, keeping them in good condition, while without this or some similar substitute our stock would inevitably suffer.

The varieties cultivated for the purpose of fodder should be those with the largest and most succulent leaves. Some of the varieties of sweet corn are usually preferred, but on this point farther and more accurate investigations are greatly needed.

It is estimated that on an average from six to eight tons of dry fodder may be procured from an acre sown in drills and properly cultivated, and that this would be equal to about four or five tons of good hay. This is a reasonable estimate, as far larger crops are often obtained.

The particular advantage of raising what are called forage plants, either to cut up green for soiling or to cure for winter use, over our ordinary mowing lands is, that they give on the same extent of land a far larger amount of nutriment for animals. They give this product immediately, or at least, in a very few months from the time of sowing, while permanent mowing lands, or the perennial grasses, require a great length of time to arrive at perfection, varying from one to four or five years. The amount of fertilizing materials drawn from the air and stored away in the soil by means of the roots, and capable of benefiting the crops of the succeeding year is very considerable, while, in the natural grasses, it remains under the turf and does not come into use till the sward is broken and submitted to culture. We may choose for forage culture plants which start up early in spring and are capable of being used even before the natural grasses have attained a size to make them particularly valuable for grazing.

Besides, the mass of manure which may be made from the product of an acre of land by the use of forage plants, owing to the increased yield, over and above what would be obtained from the same acre in the natural grasses, is an item too rarely taken into the account.

Moreover the plants usually called forage plants, like the clovers, lucerne and green corn fodder, may have some advantage over root culture, their expense being generally less, their product, dried, more easily stored, and kept with less danger of injury and decay, and the mode of feeding out to animals attended with less trouble.

Red Clover, (*trifolium pratense.*) We have given our whole attention, in the preceding pages, to what are strictly and properly called the natural grasses. We now come to consider, very briefly, the artificial. Curious as it may appear, the artificial grasses were cultivated first in point of time, in England, the red clover having been introduced and grown there about the year 1633; sainfoin, 1651; yellow clover in 1659, and white clover about the year 1700; while not one of the natural grasses was cultivated till nearly a century later, with the exception of perennial rye grass, first cultivated in 1677. About the year 1759 the custom of sowing the chaff and seed dropped from the hay stack, along with the artificial grasses and rye grass began, and soon after—between 1761 and 1764—the cultivation of Timothy and orchard grass was introduced from America. The culture of the bent grasses, the sheep's fescue and the crested dog's tail, began soon after. In 1766, the London Society for the Encouragement of Arts offered premiums for the collection of the seeds of some of the grasses then found growing wild, such as the meadow foxtail, the meadow fescue, the sweet scented vernal grass, &c., and in 1769 the same society offered additional rewards for farther investigations and experiments on the culture and comparative value of the natural grasses. But little was done, however, till the experiments undertaken by the Duke of Bedford, in 1824.

In this country the extensive and practical cultivation of the natural grasses seems to have been commenced at an earlier date than in England, for Jared Eliot, writing about the year 1750, speaks of the culture of Timothy as having been adopted sometime previously. Indeed, the necessities of our rigorous climate compelled attention to this branch of husbandry soon after the establishment of the colony, in 1620. The climate of England, on the other hand, admitted a greater degree of reliance on the wild luxuriance of nature, and this mode of management was brought over by the first settlers and attempted for some years, the few cattle they had being kept on poor and miserable swale hay, or often upon the hay obtained from the salt marshes. The death of their cattle from starvation and exposure was of very common occurrence, and not unfrequently the farmer lost his entire herd. The treatment of animals now, as they were treated during the whole of the first century of the colony, would make the owner liable to prosecution for cruelty. This treatment was, in part, owing to the poverty of the settlers, but more, probably, to the ideas and practices in which they had been early trained in a different climate. Fortunately for the poor dumb beast a more enlightened policy now governs the mass of men, and this policy has led to greater care and attention to the cultivation of the grasses.

But in this country, the culture of the natural grasses takes the precedence in point of time from the causes already indicated, and the minds of men are so influenced by the routine of ordinary practice, that the introduction of clover in the early part of the last century met with great prejudice, which is now nearly, if not quite extinct.

Red clover, though not properly included in the family of

grasses, is now not only extensively cultivated, but is found to be one of the most valuable and economical forage plants. It belongs to the pulse family, or *leguminosæ*, which includes the larger portion of forage plants called artificial grasses, in distinction from the gramineæ, the true, and often called the natural grasses. The generic name, trefoil, or trifolium, is derived from the Latin *tres*, three, and *folium*, a leaf; and the genus can generally be very readily distinguished by the number and arrangement of its leaves in three leaflets, and flowers in dense, oblong or globular heads.

Specific description: Stems ascending, somewhat hairy, leaflets oval or obovate, often notched at the end and marked on the upper side with a pale spot, heads ovate and set directly upon the stalk instead of upon branches. This species is regarded as by far the most important of the whole genus. It has sported into a number of varieties, one of which is biennial, another perennial, the latter by long cultivation becoming biennial, while the former,—as is true of most biennial and many annual plants,—assumes, to some extent, the character of a perennial and can be made to last three or four years or even more, by simply preventing it from running to seed. This plant is seen in Fig. 86, its leaf is shown in Fig. 87, and its fruit magnified in Fig. 88.

The introduction of clover into England, it is often said, produced an entire revolution in her agriculture, and indeed, when we consider how important a part it plays in our own system of farming, we can with difficulty imagine how our ancestors ever got on at all in farming without it. Be this as it may, it is certain that it led to many of the most important improvements in the rotation of crops. Clover is very properly regarded as a fertilizer of the soil. The action of its long and powerful tap roots is not only mechanical,—loosening the soil and admitting the air,—but also chemical, serving to fix the gases important to enrich the earth, and when these roots decay they add largely to that black mass of matter we call the soil. It serves, also, by its luxuriant foliage, to destroy annual weeds which would spring up on newly seeded land, especially after imperfect cultivation. But one of the most valuable uses of it, and one too often overlooked, is to shade the surface and thereby increase its fertility.

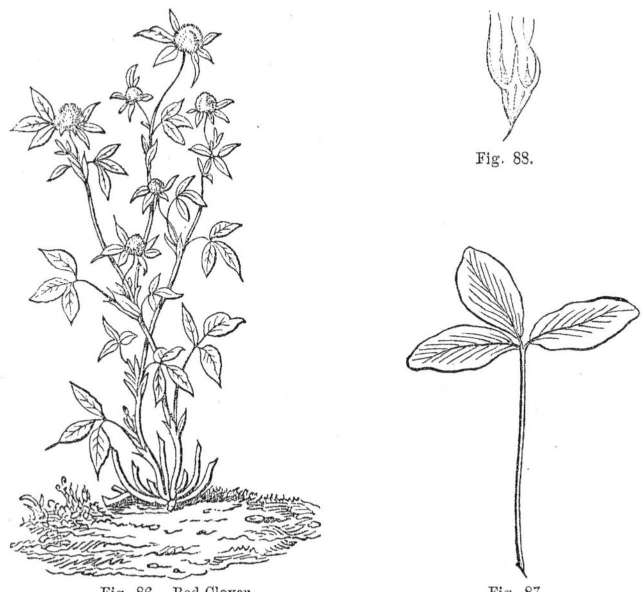

Fig. 88.

Fig. 86. Red Clover.

Fig. 87.

Clover is emphatically a lime plant, and the soils best adapted to it are tenacious or stiff loams. The careful analysis of Prof. Way found no less than 35.39 per cent. of lime in the inorganic constituents of red clover, and that of Boussingault 32.80 per cent., while intelligent practice has arrived so nearly at the same conclusion, that the term "clover soils" is now almost universally used to indicate a tenacious loam, containing more or less of lime in its composition.

Another great advantage in favor of the cultivation of clover, consists in its rapid growth. But a few months elapse from the sowing of the seed before it yields, ordinarily, an abundant and nutritious crop, relished by cattle of all kinds.

Clover seed should always be sown in the spring of the year, in the climate of New England. It is often sown upon the late snows of March or April and soon finds its way down to the soil, where, aided by the moisture of early spring it quickly germinates and rapidly shoots up its leaf stalks.

An accurate and valuable analysis of this plant, both in its green and dry state, will be found in a tabular form on a subsequent page, while a more extended notice of its culture and the mode of curing it, with the results of practical experience as to its value, will also be given in their proper place.

WHITE CLOVER, DUTCH CLOVER, HONEYSUCKLE, (*trifolium repens*,) is equally common with the red, and often forms a very considerable portion of the sward or turf of pastures and fields of a tenacious and moist soil. Specific description: Stems spreading, slender and creeping, leaves inversely heart-shaped, flower heads small, white, pods four seeded, root perennial. Flowers from May to September. Fig. 89. A magnified flower is seen Fig. 90.

White clover is widely diffused over this country and all the countries of Europe. It is indigenous probably both to England and America. When first cultivated from seed collected from wild plants, at the beginning of the last century, it was recorded of a farmer that he had "sowed the wild white clover which holds the ground and decays not." Its chief value is as a pasture grass, and it is as valuable for that purpose as the red clover is for hay or for soiling, though there are some who place a low estimate upon it. It easily accommodates itself to a great variety of soils, but grows most luxuriantly in moist grounds and moist or wet seasons. Indeed, it depends so much upon a general distribution of rains through the season, that when they are sufficiently abundant it comes in profusely even where it was not observed in other years, and hence such seasons pass under the term of "clover years." It is not apparently so much relished by stock as from its sweetness we should be led to expect, but it is, on the whole, to be cherished for permanent pastures, and improved, as it undoubtedly may be, by a proper selection and culture of varieties. For an accurate analysis of this plant the reader is referred to a subsequent page.

LUCERNE, ALFALFA, (*medicago sativa*, Fig. 91.) This genus of leguminous plants has been known and cultivated from time immemorial. This particular species, lucerne, was brought from Media to Greece in the time of Darius, about five hundred years before Christ, and its cultivation afterwards extended among the Romans, and through them to the south of France, where it has ever since continued to be a favorite forage plant. It does not endure a climate as severe as red clover, requiring greater heat and sunlight; but in a latitude equally suited to both plants it would be somewhat difficult to say which should have the preference. In some respects it is decidedly superior, as in being perennial, and consequently remaining long in the soil. I have seen fine specimens of it in South Boston, where the seed was sown in 1824, still maintaining its vigorous hold

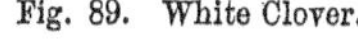

Fig. 89. White Clover.

Fig. 90.

of the soil and growing with remarkable luxuriance. The crop of lucerne is as abundant as red clover, and is equally well relished by cattle, both green and dry. Its yield of green fodder continues later in the season than that of red clover.

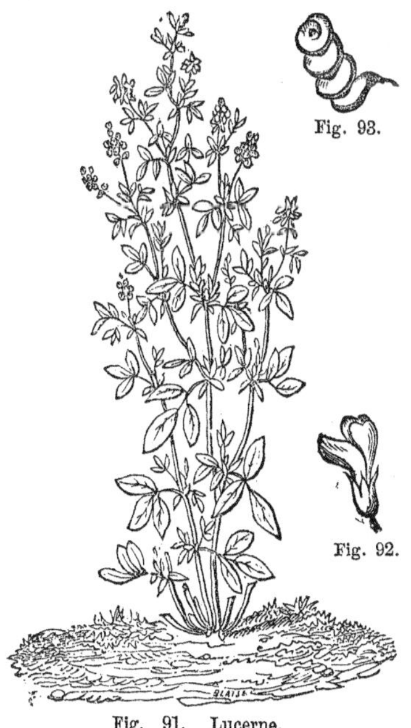

Fig. 93.

Fig. 92.

Fig. 91. Lucerne.

Lucerne sends down its tap roots in mellow soils, to enormous depths, having been found in sandy soils thirteen feet in length. The leaflets are in threes, obovate, oblong, toothed, the flowers pale blue, violet, or purple, shaped as in Fig. 92, the fruit in downy pods, having two or three twirls, as in Fig. 93.

Lucerne is cultivated in Chili and grows wild in the utmost luxuriance in the pampas of Buenos Ayres, where it is called alfalfa, which is simply the common lucerne, slightly modified by climate, and may be regarded as a variety.

The cultivation of lucerne is somewhat more difficult than

that of clover for the first year, requiring a soil thoroughly mellowed and prepared by clean and careful tillage; and the want of proper attention to this point has led to partial failures in the attempts to raise it in this country. It suffers and languishes in compact clay soils, and does not flourish in light soils lying over an impermeable subsoil, which prevents the water from running off. It will never succeed well on thin soils. But in a permeable subsoil, consisting of loam, or sand or gravel, its roots can penetrate to great depths, and being nearly destitute of lateral shoots, provided with numerous fibrous rootlets, or radical off-shoots, imbibe their moisture and nutriment in layers of soil far below the average of other plants. In this respect it differs materially from clover. For lucerne, a suitable subsoil is of the utmost consequence. For the short lived red clover, a suitable surface soil is more important; a want of care and deep tillage, especially a neglect to break through and loosen up the hard-pan wherever it exists, will inevitably lead to failure with lucerne. But when the soil is suitable, it will produce good and very profitable crops for from five to ten or twelve years, and, of course, it does not belong in the system of short rotations.

But notwithstanding the large quantity of succulent and nutritious forage it produces, its effect is to ameliorate and improve the soil rather than to exhaust it. This apparent anomaly is explained by the fact that all leguminous, broad leaved plants derive a large proportion of their nutritive materials from the atmosphere, and that a vast quantity of roots are left to decay in the soil when it is at last broken up, varying, of course, with the length of time the plant continues in the soil, while the luxuriant foliage serves to shade the soil and thus to increase its fertility. Much of this rich foliage is scattered and left to decay, as is the case with all similar plants at the time of harvesting, and the growth of the aftermath is also usually very considerable. The fact that it actually increases the fertility of the soil for other plants, has often been proved and may be regarded as fully established. A soil which would bear only a medium crop of wheat at first, produced a greatly increased quantity after being laid down to lucerne a few years till its roots had enriched the soil.

Lucerne should not follow immediately after having been

grown a few years on the same soil, and then broken up, but after the land on which it has been grown has been cultivated with some other crop or laid down to the natural grasses a length of time equal to that during which it had previously remained in lucerne, it can safely be sown again with it.

The seed of lucerne, when fresh and good, is yellow, glossy and heavy. If the seeds are white, it is an indication that they are not ripe. If they are brown, we may infer that they have been subjected to too strong a heat to separate them from their husks. In either of these cases, it is not safe to purchase or to rely upon them. The same may be said of clover, and it is desirable to try them by a simple method which will be indicated hereafter in speaking of the selection of seed. As the seeds of lucerne are somewhat larger than clover seed and the plant tillers less, it is necessary to sow a larger quantity per acre. It may be sown in the spring along with grain crops, as clover often is, and not a very large crop should be expected the first year.

Lucerne should be cut as soon as it begins to flower, or even earlier. If cut much earlier it is apt to be too watery and less nutritious and cures with greater difficulty; if later, it becomes coarse and hard with woody fibre, and is less relished by cattle. It may be cut and fed green and is an exceedingly valuable plant for soiling cattle, or it may be cut and cured and used like clover hay; but in either case, it must be cut before blossoming.

It is thought by many, that lucerne will not endure the climate of New England, but I do not think it satisfactorily proved, and I have been somewhat minute in speaking of it, in the hope of inducing more careful experiments on a scale and under circumstances sufficient to determine its relative value for us. I am the more anxious on this point from the fact that I am convinced, after much study and observation of our climate, that we should direct our labors in farming more with reference to the frequent droughts of summer to which we are liable every year, and from which there is no immediate and practicable escape except in thorough drainage and deep tillage, which most farmers are unwilling to undertake at present. "When properly managed, the number of cattle which can be kept in good condition on an acre of lucerne, during the whole season, exceeds belief. It is no sooner mown than it pushes out fresh shoots; and wonderful as the growth of clover sometimes is, in a field that has been lately mown, that of lucerne is far more rapid. Lucerne will last for many years, shooting its roots—tough and fibrous almost as those of liquorice—downwards for nourishment, till they are altogether out of the reach of drought. In the dryest and most sultry weather, when every blade of grass droops for want of moisture, lucerne holds up its stem, fresh and green, as in the genial spring."

I am convinced, also, that the failures of attempts to cultivate lucerne with us may be ascribed, in nearly every instance, to an improper selection of soils, and am inclined to think that a more accurate knowledge of the plant and a more careful observation of its habits of growth would lead to its more general adoption as an economical forage plant.

I have procured fine specimens of lucerne in various parts of this State, where it is very successfully cultivated, but on too limited a scale to determine its comparative value as a farm crop.

SAINFOIN, (*hedysarum onobrychis*,) differs from lucerne in many important particulars. It is a leguminous plant with many stems from two to three feet long, straggling, tapering, smooth, leaves in pairs of pointed, oblong leaflets, slightly hairy on the under side, flower stalks higher than the leaves, ending in a spike of crimson or variegated flowers, succeeded by flat, hard pods, toothed on the edges and prickly on the sides, root perennial, and hard and woody. Flowers in July. Fig. 94. The flower is shown in Fig. 95, and the fruit in Fig. 96.

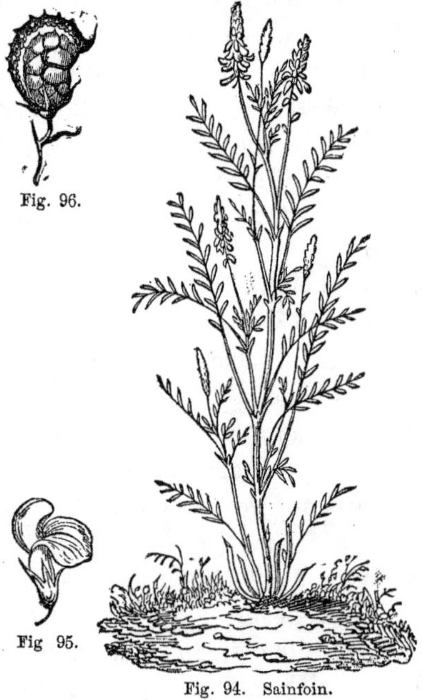
Fig. 96.
Fig 95.
Fig. 94. Sainfoin.

Experiments have been made in introducing and cultivating it in this State, but without success. It requires a calcareous soil.

In the south of France, where it flourishes best, it is considered an indispensable forage plant, improving the quality and increasing the quantity of milk when fed to milch cows, to which it may be given without producing the "hoove," to which they are subjected when allowed to feed freely on green clover and lucerne. Its stalks do not become ligneous if allowed to stand till blossoming, as those of lucerne do. The amount of fodder obtained from it is less than that from clover or lucerne, but its quality, where it can be successfully grown, is better. Its fruit or seed is said to be far more nutritious than oats. They are eagerly sought by fowls, and cause them to lay.

Sainfoin, when green and young, will not endure a severe winter, but after the second or third year will endure a considerable degree of cold. It will succeed in very dry soils, sands and gravels. It is grown with great success in some of the southern counties of England. Its seeds have been generally distributed over the country through the agency of the Patent Office, but, so far as I know, they have been followed by no marked success in the way of crops in New England.

The arrow grasses form a limited family consisting of only three species found in New England. They are arranged in the following table:—

TABLE II. *List of Arrow Grasses. (Juncagineæ.)*

Common Name.	Systematic Name.	Time of Flowering.	Place of growth.
Marsh Arrow Grass. . .	Triglochin palustre, . .	August, .	Marshes, both salt and fresh.
Sea-side Arrow Grass, . .	Triglochin maritimum, .	July, Aug. .	Salt marshes.
Tall Arrow Grass, . . .	Triglochin elatum, . .	June, July, .	Swamps in Bridgewater

The second of these, the sea arrow grass, is common in our salt marshes, having rush-like leaves of a sweetish taste, relished by cattle, and forming a very good fodder when well cured.

Many of the rushes or grass-like plants so common along the borders of our ponds, and called grasses in popular language, are readily eaten in the spring while green and full of juice. They are arranged in the following table:—

TABLE III. *List of Grass-like Rushes. (Juncaceæ.)*

Common Name.	Systematic Name.	Time of Flowering.	Place of growth.
Common Wood Rush, . .	Luzula campestris, . .	April, May, .	Fields and dry woods.
Broad-leaved Hairy Wood Rush, ...	Luzula pilosa, . . .	May, . .	Open woods, river banks
Small-flowered Wood Rush, .	Luzula parviflora, . .	July, . .	Mountains, West. Mass.
Soft Rush, ...	Juncus effusus, . . .	June, . .	Swampy grounds: common.
Slender Rush, . . .	Juncus filiformis, . .	July, . .	Wet banks and shores.
Baltic Rush, ...	Juncus balticus, . . .	July, . .	Sandy shores.
Smaller Round-headed Rush,	Juncus nodosus, . . .	July, . .	Borders of rivers and ponds.
Many-headed Rush, . .	Juncus polycephalus, . .	July, . .	Wet places.
Sharp-fruited Rush, . .	Juncus acuminatus, . .	August, .	Boggy swamps.
Brownish-fruited Rush, .	Juncus articulatus, . .	– –	Wet places.
Conrad's Rush, . . .	Juncus Conradi, . . .	July, Aug. .	Borders of ponds in sandy soil.
Toad Rush, ...	Juncus bufonius, . .	June, Aug. .	Low grounds, roadsides
Slender Rush, . . .	Juncus tenuis, . . .	June, Aug. .	Low grounds, fields.
Greene's Rush, . . .	Juncus Greenei, . . .	July, . .	Sandy borders of salt marshes.
Black Grass, ...	Juncus bulbosus, . .	August, .	Borders of salt marshes
Grass-leaved Rush, . .	Juncus marginatus, . .	July, . .	Moist, sandy swamps.
Long-fruited Rush, . .	Juncus Stygius, . . .	– –	Peat swamps.
Three-leaved Rush, . .	Juncus trifidus, . . .	July, . .	Mountain summits.

The most prominent and valuable of these plants is the

BLACK GRASS, (*juncus bulbosus*, var. *gerardi*,) an inhabitant of salt marshes. This plant has a simple, slender stem, somewhat flattened, from one to two feet high. It is considered the best product of the salt marshes and grows most luxuriantly along their borders which are only occasionally overflowed by the tides, often working its way to the uplands where the seed is scattered, in large quantities, in curing. It should be cut early, and when well cured is thought to be nearly equal in value to good English hay. Though not of itself equal in value, weight for weight, to "goose grass," (*poa maritima*, p. 49, Fig. 30,) yet the product per acre is so much larger as to make it a more desirable crop.

Most of the salt marsh plants have already been described in the natural history of the true grasses.

The "GOOSE GRASS," one of the most valuable of them, was mentioned under its synonym, Sea Spear Grass, Fig. 30, p. 49, the name "goose grass," by which it is more generally known along the shores of Essex county and Cape Cod, having been inadvertently omitted. It is generally considered one of the best products of the salt marsh when it grows in mixture with other species of plants, as the black grass, for instance, and deserves a more extended notice.

It is very well known that large tracts of salt marsh are nearly barren. Sometimes close cutting in the early morning, while the dew is on the grass and when it cuts comparatively easy, kills it out, and from that cause the marsh becomes barren. More often, however, excess of water, either upon the surface or in the soil, from the proximity of ponds which have no outlet, causes barrenness. On all such tracts goose grass springs up and dots the whole surface with circular patches of green, which in shape are very like ringworms on the human skin. This grass is seldom found alone except on these barren tracts, and upon them it grows so short and thin as seldom to be worth cutting. One will therefore never see any goose grass hay except mixed with other kinds, and generally with black grass. When these tracts begin to improve, either from draining or from any other cause, other grasses make their appearance, and the goose grass grows much more vigorous and becomes valuable. This will continue to be the case for several years, until the roots of the other grasses have taken entire possession of the soil, when the goose grass disappears almost entirely and bides its time, ready to appear again whenever from any cause its intrusive competitors cease to exist.

The hay made from the mixture of goose and other grasses —among which black grass generally predominates—is a most valuable fodder. The goose grass is so weighty that it takes but a small quantity, comparatively, for a ton, and cattle eat it with almost as much avidity as oats or any other grain. In fact, no hay is more valuable than black grass with a large admixture of goose grass, when properly cured.

The curing process requires care and time, for goose grass is as full of sap as possible, and requires a much longer exposure than black grass, while a very little wet when it is partially cured, materially injures the black grass.

We may judge of the properties of goose grass from the

fact, that in several instances within my own knowledge, cattle have died of hoove from eating it early in the spring.

It resembles in the shape of its leaves, and somewhat in its cluster-like growth, that species of garlic which used formerly to be grown in kitchen gardens called *cives*, or more properly *chives*. Its seed stalks and seeds are almost precisely like the seed stalks and seeds of the common plantain.

It grows both on high and low marshes, but is very seldom worth cutting on those tracts where it grows by itself and without the admixture of other grasses.

It is proper to state in this connection that experiments have been made to introduce this valuable grass into our fresh wet meadows, and with good success.

Most of the superior salt marsh grasses are greatly improved by ditching, while the poorer and comparatively worthless plants found there very soon die out after this operation and give place to more valuable species. It may be safely asserted that, on an average, the value of the marsh is nearly doubled by it, while the vegetable, peaty matter taken from it is sufficient, if properly used, to pay a considerable portion of the outlay.

There is also a small family of plants called the yellow eyed grasses, or the star grasses, consisting of only two species, the first of which is the Yellow Eyed Grass, (*xyris bulbosa*,) flowering in July, August and September, growing on sandy and peaty soils, and bogs near the coast; and the second, the Common Yellow Eyed Grass, (*xyris caroliniana*,) flowering in August, on sandy swamps. These are beautiful grasses, of no special agricultural value.

There is still another great family of plants which, though of no agricultural value in point of nutritive properties as compared with the true grasses, is, nevertheless, extensively used in New England for forage purposes, and consequently deserves a passing mention. I refer to the sedges, and plants constituting the coarse and innutritious herbage properly included in the term, carex, a large and prominent genus of grass-like plants, consisting in all of about four hundred and fifty species known to botanists, extensively diffused over all the damp parts of the globe, and in popular language called grasses. A few species of carex grow on sandy hills and along the sea shore, but most inhabit marshes, wet meadows, swamps, and the low, wet banks of streams and ditches, and moist woods. Somewhat over a hundred species are found in New England. None of them are of any real agricultural value, though they constitute mainly what we term "meadow hay," or more properly swale hay, in eastern Massachusetts. They are nearly destitute of mealy and saccharine principles in which many of the true grasses abound, and are eaten by cattle only when compelled by hunger, in the want of better grasses. It not unfrequently happens, however, that there is an admixture of the higher grasses among the carices or sedges, such as the fowl meadow, the bastard fowl meadow, the white top or some of the other species possessing higher nutritive qualities, and then, of course, the hay made from the swale is proportionably improved, and may thus become of considerable value for winter fodder.

The Sedges are arranged in the following table:—

TABLE IV. *List of Carices or Sedges, (Cyperaceæ.)*

Common Name.	Systematic Name.	Time of Flowering.	Place of growth.
Diandrus Sedge,	Cyperus diandrus,	Aug., Sept.,	Wet grounds.
Nuttall's Sedge,	Cyperus Nuttallii,	August,	Salt marshes.
Bristle-spiked Galingale,	Cyperus strigosus,	July to Sept.,	Swamps and low lands.
Gray's Galingale,	Cyperus Grayii,	August,	Barren, sandy soils.
Toothed Galingale,	Cyperus dentatus,	August,	Sandy swamps.
Dwarf Odorous Galingale,	Cyperus inflexus,	July to Sept.,	Banks of rivers and brooks.
Schweinitz's Galingale,	Cyperus Schweinitzii,	August,	Shores of lakes.
Common Spike-rush,	Eleocharis palustris,	August,	Swamps and low lands
Olive-fruited Spike-rush,	Eleocharis olivacea,	August,	Wet, sandy places.
Braked Spike-rush,	Eleocharis rostellata,	– –	Marshes.
Intermediate Spike-rush,	Eleocharis intermedia,	August,	Wet places.
Obtuse-headed Spike-rush,	Eleocharis obtusa,	June. July,	Bogs, borders of muddy ponds and rivers.
Large-tubercled Spike-rush,	Eleocharis tuberculosa,	August,	Sandy swamps.
Hair Club-rush,	Eleocharis acicularis,	June, July,	Muddy borders of ponds
Horsetail Rush,	Eleocharis equisetoides,	– –	Shallow water.
Robbins's Club-rush,	Eleocharis Robbinsii,	July,	Ponds and ditches.
Slender Club-rush,	Eleocharis tenuis,	June, July,	Common in wet places.
Black-fruited Club-rush,	Eleocharis Melanocarpa,	– –	Wet sand.
Dwarf Spike-rush,	Eleocharis pygmæa,	August,	Salt marshes.

TABLE IV.—*Continued.*

Common Name.	Systematic Name.	Time of Flowering.	Place of growth.
Scaly-stalked Club-rush, .	Scirpus cæspitosus, . .	July, . .	Wet mountains.
Flat-leaved Club-rush, . .	Scirpus planifolius, . .	June, . .	Woods, and in bogs.
Floating Club-rush, . .	Scirpus subterminalis, .	August, .	Sluggish streams: rare.
Chair-bottom Rush, . .	Scirpus pungens, . .	July, Aug.	Borders of salt marshes and fresh ponds.
Olney's Rush, . . .	Scirpus Olneyi, . . .	July, . .	Salt marshes.
Torrey's Rush, . . .	Scirpus Torreyi, . . .	July, Aug.	Borders of ponds.
Bulrush, ...	Scirpus lacustris, . . .	July, . .	Borders of muddy rivers and ponds.
Weak-stemmed Rush, . .	Scirpus debilis, . . .	August, .	Borders of sandy rivers and lakes.
Sea Bulrush, . . .	Scirpus maritimus, . .	August, .	Salt marshes and salt springs.
River Rush, ...	Scirpus fluviatilis, . .	July, Aug.	Borders of lakes and large streams.
Wood Rush, ...	Scirpus sylvaticus, . .	July, . .	Wet meadows.
Cluster-head Rush, . .	Scirpus polyphyllus, . .	July, . .	Swamps, shady borders of ponds.
Porter's Rush, . . .	Scirpus lineatus, . . .	July, . .	Bogs in western Mass.
Wool Grass, ...	Scirpus Eriophorum, . .	July to Sept.	Wet meadows, swamps.
Cotton Grass, . . .	Eriophorum Alpinum, .	May, June,	Peat swamps.
Harestail, ...	Eriophorum vaginatum, .	June, . .	Mossy swamps and high mountains.
Rusty Cotton Grass, . .	Eriophorum Virginicum, .	July, Aug.	Common in swamps.
Broad-leaved Cotton Grass, .	Eriophorum polystachyon, .	June, July,	Boggy meadows.
Narrow-leaved Cotton Grass,	Eriophorum gracile, . .	June to Aug.	Wet mossy swamps.
Tall Fimbristylis, . . .	Fimbristylis spadicea, . .	July to Sept.	Salt marshes: rare.
Tufted Fimbristylis, . . .	Fimbristylis autumalis, .	Aug. to Oct.	Low grounds.
Hair-like Fimbristylis, . .	Fimbristylis capillaris, .	Aug., Sept.	Common on sandy fields.
Umbrella Grass, . . .	Fuirena squarrosa, . .	August, .	Sandy, wet places.
Bald Rush, ...	Psilocarya scirpoides, . .	July, . .	Inundated swamps.
Horned Rush, . . .	Ceratoschœnus macrostachya	– –	Borders of ponds: rare.
Dwarf Hemicarpha, . .	Hemicarpha subsquarrosa, .	July, . .	Sandy borders of rivers and lakes.
White Beak-rush, . . .	Rhynchospora alba, . .	July, Aug.	Mossy swamps, common.
Small Beak-rush, . . .	Rhynchospora capillacea, .	July, . .	Swamps and marshes.
Brown Beak-rush, . .	Rhynchospora fusca, . .	July, . .	Low wet grounds: rare.
Tall, Slender Beak-rush, .	Rhynchospora gracilenta, .	– –	Low grounds.
Common Beak-rush, . .	Rhynchospora glomerata, .	July, Aug.	Boggy grounds.
Round-head Beak-rush, .	Rhynchospora cephalantha,	August, .	Sandy swamps.
Smooth Twig-rush, . .	Cladium mariscoides, . .	July, . .	Borders of ponds, bog meadows.
Sessile-spiked Nut-rush, .	Scleria reticularis, . .	August, .	Sandy swamps and borders of ponds.
Loose-flowered Nut-rush, .	Scleria laxa, ...	August, .	Sandy swamps.
Three-clustered Nut-rush, or Whip-grass, . . .	Scleria triglomerata, . .	July, . .	Swamps and moist thickets.
Few-flowered Nut-rush, .	Scleria pauciflora, . .	July, . .	Swamps and hills.

TABLE IV.—*Continued.*

Common Name.	Systematic Name.	Time of Flowering.	Place of growth.
Dwarf Verticillate Nut-rush,	Scleria verticillata, . .	June, . .	Swamps.
Slender Sedge, . . .	Carex exilis, . . .	June, July, .	Marshes in Danvers.
Few-flowered Sedge, . .	Carex pauciflora, . . .	– –	Peat swamps.
Bristle-stalked Sedge, . .	Carex polytrichoides, . .	May, . .	Low grounds & woods.
Willdenow's Sedge, . .	Carex Willdenovii, . .	May, . .	Moist, shady places.
Back's Sedge, . . .	Carex Backii, . . .	– –	Mount Tom and rocky hills.
Two-seeded Sedge, . .	Carex disperma, . . .	June, . .	Mossy swamps and mountains.
Long-rooted Sedge, . .	Carex cherelorhiga, . .	May, . .	Mossy swamps.
Oval-headed Sedge, . .	Carex cephalophora, . .	May, . .	Hill-sides and fields
Muhlenberg's Sedge, . .	Carex Muhlenbergii, . .	April, . .	Rocky hill-sides and mountains.
Dry-spiked Sedge, . . .	Carex siccata, . . .	– –	Sandy plains.
Rose Sedge, ...	Carex rosea, ...	May, . .	Moist woods and low grounds.
Retroflexed Sedge, . .	Carex retroflexa, . . .	May, . .	Open woods and moist meadows.
Bur-reed Sedge, . . .	Carex sparganioides, . .	May, . .	Low swampy grounds.
Awl-fruited Sedge, . .	Carex stipata, . . .	April, . .	Swamps, low grounds.
Fox Sedge, ...	Carex vulpinoidea, . .	May, . .	Low grounds: common
Bristly-spiked Sedge, . .	Carex setacea, . . .	June, . .	Wet meadows.
Bromus-like Sedge, . .	Carex bromoides, . . .	May, . .	Wet swamps.
Foxtail Sedge, . . .	Carex alopecoidea, . .	– –	Woods.
Sartwell's Sedge, . . .	Carex Sartwellii, . . .	– –	– –
Lesser-panicled Sedge, . .	Carex teretiuscula, . .	June, . .	Swamps: common.
Large-panicled Sedge, . .	Carex decomposita, . .	– –	Swamps.
Three-seeded Sedge, . .	Carex trisperma, . . .	June, . .	Peat swamps, wet mountain woods.
Dewey's Sedge, . . .	Carex Deweyana, . . .	June, . .	Moist woods.
White Carex, . . .	Carex canescens, . . .	May, . .	Wet meadows.
Little Prickly Sedge, . .	Carex stellulata, . . .	May, . .	Wet meadows.
Slender Cluster-spiked Sedge,	Carex tenuiflora, . . .	June, . .	Mossy swamps.
Broom-like Sedge, . . .	Carex scoparia, . . .	– –	Wet meadows and swamps.
Straw-colored Sedge, . .	Carex straminea, . . .	May, June, .	Borders of woods and fields.
Long-stalked Sedge, . .	Carex pedunculata, . .	April, . .	Rocky hills and dry woods.
Square-headed Sedge, . .	Carex squarrosa, . . .	May, . .	Low meadows, thickets
Buxbaum's Sedge, . .	Carex Buxbaumii, . .	May, . .	Mossy swamps.
Three-headed pubescent Sedge	Carex triceps, . . .	May, . .	Woods and meadows.
Green-spiked pubescent Sedge	Carex virescens, . . .	May, . .	Woods and hill-sides.
Slender Nodding Sedge, .	Carex gracillima, . . .	June, . .	Moist grounds.
Showy Sedge, . . .	Carex formosa, . . .	May, . .	Wet meadows.
Davis's Sedge, . . .	Carex Davisii, . . .	May, . .	Swamps, river banks.
Rigid Sedge, ...	Carex rigida, . . .	July, . .	Mountain summits.

TABLE IV.—*Continued.*

Common Name.	Systematic Name.	Time of Flowering.	Place of growth.
Large Bog Sedge,	Carex augustata,	May,	Swamps: common.
Smaller Bog Sedge,	Carex cæspitosa,	May,	Swamps and banks of streams.
Water Sedge,	Carex aquatilis,	June, July,	Borders of lakes and rivers.
Golden-fruited Sedge,	Carex aurea,	May, June,	Borders of swamps and brooks.
Fringed Sedge,	Carex crinita,	May, June,	Swamps, river banks.
Few-fruited Sedge,	Carex oligosperma,	June,	Mountains, borders of swamps.
Inflated Sedge,	Carex bullata,	May,	Swamps: not common.
Cylindrical-spiked Sedge,	Carex cylindrica,	– –	Swamps: common.
Bladder-fruited Sedge,	Carex utriculata,	May,	Wet swamps.
Awl-fruited Sedge,	Carex subulata,	May,	Cedar swamps.
Tall Yellow Sedge,	Carex folliculata,	June,	Swamps, peat bogs.
Swollen-fruited Sedge,	Carex intumescens,	June,	Wet grounds and open woods.
Hop Sedge,	Carex lupulina,	June,	Swamps and borders of ponds.
Rough-fruited Sedge,	Carex scabrata,	May,	Borders of brooks.
Schweitnitz's Sedge,	Carex Schweinitzii,	May,	Swamps.
Late-fruited Sedge,	Carex retrorsa,	May,	Borders of ponds and streams.
Long-pointed Sedge,	Carex tentaculata,	May,	Swamps.
Porcupine Sedge,	Carex hystricina,	June,	Swamps: common.
Cyperus-like Sedge,	Carex Pseudo-Cyperus,	June,	Swamps and sluggish streams.
Long-beaked Sedge,	Carex longirostris,	June,	Shady, rocky places.
Hairy-fruited Sedge,	Carex trichocarpa,	June,	Marshes and lakes.
Awned Sedge,	Carex aristata,	– –	Lake shores.
Umbel-spiked Sedge,	Carex umbellata,	May,	Rocky hill-sides.
Pennsylvanian Sedge,	Carex Pennsylvanica,	April,	Dry woods and hill-sides
New England Sedge,	Carex Novæ-Angliæ,	June,	Woody hills and mountains.
Slender-leaved Sedge,	Carex filiformis,	May,	Peat swamps.
Woolly-fruited Sedge,	Carex lanuginosa,	May,	Swamps and borders of ponds.
Short Woolly-spiked Sedge,	Carex vestita,	May,	Moist, sandy soils.
Pubescent Sedge,	Carex pubescens,	May,	Woods and swamps.
Mud Sedge,	Carex limosa,	June,	Mossy swamps.
Livid Sedge,	Carex livida,	June,	Mossy swamps.
Large Yellow Carex,	Carex flava,	May,	Swamps.
Œder's Sedge,	Carex Œderi,	May,	Wet limestone rocks.
Pale Pubescent Sedge,	Carex pallescens,	May,	Swamps.
Torrey's Sedge,	Carex Torreyi,	– –	Northward.
Striated Sedge,	Carex striata,	May,	Swamps.
Granular-spiked Sedge,	Carex granularis,	May,	Wet swamps: common.
Loose-flowered Sedge,	Carex laxiflora,	May,	Swamps & moist woods.

TABLE IV.—*Continued.*

Common Name.	Systematic Name.	Time of Flowering.	Place of growth.
Conical-fruited Sedge, .	Carex conoidea, ...	May, . .	Wet swamps.
Slender Wood Sedge, . .	Carex digitalis, ...	May, . .	Woods and hill-sides.
Hitchcock's Sedge, . .	Carex Hitchcockiana, . .	May, . .	Woods, hill-sides.
Small Few-fruited Sedge, .	Carex oligocarpa, . . .	May, . .	Woods.
Crooked-necked Sedge, . .	Carex tetanica, ...	May, . .	Margin of lakes and rivers.
Two-edged Sedge, . . .	Carex anceps, ...	May, . .	Woods.
Pale, Smooth Sedge, . .	Carex blanda, ...	May, . .	Swamps and dry open woods.
Crawe's Sedge, ...	Carex Crawei, ...	– –	Banks of rivers.
Plantain-leaved Sedge, . .	Carex plantaginea, . . .	April, May, .	Shady, rocky ravines.
Carey's Sedge, ...	Carex Careyana, ...	May, . .	Shady, dry woods.
Bristled-leaved White Sedge,	Carex eburnea, ...	May, . .	Limestone hills.
Fringed Sedge, ...	Carex flexilis, ...	June, . .	Moist, shady places.
Short-beaked Woody Sedge, .	Carex arctata, ...	May, . .	Moist woods, swamps.
Weak Sedge, ...	Carex debilis, ...	May, . .	Moist woods, swamps.
Millet-like Sedge, . . .	Carex miliacea, ...	May, . .	Wet swamps.
Lake Sedge, ...	Carex lucustris, ...	June, . .	Deep swamps, borders of lakes.
Tuckerman's Sedge, . .	Carex Tuckermani, . . .	– –	Wet swamps.
Washington's Sedge, . .	Carex Washingtoniana, .	– –	Near summit of Mount Washington.
Gray's Sedge, ...	Carex Grayii, ...	July, . .	Swamps and river borders.
Bog Sedge, ...	Carex acuta, ...	– –	In dense bogs in swamps
Sea Carex, ...	Carex arenaria, . .	June, July, .	Sandy sea shores.

This table includes all the species of carex known and described as inhabitants of our low lands, and is thought to be very complete. As already intimated, none of these coarse sedges are rich in nutritive elements, and none are worthy of cultivation. The farmer's care should be to eradicate them and supply their places with the higher and more nutritious grasses. This may be done by thorough draining, an operation which lies at the foundation of all successful management of low lands, and without which they are comparatively worthless, while, if properly reclaimed, they are among the best and most productive lands on the farm.

The roots of the sedges are perennial, and for the most part creeping, a few being tufted and fibrous. The stems are simple and free from joints or nodes. The leaves are linear, flat, pointed, roughish on the surface and sharp on the edges.

The grasses whose natural history has been stated in the preceding pages, might be separated into four or five distinct groups, which would facilitate the study of them; for it must have been observed that many of them possess marked peculiarities of growth.

I. We find first the bush or jungle grasses, or such as are not inclined to grow with other species, and form a close, matted turf or sward. Of these we have as examples the

Tufted Hair Grass, (*aira cæspitosa.*)
Meadow Oat Grass, (*avena pratensis.*)
Tall Fescue Grass, (*festuca elatior.*)

A few others, if sown alone, will assume somewhat the same form, in tufts or cushions, as

Sheep's Fescue, (*festuca ovina.*)
Hard Fescue, (*festuca duriuscula.*)
Orchard Grass, (*dactylis glomerata.*)

This peculiarity in the growth of the last three grasses is prevented by close pasturing, rolling and proper cultivation. These operations improve upon nature, since if left to themselves they would far more certainly assume the jungle growth, such as is often seen on poor, thin pasture soils, especially in the south-eastern parts of the State, where on the sandy soils this mode of growth is every where observable—a close, fine, matted sward being attained only by careful cultivation.

II. The aquatic or water grasses form another distinct group, and among these are the

Reed Canary Grass, (*phalaris arundinacea,*)
Common Reed Grass, (*arundo phragmites.*)
Water Spear Grass, (*poa aquatica.*)
Common Manna Grass, (*poa fluitans.*)
Rice Grass, (*Leersia oryzoides.*)
Floating Foxtail, (*alopecurus geniculatus.*)
Wild Rice, (*zizania aquatica.*)

These grasses grow mostly in water and are not cultivated with us as agricultural grasses with the exception, perhaps, of the first. Wild rice grass is sometimes cultivated and yields large crops at the South, and floating foxtail in Europe.

III. Marsh or Salt Grasses, among which we have
Salt Reed Grass, (*spartina polystachya.*)
Rush Salt Grass, (*spartina juncea.*)
Salt Marsh Grass, (*spartina stricta.*)
Black Grass, (*juncus bulbosus.*)
Beach Grass, (*ammophila arundinacea.*)
Goose Grass, (*poa maritima.*)

IV. Field or Pasture Grasses. Under this head may be included a very large number of species, all of which have been described above. These grasses might be subdivided according to the soils and situations which they naturally affect; for though a grass may sometimes be found or placed in a soil which is not naturally fitted for it, yet no species will arrive at its most perfect development on a soil not well adapted to it.

Among these might be mentioned as examples
Timothy, (*phleum pratense.*)
Meadow Foxtail, (*alopecurus pratensis.*)
Common Spear Grass, (*poa pratensis.*)
Orchard Grass, (*dactylis glomerata.*)
Perennial Rye Grass, (*lolium perenne.*)
Italian Rye Grass, (*lolium italicum.*)
Redtop, (*agrostis vulgaris.*)
Whitetop, (*agrostis alba.*)
Downy Oat Grass, (*avena pubescens.*)
Meadow Soft Grass, (*holcus lanatus.*)
Meadow Fescue, (*festuca pratensis.*)
Field Barley Grass, (*hordeum pratense.*)
Tall Oat Grass, (*arrhenatherum avenaceum.*)

V. Annual Weeds, which, though proper grasses, are often very troublesome in cultivated grounds, either on account of their creeping, underground stems, or their rapid and luxuriant growth. Thrifty farming is a ceaseless struggle against these pests, and the farmer is generally careful to keep as clear as possible of them. Among these may be named

Willard's Bromus, (*bromus secalinus.*)
Soft Brome Grass, (*bromus mollis.*)
Slender Foxtail, (*alopecurus agrestis.*)
Creeping Bent Grass, (*agrostis stolonifera.*)
Couch, or Twitch Grass, (*triticum repens.*)
Rough Stalked Meadow Grass, (*poa trivialis.*)
Annual Meadow Grass, (*poa annua.*)
Blue, or Wire Grass, (*poa compressa.*)

Of these, the last four are not always considered as weeds, since they are sometimes sown as pasture grasses; but when they appear in cultivated grounds, in gravel walks and avénues, they are exceedingly troublesome and difficult to eradicate.

Each of the groups indicated above may be considerably enlarged by a study of the natural history of the grasses presented in the foregoing pages.

Many of the grasses which have been described, possess but little value for the purposes of cultivation, it is true, but it should not be forgotten that they all have their uses, and these uses in the grand economy of nature are exceedingly important, however they may appear to our short sighted vision. No plant comes up to the sunlight or expands its beautiful leaves, that does not derive its support in part from the atmosphere, and even though its life be short, it adds materially in its decay to the vast mass of vegetable mould which covers the surface of the globe and forms the richness of the soil. This surface mould has been accumulating for ages in many localities; every plant that grew in ages past bringing down to us in a tangible form the riches with which the air that surrounded it was stored, which now lie waiting the farmers' use in meadows of exhaustless fertility, in swamps and bogs of vast, increasing utility in our agriculture, and in beds of peat, the value of which we have scarcely begun to appreciate. Thus, the grasses which are not cultivated for their direct nutritive qualities, are not without their value, and they deserve our careful study and attention.

NUTRITIVE VALUE OF THE GRASSES.

We have seen that the various species of grass differ very materially in nutritive value; that some contain the greatest quantity of nutritive matter when green or in the flower; others when the seed is ripe and the plant mature; that some yield a luxuriant aftermath, while others can scarcely be said to produce any at all; that some flourish in elevated situations and are best suited to the grazing of sheep, while others grow most luxuriantly on the low lands and in the marshes, and sustain the richest dairies; and that no soil is so sterile, no plain so barren but that a grass can be found adapted to it. Some varieties, indeed, will not endure a soil even of medium fertility, nor the application of any stimulating manure, but cling with astonishing tenacity to the drifting sands, while others prefer the heaviest clays or revel in the hot beds of ammonia; some are gregarious in their habits, requiring to be sown with other species, and if sown alone will linger along till the wild grasses spring up to their support; others are solitary, and if mixed with different species will either extirpate them, usurping to themselves the entire soil, or die and disappear. Nearly every species is distinguished for some peculiar quality, and most are deficient in some, comparatively few combining all the qualities desired by us in alternate field crops, for pastures or permanent mowing, to such an extent as to justify a general cultivation.

It is important, therefore, to learn the comparative nutritive value of each species thought to be worth cultivating.

This study is naturally attended with great difficulties. It is but recently that accurate researches have been made with a view of arriving at such positive results as would be entitled to full confidence.*

It is now very well established that the nutritive value of the food of an animal depends chiefly upon the proportion of nitrogenous substances contained in it. Without doubt, the sugar

* In 1824, a very laudable attempt was made in England by the Duke of Bedford, at Woburn Abbey, to ascertain the comparative value of most of the grasses which could then be obtained, and the results of the experiments,

which is found to be an ingredient of most vegetable substances at some periods of their growth, in some degree contributes to it also. The nitrogenous constituents of any substance, as grass or hay, for instance, may be determined with little difficulty and with great exactness, since it has been found by abundant research, that, when present, they are of nearly the same constitution, and do not vary in their combinations. The determination of the sugar is somewhat more difficult.

The constituents of plants may be divided into two classes, one class embracing all those substances of which nitrogen or azote forms a part, and the other consisting of non-nitrogenous bodies. Gluten, albumen, gelatine, casein, legumen and fibrin, belong to the former class, being nitrogenous substances, while starch, gum, sugar, woody fibre, mucilage, &c., are destitute of nitrogen, or non-nitrogenous.

Only a small quantity of nitrogen is found in vegetable substances, and it is derived, in part, at least, from the atmosphere in the form of ammonia. On the other hand, nitrogenous substances form a large proportion of the constituents of the blood of animals and appear in their whole system. As there is a constant waste in the animal and a continual formation of new tissues,—as the whole body is constantly renewed through the agency of the blood which is converted into flesh and muscle,—there must be a never failing supply of nourishment, and this nourishment for the higher animals is found, as already intimated, in the nitrogenous elements of plants.

conducted by his gardener, George Sinclair, were detailed in a volume under the title of "*Hortus Gramineus Woburnensis.*" This work, which was the first treatise worthy of mention on this subject, became the text-book on the grasses, and has been followed by most subsequent writers, down to the present time. But these experiments must be regarded as very unsatisfactory, both on account of the imperfections of the methods of arriving at the results, (though they were the best then known, and suggested by Sir Humphrey Davy,) and because each species or variety was cultivated only to a very limited extent. The produce per acre, for instance, was calculated, in most cases, from the yield of four square feet. Besides this, very great discrepancies occur in the volume which can with difficulty be accounted for.

The analyses recently made by Prof. Way, the distinguished chemist of the Royal Agricultural Society, are more reliable, in my estimation, than any which can be found, and no treatise on the grasses would be complete without giving the valuable results to which he has arrived.

For every ounce of nitrogen which the animal requires to sustain life and health, he must take into the stomach, in the shape of food, such a quantity of vegetable substances as will furnish him with an ounce of nitrogen. If we suppose one kind of hay to contain one ounce of nitrogen to the pound, and another to have only half as much, or only an ounce in two pounds, the pound which contains the ounce of nitrogen would go as far to nourish the animal—other things being equal—as the two pounds which contain only the same quantity of nitrogen. The importance of woody fibre to act mechanically in giving bulk to the food, is not, of course, to be overlooked.

Nor is this a mere deduction of theory. The experiment has frequently been made, and it is now fully established both by science and experience, that the greater the proportion of nitrogen which any vegetable contains, the smaller will be the quantity of that vegetable required to nourish the animal body, and the less nitrogen any vegetable contains, the greater will be the quantity of it required. Muscle and flesh are composed of nitrogenous principles, while fat is made up of non-nitrogenous matter. Every keeper of stock knows that to feed an animal on oil cake alone, for instance, which is but slightly nitrogenous, might fatten him, but it would not give him strength of muscle or size; while if the same animal be kept on the cereal grains, as wheat or Indian corn, alone, his size rapidly increases, his muscular system develops, and he gains flesh without increasing his fat in proportion. It was with reference to these facts that Boussingault formed his tables of nutritive equivalents, and they agree very closely with the results of practical observation.

The non-nitrogenous substances are necessary for the production of fat and to supply the animal body with heat, and thus they meet a want in the animal economy, although they do not contribute so directly to nourish and sustain the system. They are, therefore, important in the analyses of articles of food, though not so essential in determining merely their nutritive values.

From what has been said, the reader will very readily understand the following tables containing the results of the investigations of Prof. Way. The specimens of the various grasses on which his researches were made, were analyzed both in their green state as taken from the field, and after being dried at a temperature of 212° Fahr., a point at which the moisture is found to be entirely expelled and evaporation ceases, and the importance of both determinations must be obvious on a moment's reflection.

The names of the natural grasses and the dates of their collection are arranged in the following table:—

TABLE V. *Natural Grasses. Name, and Date of Collection.*

Common Name.	Botanic Name.	Date of collection.	Character of the Soil.
Sweet-scented Vernal Grass, .	Anthoxanthum odoratum, .	May 25,	Calcareous loam.
Meadow Foxtail Grass, . .	Alopecurus pratensis, . .	June 1,	Calcareous loam, gravelly subsoil.
Tall Oat Grass, ...	Arrhenatherum avenaceum, .	July 17,	Forest marble loam.
Yellow Oat Grass, . . .	Avena flavescens, . . .	June 29,	Forest marble loam.
Downy Oat Grass, . . .	Trisetum pubescens, . .	July 11,	Dry calcareous loam.
Common Quaking Grass, . .	Briza media, ...	June 29,	Forest marble.
Upright Brome Grass, . .	Bromus erectus, . . .	June 23,	Calcareous loam.
Soft Brome Grass, . . .	Bromus mollis, . . .	May 8,	Stiff loam.
Crested Dog's-tail Grass, . .	Cynosurus cristatus, . .	June 21,	Calcareous loam.
Orchard Grass, ...	Dactylis glomerata, . . .	June 13,	Calcareous loam on gravel.
Orchard Grass, seeds ripe, .	Dactylis glomerata, . . .	July 19,	Calcareous loam.
Hard Fescue Grass, . . .	Festuca duriuscula, . .	June 13,	Dry calcareous loam.
Meadow Soft Grass, . . .	Holcus lanatus, . . .	June 29,	Calcareous loam.
Barley Grass, ...	Hordeum pratense, . . .	July 11,	Calcareous loam on gravel.
Perennial Rye Grass, . .	Lolium perenne, . . .	June 8,	Calcareous rubbly loam
Italian Rye Grass, . . .	Lolium italicum, . . .	June 13,	Forest marble loam.
Timothy, ...	Phleum pratense, . . .	June 13,	Forest marble loam.
Annual Spear Grass, .	Poa annua, ...	May 28,	Loam, with gravelly subsoil.
June Grass, ...	Poa pratensis, ...	June 11,	Dry calcareous loam.
Rough-stalked Meadow Grass, .	Poa trivialis, ...	June 18,	Calcareous loam.
Grass from a watered or irrigated meadow, ...	First Crop, ...	April 30,	Calcareous loam.
Grass from a watered or irrigated meadow, ...	Second Crop, ...	June 26,	Calcareous loam.
Annual Rye Grass, . . .	- - -	June 8,	Calcareous rubbly loam

In the same manner, the name and date of collection of each specimen of artificial grass, analyzed, are arranged in table VI.

TABLE VI. *Artificial Grasses. Name, and Date of Collection.*

Common Name.	Botanic Name.	Date of collection.	Character of Soil.
Red Clover, ...	Trifolium pratense, . .	June 7,	Tenacious loam.
Perennial Clover, . . .	Trifolium perenne, . .	June 4,	Calcareous loam.
Crimson Clover, . . .	Trifolium incarnatum, .	June 4,	Calcareous loam.
Cow Grass, . . .	Trifolium medium, . .	June 7,	Tenacious loam.
Cow Grass, 2d lot, . .	Trifolium medium, . .	June 21,	Calcareous loam.
Hop trefoil, ...	Trifolium procumbens, .	June 13,	Calcareous loam.
White Clover, . . .	Trifolium repens, . .	June 18,	Forest loam.
Common vetch, . . .	Vicia sativa, . . .	June 13,	Forest loam.
Sainfoin, ...	Onobrychis sativa, . .	June 8,	Dry loam.
Lucerne, or Alfalfa, . .	Medicago sativa, . . .	June 16,	- -
Black Medick, or Nonsuch, .	Medicago lupulina, . .	June 6,	Calcareous loam.

The inquiries of Prof. Way were directed to ascertain

1. The proportion of water in each grass as taken from the field.

2. The proportion of albuminous or flesh-forming substances, including, without distinction, all the nitrogenous principles.

3. The proportion of oily or fatty matters which may be called *fat-forming principles.*

4. The proportion of elements of respiration, or heat producing principles, among which are included starch, gum, sugar, pectic acid, &c.; all the non-nitrogenous substances indeed, except fatty matters and woody fibre.

5. The proportion of woody fibre.

6. The amount of mineral matter or ash.

The specimens were picked out, plant by plant, each specimen by itself, from fields in which they were growing naturally, or mixed in the ordinary mode of cultivation, and were not raised expressly for analysis.

These tables of analyses, containing as they do the results of profound investigation, and forming as they do one of the most important contributions recently made to the science of agriculture, are worthy of careful study and will be found to be full of the most valuable practical suggestions.

The results of the analysis of the natural grasses in the green state, are arranged in table VII. as follows:—

TABLE VII. *Analysis of Natural Grasses.* (100 *parts as taken green from the field.*)

Name of Grass.	Water.	Albuminous, or flesh-forming principles.	Fatty Matters.	Heat-producing principles—starch, gum, sugar, etc.	Woody Fibre.	Mineral matter, or ash.
Sweet-scented Vernal,	80.35	2.05	.67	8.54	7.15	1.24
Meadow Foxtail,	80.20	2.44	.52	8.59	6.70	1.55
Tall Oat Grass,	72.65	3.54	.87	11.21	9.37	2.36
Yellow Oat Grass,	60.40	2.96	1.04	18.66	14.22	2.72
Downy Oat Grass,	61.50	3.07	.92	19.16	13.34	2.01
Quaking Grass,	51.85	2.93	1.45	22.60	17.00	4.17
Upright Brome Grass,	59.57	3.78	1.35	33·19		2.11
Soft Brome Grass,	76.62	4.05	.47	9.04	8.46	1.36
Crested Dog's-tail,	62.73	4.13	1.32	19.64	9.80	2.38
Orchard Grass,	70.00	4.06	.94	13.30	10.11	1.59
Orchard Grass, seeds ripe,	52.57	10.93	.74	12.61	20.54	2.61
Hard Fescue Grass,	69.33	3.70	1.02	12.46	11.83	1.66
Meadow Soft Grass,	69.70	3.49	1.02	11.92	11.94	1.93
Barley Grass,	58.85	4.59	.94	20.05	13.03	2.54
Perennial Rye Grass,	71.43	3.37	.91	12.08	10.06	2.15
Italian Rye Grass,	75.61	2.45	.80	14.11	4.82	2.21
Timothy Grass,	57.21	4.86	1.50	22.85	11.32	2.26
Annual Spear Grass,	79.14	2.47	.71	10.79	6.30	.59
June Grass,	67.14	3.41	.86	14.15	12.49	1.95
Rough-stalked Meadow Grass,	73.60	2.58	.97	10.54	10.11	2.20
Grass from Irrigated Meadow,	87.58	3.22	.81	3.98	3.13	1.28
Grass from Irrigated Meadow, 2d crop,	74.53	2.78	.52	11.17	8.76	2.24
Annual Rye Grass,	69.00	2.96	.69	12.89	12.47	1.99

A glance at the first column of table VII. will show a striking difference in the percentage of water, it being as high as 80 in some instances, while it falls as low as 60, and in one instance to 51, without considering the second specimen of orchard grass—in which the seed was allowed to ripen, when, of course, the amount of water would be much less than at the period of flowering—or the irrigated grasses.

It will be noticed that those grasses which come earliest into flower are generally the most succulent, though this is not uniformly the case.

It will be seen that the sweet-scented vernal grass and the meadow foxtail contain but 20 parts in 100, of dry, solid matter, while the yellow oat and the downy oat grasses contain nearly double, or about 40 per cent. This difference, though of no great importance in itself, is of some interest in showing that to judge of the quantity of hay a given burden of grass will produce, it is necessary to consider the species of grass which mainly composes the meadow, since it is evident that a given weight of one variety might make double the quantity of the same weight of another.

But the chief interest of the table is to be found in columns three, four and five. The albuminous or flesh forming principles will be found to be double in some instances what they are in others; and in accordance with the principles laid down in the explanatory remarks which precede the tables, some would appear to be more than twice as nutritive as others, but it should be borne in mind that these differences depend in part on the variations in the quantity of water, and that the real differences will appear more apparent in the dried specimens.

A glance at table VIII. will show that the percentage of water in the artificial grasses as taken from the field, is greater than that of the natural grasses under the same circumstances. The percentage of albuminous or flesh forming principles is generally, though by no means uniformly, less than that of our best grasses. Compare red clover, for instance, with Timothy, and the first striking peculiarity is the difference in the amount of water, in the one case exceeding 81 per cent., leaving but 19 per cent. of solid matter from which the flesh forming and other nutritive substances must be drawn, while in Timothy the water amounts to only little over 57 per cent., leaving 43 per cent. of solid substances containing nutritive principles. This is an important difference to begin with. The percentage of flesh forming principles of the two plants does not, at first sight, appear to differ very materially, the clover containing 4.27 the Timothy 4.86; but a little consideration of the exceeding value of this constituent, will show that the latter has an important advantage in this respect over the clover. In fat-forming principles, the Timothy is more than twice as rich as clover, while in heat-producing principles—also very valuable—Timothy far surpasses clover, the one producing 22.85 per cent., and the other only 8.45 per cent. Of waste and useless matter in the shape of woody fibre, Timothy contains the largest per cent., while the larger quantity of mineral matter shows it also to be a greater exhauster of the soil. The most valuable practical deductions of a similar nature may be made by comparing these tables.

TABLE VIII. *Analysis of Artificial Grasses.* (100 *parts, as taken from the field*).

Name of Plant.	Water.	Albuminous, or flesh-forming principles.	Fatty Matters.	Heat-producing principles—starch, gum, sugar, etc.	Woody fibre.	Mineral matter, or ash.
Red Clover,	81.01	4.27	.69	8.45	3.76	1.82
Perennial Clover,	81.05	3.64	.78	8.04	4.91	1.58
Crimson Clover,	82.14	2.96	.67	6.70	5.78	1.75
Cow Grass,	74.10	6.30	.92	9.42	6.25	3.01
Cow Grass, 2d specimen,	77.57	4.22	1.07	11.14	4.23	1.77
Hop Trefoil,	83.48	3.39	.77	7.25	3.74	1.37
White Clover,	79.71	3.80	.89	8.14	5.33	2.08
Common Vetch,	82.90	4.04	.52	6.75	4.68	1.11
Sainfoin,	76.64	4.32	.70	10.73	5.77	1.84
Lucerne, or Alfalfa,	69.95	3.83	.82	13.62	8.74	3.04
Black Medick, or Nonsuch,	76.80	5.70	.94	7.73	6.32	2.51

It will be seen in table IX. that in the case of orchard grass and the irrigated meadow, the seeds were ripened, and they should not, therefore, be compared with other grasses taken in the blossom, without considering this fact. It will be seen, too, that the specimens analyzed were in the dry state, much drier than they could be made by the ordinary process of hay making; for however perfectly the hay is cured it will still contain a very considerable percentage of water, and if artificially dried, as in the trials given above, and then exposed to the air, it will absorb from 10 to 15 per cent. of water, showing that no hay is absolutely dry by any ordinary processes. In England, the percentage of water in well made hay is about 16, and hay artificially dried will absorb that amount if exposed again to the air. I do not think the percentage here would be so large, for obvious reasons. In the analysis of the hay of the reed canary grass, made by Prof. Horsford and given on a preceding page, the percentage was but 10.24. That was a well-cured specimen, taken after it had passed the period of blossoming, and the amount of water is, perhaps, slightly below the average.

TABLE IX. *Analysis of Natural Grasses.* (100 *parts of the grass dried at* 212° *Fahr.*)

Name of Grass.	Albuminous, or flesh-forming principles.	Fatty Matters.	Heat-producing principles—starch, sugar, gum.	Woody Fibre.	Mineral Matter, or ash.
Sweet-scented Vernal Grass, ...	10.43	3.41	43.48	36.36	6.32
Meadow Foxtail, ...	12.32	2.92	43.12	33.83	7.81
Tall Oat Grass, ...	12.95	3.19	38.03	34.24	11.59
Yellow Oat Grass, ...	7.48	2.61	47.08	35.95	6.88
Downy Oat Grass, ...	7.97	2.39	49.78	34.64	5.22
Quaking Grass, ...	6.08	3.01	46.95	35.30	8.66
Upright Brome Grass, ...	9.44	3.33	82·02		5.21
Soft Brome Grass, ...	17.29	2.11	38.66	36.12	5.82
Crested Dog's-tail, ...	11.08	3.54	52.64	26.36	6.38
Orchard Grass, ...	13.53	3.14	44.32	33.70	5.31
Orchard Grass, seeds ripe, ...	23.08	1.56	26.53	43.32	5.51
Hard Fescue Grass, ...	12.10	3.34	40.43	38.71	5.42
Meadow Soft Grass, ...	11.52	3.56	39.25	39.30	6.37
Meadow Barley Grass, ...	11.17	2.30	46.68	31.67	6.18
Perennial Rye Grass, ...	11,85	3.17	42.24	35.20	7.54
Italian Rye Grass, ...	10.10	3.27	57.82	19.76	9.05
Timothy, ...	11.36	3.55	53.35	26.46	5.28
Annual Spear Grass, ...	11.83	3.42	51.70	30.22	2.83
June Grass, ...	10.35	2.63	43.06	38.02	5.94
Rough-stalked Meadow Grass, ...	9.80	3.67	40.17	38.03	8.33
Grass from irrigated meadow, ...	25.91	6.53	32.05	25.14	10.37
Grass from irrigated meadow, 2d crop, .	10.92	2.06	43.90	34.30	8.82

It will be seen that a great difference exists in the valuable constituents of the grasses analyzed in this table, ranging as follows:—

	Lowest.	Highest.	Average.
Flesh-forming principles, . .	6.08	17.29	11.68
Fat-producing principles, . .	2.11	3.67	2.89
Heat-giving principles, . .	38.03	57.82	47.92

TABLE X. *Analysis of Artificial Grasses.* (*In* 100 *parts of the grass dried at* 212° *Fahr.*)

Name of Plant.	Albuminous, or flesh-forming principles.	Fatty Matters.	Heat-producing principles—starch, sugar, gum, etc.	Woody fibre.	Mineral matter, or ash.
Red Clover, ...	22.55	3.67	44.47	19.75	9.56
Perennial Clover, ...	19.18	4.09	42.42	25.96	8.35
Crimson Clover, ...	16.60	3.73	37.50	32.39	9.78
Cow Grass, ...	24.33	3.57	36.36	24.14	11.60
Cow Grass, 2d specimen, ...	18.77	4.77	49.65	18.84	7.97
Hop Trefoil, ...	20.48	4.67	43.86	22.66	8.33
White Clover, ...	18.76	4.38	40.04	26.53	10.29
Common Vetch, ...	23.61	3.06	39.45	27.38	6.50
Sainfoin, ...	18.45	3.01	45.96	24.71	7.87
Lucerne, or Alfalfa, ...	12.76	2.76	40.16	34.21	10.11
Black Medick, ...	24.60	4.06	33.31	27.19	10.84

A glance at this table will show that the different principles in the artificial grasses vary to a great extent, as follows:—

	Lowest.	Highest.	Average.
Flesh-forming principles, . .	12.76	24.60	18.68
Fat-producing principles, . .	2.76	4.77	3.76
Heat-giving principles, . .	33.31	49.65	41.48

The difference in composition exhibited in the natural grasses of table IX. are very marked, and of course, the value of the grasses as compared with each other must vary greatly. Still, the practical value of a grass depends somewhat upon circumstances which cannot be analyzed, such as the period at which it arrives at maturity, and the particular soil and location of the farmer. It might happen that a grass not in itself so rich in nutritive qualities as another, would be preferred on account of its coming to maturity just at the time when the farmer most needed it. But the particular value of this table is, that it shows the comparative nutritive qualities of the grasses, since all the specimens were collected and investigated in the same manner, at the same period of growth,—or as nearly as possible,—when in the flower, so that whatever sources of error might exist to modify the results, they would naturally apply to all alike.

The grasses from the irrigated meadow consisted principally of June, or Kentucky blue grass, rough stalked meadow grass, perennial rye grass, meadow soft grass, barley grass, meadow oat grass and a few other species, and it will be noticed that in combination they abound in flesh and fat-forming principles to a greater extent than we should be led to suppose from the composition of any one of them alone.

Our favorite Timothy compares very favorably with the other grasses, containing a less percentage of useless matter as woody fibre, than any other, except Italian rye grass and crested dog's-tail, a grass not common with us, and the irrigated grasses. In point of soluble, heat-producing principles, sugar, gum and starch, it is surpassed by the Italian rye grass, but by no others. The analyses of this grass in its green and dry states in tables VII. and IX., fully justify the preference which we have long shown for the use of Timothy; for, as taken from the field at the time of blossoming, it will be found to contain less water, (table VII.,) a greater percentage of flesh and fat-forming principles, and less useless matter in the shape of woody fibre, than most of the other grasses. The deductions of science certainly correspond, in this case, with the results of practice.

A comparison of tables VII. and IX. with tables VIII. and X. will show the comparative advantages of the use of the artificial grasses, in point of albuminous or flesh-forming principles and fatty matters. The carbonaceous or heat-producing principles remain nearly the same throughout, while the percentage of waste matter or woody fibre is less than in the natural grasses. This is an important fact, worthy of the careful consideration of the farmer.

In the sixth column of table IX. will be found the percentage of ash of each of the grasses analyzed. Table XI. contains a still further analysis of this ash, which gives all the inorganic constituents which the plant derives from the soil and the manures furnished to it. It is important and suggestive to one who will examine it carefully, as indicating the kind of manure which in many cases it may be desirable to apply.

The first peculiarity which plainly appears from a glance at the ash analyses, is the very large percentage of silicates and

TABLE XI. *Analysis of the Ash of some of the Natural and Artificial Grasses.*

Common Name.	Ash in 100 parts of dried grass.	Silica.	Phos. Acid.	Sulph. Acid.	Carb. Acid.	Lime.	Magnesia.	Peroxide of iron.	Potash.	Soda.	Chloride of Potassium.	Chloride of Sodium.
Meadow Foxtail, ...	7.81	38.75	6.25	2.16	.65	3.90	1.28	.47	37.03	–	9.50	–
Sweet-scented Vernal, . .	6.32	28.36	10.09	3.39	1.26	9.21	2.53	1.18	32.03	–	7.03	4.90
Downy Oat Grass, . . .	5.22	36.28	10.82	3.37	–	4.72	3.17	.72	31.21	–	4.05	5.66
Upright Brome Grass, .	5.21	38.48	7.53	5.46	.55	10.38	4.99	.26	20.33	–	10.63	1.38
Soft Brome Grass, . . .	5.82	33.34	9.62	4.91	9.07	6.64	2.60	.28	30.09	.33	–	3.11
Crested Dog's-tail, . . .	6.38	40.11	7.24	3.20	–	10.16	2.43	.18	24.99	–	11.60	–
Orchard Grass, ...	5.31	26.65	8.60	3.52	2.09	5.82	2.22	.59	29.52	–	17.86	3.09
Orchard Grass, with seeds ripe, .	5.51	32.18	6.41	3.96	2.88	8.14	3.47	.23	33.06	–	4.87	4.76
Hard Fescue Grass, . . .	5.42	28.53	12.07	3.45	1.38	10.31	2.83	.78	31.84	–	8.17	.62
Meadow Soft Grass, . . .	6.37	28.31	8.02	4.41	1.82	8.31	3.41	.31	34.83	–	3.91	6.66
Meadow Barley Grass, . .	5.67	56.23	6.04	4.29	–	5.04	2.42	.66	20.26	3.40	–	1.66
Perennial Rye Grass, . . .	7.54	27.13	8.73	5.20	.49	9.64	2.85	.21	24.67	–	13.80	7.25
Annual Spear Grass, . . .	2.83	16.03	9.11	10.18	3.29	11.69	2.44	1.57	41.86	–	.47	3.35
June Grass, ...	5.94	32.93	10.02	4.26	.40	5.63	2.71	.28	31.17	–	11.25	1.31
Rough-stalked Meadow Grass, .	8.33	37.50	9.13	4.47	.29	8.80	3.22	.29	29.40	–	6.90	–
Timothy, ...	5.29	31.09	11.29	4.86	4.02	14.94	5.30	.27	24.25	–	.70	3.24
Annual Rye Grass, . . .	6.45	41.79	10.07	3.45	–	6.82	2·59	.28	28.99	.87	–	5.11
Yellow Oat Grass, . . .	5.28	35.20	9.31	4.00	–	7.98	3.07	2.40	36.06	.73	–	1.25
Red Clover, ...	9.56	.59	6.71	1.85	23.47	22.62	4.08	.26	36.45	–	2.39	1.53
White Clover, ...	–	3.68	11.53	7 21	18.03	26.41	8.15	1.96	14.33	3.72	–	4.95
Sainfoin in flower, . . .	6.37	3.22	9.35	3.28	15.20	24.30	5.03	.61	31.90	–	6.24	.78
Sainfoin in seed, ...	6.50	3.49	7.97	2.33	17.36	29.67	4.59	.58	29.61	1.25	–	3.12
Italian Rye Grass in flower, .	6.97	59.18	6.34	2.82	–	9.95	2.23	.78	12.45	3.98	–	2.27
Italian Rye Grass in seed, . .	6.40	60.62	6.32	1.31	–	12.29	2.64	.30	10.77	.13	–	5.58

potash contained in the natural grasses, and the very small comparative percentage of silica in the artificial grasses, the red and white clovers. The large percentage of lime and carbonic acid attract our attention in the latter. This table is exceedingly valuable as suggesting the proper course of manuring for the most successful cultivation of the various crops contained in it.

If now we cast our eye at the analysis of some of our com-

TABLE XII. *Analysis of Specimens of Weeds, as taken from the field, and when dried.*

Name of Plant.	Date of collection	Water.	Albuminous matter.	Fatty matter.	Heat-producing principles.	Wood fibre.	Ash.
Ox-eye Daisy, (*Crysanthemum leucanthemum*,)	June 23,	71.85	2.12	.999	12.64	10.51	1.86
Yellow Buttercup, (*Ranunculus acris*,) .	June 13,	83.15	1.18	.507	6.26	3.00	.91
Sorrel, (*Rumex acetosa*,).	July 4,	75.37	1.90	.545	7.62	13.04	1.51
DRIED SPECIMENS OF THE SAME.							
Ox-eye Daisy, ...	– –	–	7.53	3.49	45.02	37.33	6.63
Buttercup, ...	– –	–	9.98	4.28	52.69	25.34	7.71
Sorrel, ...	– –	–	7.71	2.19	46.82	37.16	6.12

mon weeds, we shall see how far superior the cultivated grasses are in nitrogenous or nutritive principles.

The albuminous principles are very much less than in either the natural or the artificial grasses.

A line of investigation, both scientific and practical, equally interesting and valuable with the foregoing, would lead into the comparative nutritive equivalents of hay and other feeding substances. This is not the place to discuss that subject in full, the line of our present inquiry embracing only the comparative nutritive values of the grasses themselves. For convenience of reference, however, I subjoin the following table, (XIII.,) embracing the results of the profoundest researches of many distinguished chemists and practical men, both in the laboratory and the barn. Boussingault and others in France, and Fresenius, Thaer and others in Germany, have devoted to these and similar investigations the best part of their lives.

It is necessary to remark that tables of nutritive equivalents are liable to imperfections, on account of sources of error which must exist in the nature of things, as difference of soil, climate, season, imperfection of methods of analysis, &c.; but making all allowance for these, and admitting that the table cannot be absolutely, and literally correct or perfect, it possesses great practical value and interest as giving a good general idea of the relative value for feeding purposes, of various agricultural products.

In regard to the nutritive value, as based on the amount of nitrogen or nitrogenous compounds, it may be remarked that the latest and most careful experiments, conducted by most experienced and competent experimenters, tend to show that this basis is correct, so far as it can be applied to substances so analogous in composition that they can be included in one group; as for example, the different root crops possess a nutritive value in proportion to the amount of nitrogen they contain, but the nutritive value of a root ought not to be compared with a succulent vegetable, like clover, for instance, by the proportion of nitrogen in each, merely, without taking into consideration other properties. In other words, roots may be compared with each other on that basis merely, and grasses with each other, and leguminous plants with each other, but not root crops and grasses. This fact is alluded to as a possible source of error in some of the earlier researches of Boussingault, and not as materially affecting the practical value of the table.

The mode of using table XIII. is very simple. Good upland meadow hay,—or what would be called in New England, good English hay,—is taken as a standard of comparison. Now if we wished to produce the same results with carrots as with one hundred pounds of good, average English hay, we must use, according to Boussingault's column of equivalents, 382 pounds of carrots, or for each pound of hay, 3.82 pounds of carrots, and according to the practical experiments mentioned, 366 pounds, 250 pounds, 225 pounds, 300 pounds, and so on, to each 100 pounds of hay.

According to the theoretical values of Boussingault, 100 pounds of hay are equal in feeding qualities to 65 pounds of barley, 60 pounds of oats, 58 pounds of rye, or 55 pounds of wheat. While, according to the experiments of Thaer, 100 pounds of hay produced the same effect as 76 pounds of barley, 86 pounds of oats, 71 pounds of rye, 64 pounds of wheat.

With regard to the analyses of tables VII., VIII., IX. and X., some allowance should undoubtedly be made for difference of climate, since it is well known that grasses, as well as other plants, grown rapidly in a hot sun, which we usually have in the months of May, June and July, contain a much larger amount of nutritive and saccharine matter than those grown slower and in a greater amount of available moisture both in

TABLE XIII. *Nutritive Equivalents. (Practical and Theoretical.)*

ARTICLES OF FOOD.	THEORETICAL VALUES. Boussingault.				THEORETICAL VALUES. Fresenius.		Practical values, as obtained by experiments in feeding, according to						
	Water in 100 parts.	Nitrogen in 100 parts of dried substance.	Nitrogen in 100 parts of undried substance.	Nutritive equivalent.	Relative proportion of nitrogenized to non-nitrogeniz'd substances.	Nutritive equivalent.	Block.	Petri.	Meyer.	Thaer.	Pabet.	Schwertz.	Schweitzer.
English Hay,	11.0	1.34	1.15	100	–	100	100	100	100	100	100	100	100
Lucerne,	16.6	1.66	1.38	83	–	–	–	90	–	90	100	100	–
Red Clover Hay,	10.1	1.70	1.54	75	1 to 6.08	77.9	100	90	–	90	100	100	–
Red Clover (green),	76.0	–	.64	311	–	–	430	–	–	450	425	–	–
Rye Straw,	18.7	.30	.24	479	1 to 24.40	527 7-12	200	500	150	666	350	–	267
Oat Straw,	21.0	.36	.30	383	1 to 12.50	445 5-12	200	200	150	190	200	400	200
Carrot Leaves (tops),	70.9	2.94	.85	135	–	–	–	–	–	–	–	–	–
Swedish Turnips,	91.0	1.83	.17	676	–	–	–	300	–	300	250	200	–
Mangold Wurzel,	–	–	–	–	1 to 7.26	391⅓	366	400	250	460	250	333	366⅔
White Silician Beet,	85.6	1.43	.18	669	–	–	–	–	–	–	–	–	–
Carrots,	87.6	2.40	.30	382	1 to 7.84	542.1	366	250	225	300	250	270	300
Potatoes,	75.9	1.50	.36	319	1 to 9.00	330 5-12	216	200	150	200	200	200	200
Potatoes kept in pits,	76.8	1.18	.30	383	–	–	400	–	–	–	–	–	–
Beans,	7.9	5.50	5.11	23	1 to 2.8	34 5-12	30	54	50	73	40	–	30
Peas,	8.6	4.20	3.84	27	1 to 2.14	34⅓	30	54	48	66	40	Boussingault. 59	30
Indian Corn,	18.0	2.00	1.64	70	1 to 6.55	–	–	52	–	–	–		–
Buckwheat,	12.5	2.40	2.10	55	1 to 6.05	93 5-12	–	64	–	–	–	–	–
Barley,	13.2	2.02	1.76	65	1 to 4.25	–	33	61	53	76	50	–	35
Oats,	12.4	2.22	1.92	60	1 to 4.08	58 11-12	39⅓	71	–	86	60	–	37½
Rye,	11.5	2.27	2.00	58	1 to 4.42	58 1-16	33	55	51	71	50	–	33⅓
Wheat,	10.5	2.33	2.09	55	1 to 2.42	38 5-6	27	52	46	64	40	–	30
Oil-cake (Linseed),	13.4	6.00	5.20	22	–	–	42	108	–	–	–	–	43

the atmosphere and the soil, which is ordinarily present in the climate of England. Every observing farmer knows that grasses grown on our low, reclaimed swamp lands, for instance, make less milk, and less flesh and fat in animals, than the same species grown on our dry, upland soils. The same difference must exist, to some extent, between our grasses and the grasses grown in a comparatively moist climate, where they have the advantage of more frequent rains, which push them to a more complete development and give them greater luxuriance, increasing, of course, the quantity of their produce, while their quality cannot be improved in the points alluded to. This subject will come more properly under discussion in treating of the

INFLUENCE OF THE SEASONS.

We now come to consider the influence which the season or the climate has upon the quantity and nutritive quality of grass. Before entering upon this topic, it is proper to remark, that in order to bring together the practical wisdom and judgment of some of the best farmers in the State, as well as to be able to present some statistical information in regard to the product of grass and hay for the past season, I directed the following circular to one or more farmers in every town in Massachusetts, asking for replies from each.

BOARD OF AGRICULTURE, STATE HOUSE,
Boston, Sept. 1, 1856,

DEAR SIR:—Will you have the goodness to reply to the following inquiries in reference to the grass and hay crop of your town, according to the best of your judgment and experience? If circumstances prevent your giving it personal attention, will you be kind enough to put it into the hands of some one interested in the subject in your neighborhood, who will do me the favor to answer it?

1. What was the estimated yield of grass and hay in your town this season, as compared with others? If above or below the average, how much?

2. What, in your opinion, is the effect of a wet or a dry season on the quality of grass and hay? Is grass grown in the shade as good as that grown in the sun, and what is the difference?

[This question embraces the intrinsic value of hay this season as compared with the crops of 1854 and 1855, both comparatively dry seasons, while this has been unusually wet in most parts of the State.]

3. In what month do you prefer to seed down land designed for mowing, and what is the reason of your preference?

4. What varieties of grass seed do you usually sow for mowing, and what for permanent pasturage, and in what quantities and proportions, per acre?

5. Do you prefer to sow grass seed alone in either case, or with some variety of grain? If the latter, why, and with what grain?

6. Have you cultivated or raised orchard, fowl meadow, or blue joint grasses, and with what result as compared with the yield and value of other grasses?

7. At what stage of growth do you prefer to cut grass to make into English and into swale hay, and what is the reason for your preference?

8. What is the best mode of making hay from Timothy, from red-top, and from wet meadow grass, and at what state of dryness do you consider it made, or fit to get into the barn?

[This question embraces, to some extent, the time taken to make it under ordinary circumstances of good weather, &c. This, of course, varies greatly, but some farmers would dry grass cut in the blossom two good hay days, while others would prefer to cure it less, and get it in on the day it was cut.]

9. Will you state in detail how you make or cure clover, and how, when so cured, it compares in value with other kinds of hay to feed out to farm stock?

10. Have you used hay caps, and if so, with what result, in point of economy? How were they made and at what cost?

11. Have you used a mowing machine, and if so, what patent, with what power, and with what advantage?

12. At what height from the ground do you prefer to have your grass cut, and why?

13. Have you used a horse-rake, and if so, what patent, and with what advantage?

14. Do you feed off the after growth of your mowing lands in the fall? Do you think it an injury or a benefit to the field to feed it off?

15. Do you top-dress your mowing or pasture lands, and if so, what manure do you prefer to use, at what time, and in what quantities do you apply it?

16. What is the best mode of renovating old worn out pasture lands?

17. If you have any experience in ditching and draining wet meadow, or ditching or diking salt marsh, will you state the result, and the comparative value of the grass before and after the operation?

18. What are the most valuable varieties of salt marsh grasses, and how does the hay made from them compare in value with good English hay?

17

19. Have you any experience in irrigating mowing or pasture lands, and if so, what is the result?

20. Do you prefer to salt your hay when putting into the barn, and if so, what quantity do you use, per ton?

21. What do you consider the best mode of destroying couch or twitch grass?

22. What is the best mode of destroying the white weed or ox-eye daisy?

23. Will you give any other details not suggested by the above, which, in your opinion, may be considered important, in regard to this crop, and particularly if you have experimented with any varieties of grass not in general cultivation, such as lucerne or alfalfa, rye grass, brome grass, Kentucky blue grass, &c., will you state the results as fully as possible? If you have any varieties of grass found to be valuable but not in general cultivation, the names of which are not known to you, will you send them to this office where the names will be given?

Very respectfully, your obedient servant,

CHARLES L. FLINT,

Secretary of the Board of Agriculture.

I am indebted to the kindness of many enterprising and intelligent farmers for full and valuable answers from more than two hundred towns in the State, and these alone would make a valuable volume of themselves. I can, of course, do no more than extract from them as freely as space will permit, which I shall do at greater length in the subsequent sections.

No crop, perhaps, is more dependent on the seasons than the grasses. Every farmer knows that a moist spring, with rains evenly distributed over the months of April, May and June, will insure him the most luxuriant crops of grass and hay; and he knows, also, that a dry, cold spring is fatal to their rapid and healthy development, and that he must, in such a spring, expect a comparatively small crop. These and many similar facts are familiar to the commonest practical observation.

It has also been found by observation that the grasses will vegetate when the temperature of the air is above the freezing point of water, 32° Fahrenheit, provided the temperature of the soil ranges from 35° to 40,° while a lower temperature checks their growth. Vegetation, at temperatures higher than these, depends much on the amount of moisture and heat, both of the soil and the atmosphere. Grass will not vegetate when the temperature of the air is higher than 66° unless the soil is very moist. When the vapor of the air is at its maximum, or when the air is saturated with moisture, vegetation advances with the greatest rapidity, and this most frequently happens with us in the earlier growing months, April, May and June. But when the moisture in the atmosphere is slight, and the soil becomes dry, and the subsoil is porous, the turf of our fields and pastures suffers from the drought, and scarcely a year passes over us when this does not happen.

A writer in the Journal of the Royal Agricultural Society, (quoted in the Farmers' Magazine, Vol. ix., No. 5, Third Series,) after many careful observations, comes to the conclusion, First. That the growth of grass is always proportionate to the heat of the air, if a sufficiency of moisture be present in the atmosphere. Second. That in the climate of England the moisture present is rarely sufficient to allow the temperature to have full effect, when that temperature exceeds 56°, but that if moisture be artificially supplied, as by irrigation, to catch water meadows, that then vegetation will still proceed in proportion to the heat. Third. That when the temperature of the air is between 36° and 41°, the grass will only vegetate with a fifth part of the force that it will when the temperature is 56°. Thus the land that will keep ten sheep per acre in the latter case, will only keep two in the former. That from 41° to 46° its growth is two-fifths, or double that of its growth when the temperature is under 41°, and it will then keep four sheep instead of two. Again, from 46° to 50°, its growth will rise to seven-tenths, or it will keep on the same ground from five to seven sheep, and from 50° to 66°, it generally,—unless assisted by an artificial addition of moisture—arrives at its maximum; but if the month of June be very moist, it will continue to grow with an increase of force up to 60°.

Our climate is very different from that of England. The evaporation from the soil is ordinarily very much more rapid, and the actual amount of moisture in the air is greater, since it is well established that the evaporation is in proportion to the height of the temperature and the extent of water or land surface; that in the temperate zones it amounts to about thirty-seven inches a year, while in the tropics it rises to from ninety to one hundred inches, and that the atmosphere when at the freezing point contains about a two-hundredth part of its weight of water, while at 52° it contains a hundredth part, or twice as much; at 74°, a fiftieth part, or four times as much, and at 98°, a twenty-fifth part, or eight times as much, and so on in that ratio. Now although the mean annual temperature of the two countries is about the same,—it being near London about 48° 5′, and at Boston 48° 9′,—yet the temperature of the growing months of the two countries presents a marked difference, the mean temperature of every one being with us much higher. But the climate of England is proverbially moist, notwithstanding that the mean annual fall of rain near London is only little over twenty-five inches, while the quantity which falls at Boston is over forty-two inches. The amount of sensible moisture of the atmosphere is greater in England than here, though the actual amount existing in our atmosphere must exceed that of the atmosphere even in the eastern part of England. Our soil is consequently dryer, and unless we have frequent rains vegetation suffers sooner, and the growth of grass is liable to be checked for the want of moisture. This actually happens more or less nearly every year. But the spring of the past year was an exception, for the quantity of rain in most parts of the State was no only somewhat larger than usual, but it was well distributed over the spring months; that is, it fell frequently and in small quantities. This, as is usually the case, caused an early and remarkably luxuriant growth of grass, while the quality was not generally considered so good as the average. It may be laid down as a well-fixed principle, that the grass crop is better from large quantities of rain falling at once and at longer intervals,—provided it does not come in torrents to prostrate the crop, and that the intervals are not so long as to produce droughts, which are always attended with deleterious effects,—than from smaller quantities falling with greater frequency. The quantity in the latter case will not ordinarily be so great as in the former, but it is more than compensated, it is thought, by the increased value. More accurate statistics will throw light on this subject.

As a means of comparison, the following table of the mean monthly temperature and rain at the observatory at Cambridge, during the growing months of 1854, '55 and '56, will be found convenient. The observations were made four times a day, at sunrise, 9 A. M., 3 and 9 P. M. The latitude being 42° 22′ 48″, the longitude 71° 1′.

Months.	Mean Temp. in 1854.	Rain in 1854.	Mean Temp. in 1855.	Rain in 1855.	Mean Temp. in 1856.	Rain in 1856.
				Inches.		Inches.
March, . . .	33°.1	2.949	32°.31	1.159	26°.98	0.970
April, . . .	42°.9	4.842	44°.08	3.990	45°.82	3.732
May, ...	57°.7	5.453	53°.40	1.501	52°.55	6.732
June, . . .	65°.9	3.585	65°.48	3.581	68°.08	2.869
July, ...	72°.9	3.239	72°.24	4.845	72°.76	4.243
August, . . .	68°.6	0.351	67°.31	2.270	67°.31	14.981
September, . .	61°.4	4.36 0	61°.45	1.216	62°.98	–

The mean temperature and the rain at Amherst, during the growing months of 1856, was as follows:—

Temperature.		Amount of Rain.		Average of 18 years.
	Fahr.		Inches.	Inches.
March, ...	25°.88	March, ...	1.118	3.05
April, ...	46°.44	April, ...	2.510	3.27
May, ...	55°.58	May, ...	5.313	3.91
June, ...	68°.66	June, ...	1.920	3.22
July, ...	72°.93	July, ...	1.955	4.05
August, ...	66°.19	August, ...	12.132	4.40
September, ...	60°.79	September, ...	3.472	3.26

The first of these places represents the eastern section of the State, the second, the western; and observations made at Boston, at Bradford, at Salem and elsewhere in the eastern part, do not materially differ from those at Cambridge, while the observations at Williamstown and at Albany, N. Y., do not differ materially, so far as practical deductions are concerned, from those at Amherst.

The amount of rain at Worcester, in the central section, in 1854, '55 and '56, was as follows:—

Months.	1854.	1855.	1856.	Average for 15 years.
	Inches.	Inches.	Inches.	Inches.
March,	3.45	.23	1.69	3.29
April,	6.69	5.39	3.34	3.98
May,	6.78	1.64	6.55	4.36
June,	3.05	4.19	1.44	2.93
July,	5.68	9.40	2.68	3.70
August,	.35	4.06	13.14	5.58
September,	5.53	.20	3.39	3.47

The amount of rain at Providence, R. I., on our southern border, was as follows:—

Months.	For 1856.	Average of 25 years.
	Inches.	Inches.
April,	2.80	3.57
May,	4.10	3.33
June,	2.47	2.95
July,	4.20	2.91
August,	5.75	3.70
	19.32	16.46.

The amount of rain which fell at Bradford, in Essex county, in the month of August alone, was sixteen inches, the greatest, probably, ever known in one month in New England, while at Nantucket it was but a fraction over one inch; so that while the vicinity of Boston and the eastern part of the State, generally, was abundantly supplied, the wet meadows being flooded, and thousands of tons of swale hay ruined, the island of Nantucket and some parts of Barnstable and Plymouth counties were suffering severely from drought, vegetation being entirely parched up.

So great is the dependence of the grasses upon heat and moisture combined, that, knowing the results of observations of the thermometer and the rain gauge in any section, during the three growing months of April, May and June, one might predict with great certainty the results of the harvest in that section; and, on the other hand, the returns of practical farmers in different sections of the State, indicate so clearly and uniformly the excess above the average, or the partial failure of the crop, that a meteorological map of the State might be constructed from them.

As might be expected, therefore, from what has already been said, the yield of grass and hay throughout most parts of this State during the past year, has been somewhat above the average, the best judges estimating the excess variously from one-eighth to one-half, and it has, doubtless, in some localities, reached this latter estimate, though the general average was not, probably, over an eighth above that of other years.

It may be inferred, also, from what has been said, that the quality was not quite equal to the average, and this was unquestionably the case, where the excess in quantity was due to the excess of moisture and the rains.

The remarks of an experienced, practical farmer of Kentucky, express very well the general estimate made by our farmers in reply to the second question proposed in the above circular. "Just so far," says he, "as there is shade, is the grass deficient in saccharine and nutritious qualities; that grass which is most exposed to the sun being best. Woodland pastures will keep young stock growing and old ones on foot, but will not fatten them. A three-year old Durham will get 'stall fat' in a year on *open* blue grass." And so a farmer of Hampshire county, says: "Grass grown in the shade is lighter and does not contain so much nutriment. Wet seasons increase the weight and bulk of the crop, but the same weight does not contain the amount of nutritive matter of hay raised in a dry season. And another of Worcester county: "Hay grown in a dry season contains more nutriment. This is particularly noticeable in the condition of cattle in the spring following a dry season. I do not consider grass grown in a dense shade worth over half price;" while a farmer of great observation, in Middlesex county, says: "From an experience of fifty years in making hay, and thirty-five in feeding it out and selling it, I should say that in a wet season I never found any thing like so much heart or nutriment in hay as in a dry one. Grass grown under a thick, shady tree is not worth one-half as much as that grown in the sun. The grass this year in this town was well set in the spring and grew very quick when the warm weather came on, but still we had much good, warm sun to bring it to maturity, and I think it will spend pretty well, but probably not quite as well as the same bulk last year. Since the fifth of September we cut our salt hay in this town and never found it cleaner or better, and I think it will spend well." And another practical farmer remarks: "I think grass and hay are not so good in a wet season. We lose about one-third in the quality of what we gain in the quantity. Grass grown in the shade is not worth more than two-thirds as much as that grown in the sun."

It is not necessary to multiply the authorities of practical farmers on this point, since they uniformly coincide with the testimony given above, and it may be regarded as fully established as the result both of scientific investigations and of practical experience, that both the quantity and the quality of grass are in proportion to the heat or sunlight and the moisture in which it is grown.

What has been said will explain the suggestion in the last section with respect to the allowance which it may be proper to make in the analyses of grass grown in a climate of less heat and less sunshine than our own. It will also lead to the conclusion that our own grasses grown on low, moist lands, are neither so sweet nor so nutritious as the same species grown on higher and dryer soils; and it is a fact which has fallen under the observation of practical farmers, that the grasses on low lands do not produce so much nor so good a quality of milk, nor so much fat in animals as the same species of grass grown on upland soils.

Closely connected with the influence of the seasons is the

TIME FOR SOWING GRASS SEED.

More than sixty years ago careful experiments were made in this State, in the hope of obtaining such information as would settle the question as to the best time of sowing grass seed, and the practice of seeding down in the fall was then commenced by a few individuals. At and before that time, the practice of sowing in the spring was universal, and the same custom has generally prevailed till within a very few years. Both the practice and the opinion of the best practical farmers among us have changed to a considerable extent, and it is now commonly thought best to sow grass seed in the fall, early in September, if possible, mixing no grain or any thing else with it, though there are, and always will be, some cases where the practice of sowing in the spring with grain is convenient and judicious. There can be no doubt that it is, in most cases, an injury to both crops to sow them together. The following statement of an experienced and successful farmer will enable us to comprehend how the change was brought about, though others had tried the same experiment long before him. "More than twenty years ago we had several dry summers, in the springs of which I had sown grass seed with rye, barley and sometimes wheat and lost most of my seed by the drought. I could scrape it up, the plants being dead and dry, when small. Since that time I have universally ploughed after haying and sowed Timothy grass and redtop."

Other farmers probably experienced the same difficulty and came to the same conclusion. Our seasons differ greatly to be sure, but it is now well understood that we must calculate on a drought in some part of the summer, and grass will suffer more from drought than from frost. Hence the propriety of fall sowing. There are some localities, undoubtedly, where spring sowing with grain is best, on the whole, as in the south-eastern sections of the State, along the coast, where on account of the proximity of the sea, the ground is often but slightly covered and protected with snow; yet even there, some farmers say it is better to seed in August and September. Few general rules are of universal application in agriculture, and the farmer must constantly exercise sound judgment and common sense. One practical farmer of Essex, in answer to the circular, says: "I prefer August, because I think it less liable to winter-kill than summer-kill. And another greater reason is, that in fall seeding I get rid of a crop of weeds, while in spring seeding my ground is seeded with them." An experienced farmer of Hampshire county, writes: "I rather prefer the last week in August for seeding down land. The reason is, that we frequently have a summer drought which kills out the young grass." One of the best farmers of Middlesex, says: "When sown alone I prefer from the 20th of August to the 20th of September. If sown sooner, the summer droughts are apt to injure the young blades; if later, they do not have a chance to expand and arrive at that degree of maturity necessary for a good crop the ensuing season." He says, also, that if in any case it is found necessary to sow with grain, it should be in the spring and not in the fall. An experienced practical farmer of Essex county, recommends "The latter part of August and the month of September for seeding down land to grass for mowing, unless that season should be very dry; in that case, sow so soon after a rain as may be. I do not think it advisable to sow grass seed when the earth is very dry, as some of it may, by the moisture brought up in preparing the land, sprout, but not having continued moisture to support it, will wither away, while some of the lighter seeds will, perhaps, swell by moisture, but fail to sprout for a lack of nourishment, and consequently perish, while others will be blown away by the winds. The plant from seed sown in August or September, if the season is moist, will take deep root and be prepared to withstand the changes of winter. Grass seed sown with grain in the spring is liable to be killed in the hot days of July and August, about the time of cutting the grain, particularly on light, sandy or gravelly lands. Clover should be sown in the spring as soon as convenient after the frost is out of the ground, on land seeded down the preceding autumn, probably, rather than sooner, in the autumn, as the winter is often too severe for the tender roots."

A farmer of Worcester county, says: "On moist land I prefer to turn over the green sward after haying, with a Michigan plough, and seed in August, after spreading on a coat of manure to give the grass an early start." A farmer of Franklin county, writes: "I consider the month of August as the best time to seed down land for mowing, with the exception of clover, and that I sow early in spring." Another from Hampden: "I think August or the early part of September is the best time to seed down grass land, as in the fall of the year it will get root and not be burned up by the sun, as it would be in spring." Another says: "I sow from the middle of August to the middle of September. If sown in spring with oats or other grain, the young grass is liable to be summer-killed, either choked by the ranker growth of the grain, or scorched by the hot sun when the grain is taken off. If sown in spring without grain there is one season lost."

A farmer on the Connecticut River states, that "If the season is not too dry, August is a good month to seed for mowing. Have had very good success in seeding with turnips, or grass seed alone, in August or September, to mow the next year; but the usual practice here is to seed with wheat or rye in September or October. Some seed in spring with oats, but generally it does not do well. Clover is more often sown in the spring, because it winter-kills." Another, writing from the northern part of Worcester county, says: "There is a difference of opinion among farmers in this region on this subject; some prefer to sow the grass seed with the spring grain in May, while others prefer to sow in August. The latter, no doubt, is the best practice, if the ground is sufficiently moist."

A very successful farmer of Berkshire, advises, "August or September. I have sown in the month of October with good success. Seed sown in August obtains more root than when sown later, and consequently, is not as liable to winter-kill. It also starts earlier the succeeding spring, thereby keeping down the weeds. Much of our moist meadow lands,—too wet for hoed crops, and producing but light crops of grass, and that of an inferior quality,—may be made to produce well by ploughing and seeding. Let them be ploughed deep in August or September, the surface well-harrowed and covered with a light coat of compost, ashes or barnyard manure, and seeded, and the next year the crop will repay all expense." But on the other hand, a practical farmer on the island of Martha's Vineyard, Duke's county, says: "I prefer seeding down land designed for mowing, in April, for the reason that if sown in March the ground becomes so compact from the effects of heavy rains that the seed does not come up well, and if sown in August or September the grass does not attain that degree of maturity to enable it to withstand the frequent freezing and thawing of the succeeding winter. We usually have but little snow to protect the young grass on this island. The objection to sowing grass seed after English harvest will not probably apply to those places where the winters are less changeable."

Another says: "I have sown grass seed in the months of March, April, May, August, September and October. On a rich, compact, retentive soil, seed has done well sown in April or May, but I prefer to seed my land of any description in August, or on a light snow in March. My reason is, that when I have seeded my ground in the spring I have sown rye or oats with the grass seed generally; if not, a crop of weeds would come up and usurp the place of the grasses and choke them out, and a hot and dry July and August would exterminate what escaped the oats and weeds."

Thus, the opinions and practice of farmers is divided on this question, each one being influenced in part by the character of his land and his crops. But it will be found that no season is without its exposure to loss, for if we sow in autumn and have an open and severe winter with frequent changes from comparatively warm and thawing weather to excessive cold, the young grass will be likely to suffer, while if we sow in spring with some kind of grain, as oats, barley or rye, and have a drought in spring or summer, as we generally do, the grass may be injured and may be entirely killed. No invariable rule for all soils and seasons can be given. But the weight of authority seems to fix upon early autumn as the best season to sow grass seed; sowing it alone without a grain crop, and the losses from proper seeding down, at that season are probably considerably less, in an average of years, than those which arise from spring sowing with grain.

But whatever time may be chosen for sowing, it is very important that the seed bed should have been thoroughly tilled and properly prepared and manured. But instances have fallen under my immediate observation where land which had become "hide-bound" and worn out, producing but a light crop of grass, was very much benefited by being turned over in September and having a dressing of compost harrowed in, grass seed being then sown alone. The crop even of the next year was much greater than that of previous years and nearly paid for the labor of ploughing and seeding by its increase.

No rule in regard to the time of seeding down land, which should be found to work best in one latitude, would necessarily apply in a different climate, and under different circumstances.

After having determined upon the time of sowing, the next question in the farmer's mind is as to the

SELECTION OF SEED.

In general, too little attention is paid to the selection of seeds, not only of the grasses, but of other cultivated plants. The farmer cannot be sure that he has good seed unless he raises it for himself or uses that raised in his neighborhood. He too often takes that which has passed through several hands, and whose origin he cannot trace. Bad or old seed may thus be bought, in the belief that it is good and new, and the seller himself may not know any thing to the contrary. The buyer, in such cases, often introduces weeds which are very difficult to eradicate. The temptation to mix seeds left over from previous years with newer seed, is very great, and there can be no doubt that it is often done on a large scale. In such cases the buyer has no remedy. He cannot return the worthless article, and the repayment of the purchase money, even if he could enforce it, would be but poor compensation for the loss of a crop. The seeds of some plants retain their vitality much longer than others. Those of the turnip, for instance, will germinate as well, or nearly as well, at the age of four or five years as when only one or two years old. But the seeds of most of the grasses are of very little value when they have been kept two or three years, and hence the importance of procuring new and fresh seeds, and guarding against any mixture of the old and worthless with the new, as carefully as possible.

It is easy to tell whether the germinative power of grass or any other seed still remains, by the following simple method, and if the buyer should be willing to try it, he might purchase only a small quantity at first, and afterwards obtain his full supply with more confidence if the trial showed it to be good. Take two pieces of thick cloth, moisten them with water and place them one upon the other in the bottom of a saucer. Place any number of seeds which it is desired to try, upon the cloth, spreading thin, so as not to allow them to cover or touch each other. Cover them over with a third piece of cloth similar to the others and moistened in the same manner. Then place the saucer in a moderately warm place. Sufficient water must be turned on from time to time to keep the three thicknesses of cloth moist, but great care must be taken not to use too much water, as this would destroy the seed. There should be only enough to moisten the cloths, and not enough to allow any to stand in the saucer. Danger from this source may be avoided in a great measure, however, by tipping up the saucer so as to permit any superfluous water in the saucer to drain off. The cloth used for covering may be gently raised each day to watch the progress of the swelling or the moulding of the seeds. The good seed will be found to swell gradually, while the old or poor seed, which has lost its germinating power, will become mouldy in a very few days. In this way, also, any one can judge whether old seed is mixed with new. The latter will germinate much more quickly than the former. He can judge, besides, of the quantity which he must sow, since he can tell whether a half, or three-fourths, or the whole will be likely to germinate, and can regulate his sowing accordingly. The seeds of the clovers, if they are new and fresh, will show their germs on the third or fourth day; other seeds will take a little longer, but till they become coated with mould there is hope of their germinating. As soon as the mould appears it is decisive, and the seed that moulds is worthless.

MIXTURES OF GRASS SEED.

It is difficult to overestimate the importance to the farmer of a good selection and proper mixture of grass seeds for the various purposes of cultivation, for mowing, for soiling, for permanent pasturage, or for an alternate crop.

Doubtless the varieties of seed usually sown in this State, consisting almost exclusively of Timothy and redtop, with a mixture of red clover, are among the best for our purposes, and their exclusive use is, in a measure, sanctioned by the experience and practice of our best farmers; yet, it would seem very strange indeed, if this vast family of plants, consisting of thousands of species and varieties, and occupying, as already intimated, nearly a sixth part of the whole vegetable kingdom, could furnish no more than two or three truly valuable species.

When we consider also, that some species are best adapted to one locality, and others to another, some reaching their fullest and most perfect development on clay soils and some on lighter loams and sands, we cannot but wonder that the practice of sowing only Timothy and redtop on nearly all soils, clays, loams and sands indiscriminately, both on high and low land, should have become so prevalent. It is equally remarkable that while but very few of our grasses, and these for the most part species peculiar to sterile soils, flourish alone, but nearly all do best with a mixture of several species, it should so constantly have been thought judicious to attempt to grow only two prominent species together with merely an occasional addition of an annual or a biennial clover, which soon dies out. When this course is pursued, unless the soil is rich and in good heart, the grass is likely to grow thin and far between, producing but half or two-thirds of a crop, whereas the addition in the mixture of a larger number of species, would have secured a heavier burden of a better quality. These considerations, it seems to me, indicate the true direction in which the farmer who wishes to "make two spires of grass grow where one grew before" without impoverishing the soil, should turn his attention.

I hold this proposition to be indisputable, that any soil will yield a larger and more nutritious crop if sown with several kinds of nutritious grasses, than when sown with only one or two species. Indeed, it is a fact well established by careful experiment, that a mixture of only two or three species of grasses and clover, will produce a less amount of hay than can be obtained by sowing a larger number of species together. There may be some exceptions to this rule, as in cases where the yield of Timothy and redtop, owing to the peculiar fitness of the soil for these grasses, is as great as can stand on the ground covered by them.

But it is nevertheless true, that if we sow but one kind of grass, however abundantly the seed may be scattered, or on whatever soil it may be, or under however favorable influences, yet only a part of the plants will flourish; vacant spaces will occur throughout the piece which will be filled up after a time by grasses of an inferior quality, weeds or mosses. This is the case in some degree also, where only two, or a small number of species are sown; while if a mixture made up of a larger number of kinds of seed is used, the plants will cover the entire surface and produce a far better quality of herbage.

In sowing such a mixture of several different species, we do but follow nature, who after all, will generally be found to be the best teacher, for wherever we cast our eyes over an old, rich, permanent pasture, we ordinarily see from fifteen to twenty species of grass or forage plants growing in social profusion. If the soil be very poor, as a cold, hard clay, or a barren sand, perhaps two or three varieties will suffice, but on good soils a larger number will be found to be far more profitable. Especially is this the case where the land is to be left in grass for some years and eventually be pastured, as is frequently done in New England, for it is then desirable to have grasses that reach their maturity at different times, as a constant succession of good feed throughout the season may thus more surely be obtained. It is well known that there is no month of spring or summer in which some one of the grasses does not attain to its perfection, if we except the month of March. For good soils, eight or ten species of the grasses or six or eight of the grasses proper and one or more of other herbage plants would probably be found to be profitable.

I am aware that the prevailing practice is decidedly against the use of any thing but Timothy, redtop and clover, and that very large crops of these grasses are often raised, but it is nevertheless true that we obtain on an average less than a ton to the acre, while with the same culture and a larger number of species we ought to get double that quantity.

Before proceeding to consider the proportions in which the different species should be mixed, it may be well to refer to the mode generally adopted for estimating the quantities of seeds their relative weight. And I may remark here that the prevailing practice of buying and sowing grass seeds by measure rather than by weight, seems injudicious to say the least. It is well known that old or poor seed weighs less than that which is fresh and new. Now if a farmer buys by weight, even if he does get an old or inferior quality of seed, he gets a much larger number of seeds, and this larger quantity of seed which he receives for his money, may make up for the inferior quality, and he will have a larger number of seeds capable of germination than he would have if he bought by measure. It is to be regretted that it has become so nearly universal to purchase by measure, though as this course is for the seller's advantage, it may be difficult to change the custom.

The following table, containing the weight per bushel of the seeds of the most important agricultural grasses, has been prepared chiefly from a valuable treatise on the grasses by the Messrs. Lawson, of Edinburgh, who have paid much attention to this subject, and whose experience and observation in the practical culture of the grasses has probably been larger and more extensive than those of any other seedsmen.

This table will be found to be exceedingly valuable for reference.

Column 1 contains the common names of the grasses.

Column 2, the average number of pounds in a bushel of the seeds.

Column 3, the average number of seeds *in an ounce.*

Column 4 shows the depth of soil in inches and fractions of an inch at which the greatest number of seeds germinate.

Column 5 shows the depth of soil in inches and fractions of an inch at which only one-half the seeds germinated.

Column 6 shows the least depth of soil in inches or fractions of an inch at which none of the seeds germinated.

Column 7 shows the average percentage of loss in the weight of the grass in making into hay, when cut in the time of flowering.

The weight of seeds varies, of course, somewhat, from that stated in the above table, according to their quality. Those given in the table are the average weights of good, merchantable seed. In some States, as in Wisconsin, for instance, the legal weight of Timothy seed is forty-six pounds to the bushel. The weight of a bushel will depend in part, also, upon the thoroughness with which it is cleaned. The seeds of the different varieties of rye grass differ in weight, varying from twenty to thirty pounds per bushel; but the average is about twenty-six pounds.

TABLE XIV. *Weight of Grass Seeds, and depth of Covering.*

1.	2.	3.	4.	5.	6.	7.
Whitetop,	13	500,000	0 to $\frac{1}{4}$	$\frac{1}{2}$ to $\frac{3}{4}$	1	.65
Redtop,	12	425,000	–	–	–	.63
Hassock Grass,	14	132,000	0 to $\frac{1}{2}$	$\frac{3}{4}$ to 1	$2\frac{1}{4}$	.65
Meadow Foxtail,	5	76,000	0 to $\frac{1}{2}$	1 to $1\frac{1}{4}$	$2\frac{1}{4}$	.57
Sweet-scented Vernal,	6	71,000	0 to $\frac{1}{2}$	1 to $1\frac{1}{4}$	2	.45
Tall Oat Grass,	7	21,000	$\frac{1}{2}$ to $\frac{3}{4}$	$1\frac{1}{2}$ to $1\frac{3}{4}$	4	–
Slender Wheat Grass,	10	15,500	0 to $\frac{1}{4}$	$\frac{1}{2}$ to $\frac{3}{4}$	2	–
Crested Dog's-tail,	26	28,000	–	–	–	–
Orchard Grass,	12	40,000	0 to $\frac{1}{4}$	$\frac{3}{4}$ to 1	$2\frac{1}{4}$	.29
Hard Fescue,	10	39,000	0 to $\frac{1}{4}$	$\frac{3}{4}$ to 1	$2\frac{1}{4}$	–
Tall Fescue,	14	20,500	0 to $\frac{1}{4}$	1 to $1\frac{1}{4}$	$2\frac{3}{4}$	.52
Sheep's Fescue,	14	64,000	0 to $\frac{1}{4}$	$\frac{3}{4}$ to 1	2	.65
Meadow Fescue,	14	26,000	0 to $\frac{1}{2}$	$\frac{3}{4}$ to 1	$2\frac{1}{2}$	.60
Slender, or Spiked Fescue,	15	24,700	–	–	–	–
Red Fescue,	10	39,000	–	–	–	–
Reed Meadow Grass,	13	58,000	$\frac{1}{4}$ to $\frac{1}{2}$	$\frac{3}{4}$ to 1	$2\frac{1}{4}$	.30
Common Manna Grass,	15	33,000	–	–	–	.35
Meadow Soft Grass,	7	95,000	$\frac{1}{4}$ to $\frac{1}{2}$	$\frac{3}{4}$ to 1	$2\frac{1}{2}$	.73
Italian Rye Grass,	15	27,000	0 to $\frac{1}{4}$	1 to $1\frac{1}{4}$	$3\frac{1}{4}$	–
Perennial Rye Grass,	18 to 30	15,000	$\frac{1}{4}$ to $\frac{1}{2}$	$1\frac{1}{2}$ to $1\frac{3}{4}$	$3\frac{1}{2}$	.50
Millet Grass,	25	80,000	$\frac{1}{4}$ to $\frac{1}{2}$	1 to $\frac{1}{4}$	$2\frac{3}{4}$	.38
Reed Canary Grass,	48	42,000	–	–	–	.32
Timothy,	44	74,000	0 to $\frac{1}{4}$	$\frac{3}{4}$ to 1	2	.50
Wood Meadow Grass,	15	173,000	–	–	–	.31
June, or Spear Grass,	13	243,000	–	–	–	.57
Rough-stalked Meadow Grass,	15	217,000	0 to $\frac{1}{4}$	$\frac{1}{2}$ to $\frac{3}{4}$	$1\frac{1}{2}$	.72
Beach Grass,	15	10,000	$\frac{1}{2}$ to 1	$1\frac{1}{2}$ to $1\frac{3}{4}$	4	–
Yellow Oat Grass,	$5\frac{1}{2}$	118,000	0 to $\frac{1}{4}$	$\frac{3}{4}$ to 1	2	–
Red Clover,	64	16,000	0 to $\frac{1}{2}$	$1\frac{1}{4}$ to $1\frac{1}{2}$	2	–
Perennial Clover,	64	16,000	0 to $\frac{1}{2}$	$1\frac{1}{4}$ to $1\frac{1}{2}$	2	–
White Clover,	65	32,000	0 to $\frac{1}{4}$	$\frac{1}{2}$ to $\frac{3}{4}$	$1\frac{1}{2}$	–
Lucerne,	60	12,600	–	–	–	–
Sainfoin,	26	1,280	$\frac{3}{4}$ to 1	2 to $2\frac{1}{4}$	$4\frac{1}{4}$	–

The number of seeds of each species in a pound, may be found, of course, by multiplying the numbers in column three by sixteen, the number of ounces in a pound. It is obvious, however, that these numbers must vary, like the number of pounds in a bushel, for it is evident that the lighter the seed, the greater will be the number of seeds in a pound. The numbers stated are the average obtained by careful and repeated trials.

The results obtained in columns 4, 5 and 6, were obtained by careful experiment, and will be found to be very suggestive.

The fact that the soil used in the experiments to ascertain the proper depth of covering was kept moist during the process of germination, though freely exposed to the light, accounts for the large number of seeds germinated without any covering whatever. In ordinary field culture some slight covering is desirable ; but the figures in column 6 show the important fact that in our modes of sowing and covering there must be a great loss of seed from burying too deep, though the depth should be governed somewhat by the nature of the soil, as its usual moisture or dryness.

I have already expressed my opinion that we limit our mixtures to too few species, thus failing to arrive at the most profitable results, and have said that, in a piece of land seeded with one or two favorite grasses only, small vacant spaces will be found, which, in the aggregate will diminish very considerably the yield of an acre, even though they may be so small as not to be perceived. It might be thought that this could be avoided by putting into the ground a very large number of seeds. But a knowledge of the quantities of seed ordinarily used in this State for sowing, and an inquiry as to the number of plants necessary to cover the ground with a thick coating of grass, will show that this is not the case. I have in my possession letters from some of the best farmers in Berkshire, Plymouth and other counties of the Commonwealth, in which they state it to be the prevailing practice to sow a bushel of redtop, a half bushel of Timothy, and from four to six pounds of red clover to the acre. Some of them vary the proportions a little, as by the use of one peck of Timothy and a larger quantity of clover, but the general practice is to use nearly the quantities stated, some even using a considerable larger quantity. Now if we examine the table we shall find that in an ounce of redtop seed there are 425,000 grains. In a pound there are 6,800,000 seeds; in a bushel, or twelve pounds, there are 81,600,000 seeds. Now take only one peck of Timothy seed to mix with it. In an ounce of Timothy grass seed there are 74,000 grains. In a pound there are 1,204,000 grains. In eleven pounds, or a peck, there are 13,244,000 seeds, and if we take but four pounds of clover, which is below the average quantity used, we shall find by the same process that we have 1,024,000 seeds. If now we add these sums together, we shall find that we have put upon the acre no less than 95,868,000 seeds! This gives over 15 seeds to the square inch, or about 2,200 seeds to the square foot!

Again, one of the most intelligent farmers of Middlesex county, a practical man, uses five pecks of redtop and twelve quarts of Timothy seed per acre, for mowing lands, and an addition of five pounds of white clover for pastures, making no less than 124,426,000 seeds per acre. There must be, evidently, an enormous waste of seed, or an extensive destruction of plants, for if we take nature for our guide, we shall not find any thing like that amount of plants on an inch or a foot of our grass lands. Now let us see from a very careful trial how many plants and how many species are to be found in a square foot.

TABLE XV. *Average number of Plants and Species to the square foot of Sward.*

CHARACTER OF THE TURF.	Whole number of plants on the square foot.	Natural grasses.	Clover, and other plants.	Distinct species.
1. A square foot taken from the richest natural pasture, capable of fattening one large ox or three sheep to the acre, was found to contain	1,000	940	60	20
2. Rich old pasture, capable of fattening one large ox and three sheep, per acre, ...	1,090	1,032	58	–
3. Another old pasture contained	910	880	30	12
4. An old pasture of a damp, moist, and mossy surface, . . .	634	510	124	8
5. A good pasture, two years old, laid down to rye grass and white clover, ...	470	452	18	2
6. A sod of narrow-leaved meadow grass, (poa angustifolia,) six years old, ...	192	–	–	1
7. A sod of meadow foxtail by itself, six years old, ...	80	–	–	1
8. Rye Grass by itself, same age, ...	75	–	–	1
9. Meadow, irrigated and carefully managed, ...	1,798	1,702	96	–

These plants in each instance were counted with the utmost care by a farmer now living in this State, then in the employ of Mr. Sinclair, and the correctness of his results may be relied on.

Now it is a well known fact that the sward of a rich old pasture is closely packed, filled up, or interwoven with plants and no vacant spaces occur. Yet, in a closely crowded turf of such a pasture, only one thousand distinctly rooted plants were found on a square foot, and these were made up of twenty different species. The soil should be supplied with a proper number of plants, else a loss of labor, time and space will be incurred; but however heavily seeded a piece may be with one or two favorite grasses, small vacant spaces will occur, which, though they may not seem important in themselves, when taken in the aggregate, will be found to diminish very considerably the yield of an acre, even if they are so small as not to be perceived. And undoubtedly some allowance should be made for the seeds and young plants destroyed by insects, birds and various accidental causes; but even after all deductions for these, we see that in this State, at least, there is no deficiency in the quantities of seed used, and the imperfectly covered ground cannot be explained in this way.

The above table is also important as an illustration of the truth of my general proposition. It shows that in those pastures where few species were found together, whether in old, natural pastures or in artificial meadows, the number of plants on a given space was proportionably small. Sinclair, too, who had observed carefully and extensively, writes on this point in regard to the practice of overseeding, as follows: "When an excess of grass seed is sown, the seeds, in general, all vegetate, but the plants make little, if any progress, until from the want of nourishment to the roots, and the confined space for the growth of the foliage, a certain number decay, and give the requisite room to the proper number of plants; and that will be according as there are a greater or less variety of different species of grasses combined in the sward."

It is proper to make some allowance for bad seed, it is true, but our practice is defective and uneconomical. In the examination of the rich and productive pasture turf, from twelve to twenty species were found closely mixed together, and there were six or seven plants to the square inch. We sow seed enough, frequently, for fifteen plants to the inch, but rarely obtain above two or three, and very frequently even less than that.

The difficulty of procuring the seed, and its expense, have been the strongest objections to the use of many species. A demand for these species, however, would soon remove this difficulty, and varieties would be kept for sale in Boston at a reasonable price. When it is considered that the additional expense of sowing a field or permanent pasture with a greater number of species will be, comparatively, very small, while the additional yield will be proportionably large,—if the result is as favorable as the opinion of many who have made the trial would lead us to expect,—every farmer must admit that it is for his interest to try the experiment, on a small scale, at least.

It will be evident, after a moment's reflection, that very different mixtures, both as regards the species and the relative quantities of each, will be desirable for different soils; that dissimilar mixtures would be required for alternate cropping or laying down land for only a year or two, and for permanent pasture. In our pratice it is most common to seed down for some years, and not unfrequently this is done with the design of cutting the grass for hay for a few years and then pasturing the field, in which case our seeding down assumes the character of laying down for permanent pasturage. Equally good, but very different mixtures might be made, also, for the same soils by different individuals who had different objects in view, some desiring a very early crop, some wishing to select species which resist the access of profitless weeds, and others to cultivate those varieties which exhaust the soil the least. Each of these mixtures may be best adapted to the specific object of the farmer who makes it, and if composed of a sufficient number of species, may be good and truly economical.

The practice with many in New England has already been alluded to as consisting usually of one bushel, or twelve pounds of redtop, a half a bushel, or twenty-two pounds of Timothy, and from four to six or eight pounds of clover. The practice of good farmers varies but little from this mixture.

The following tables are recommended by Lawson & Son, of Edinburgh. Only a few of the mixtures have been sufficiently tried in this country, and they may need some modification to meet the exigencies of our severe droughts. It may be proper to remark here that the climate of Scotland, in some respects, does not differ much from our own. The latitude of Edinburgh is 55° 57′, that of Boston, 42° 21′; while the mean annual temperature of the former is 47°.1 Fahr., that of the latter, 48°.9, showing a very slight difference. But our summers are hotter, and we are annually liable to the most severe and parching droughts, such as are not often felt in Scotland.

The quantities are stated in pounds. If any one is desirous of reducing them to measures he may easily do so by the use of table XIV., which gives the weight per bushel of each species.

TABLE XVI. *For Permanent Pasture.*

Meadow Foxtail,	2 pounds.
Orchard Grass,	6
Hard Fescue,	2
Tall Fescue,	2
Meadow Fescue,	2
Italian Rye Grass,	6
Perennial Rye Grass,	6
Timothy,	4
Redtop,	2
Rough stalked Meadow Grass,	3
Red Clover,	2
Perennial Clover,	3
White Clover,	5—45

Here we have a considerable number of species, and according to table XIV., over 45,500,000 seeds. Thus, though we use less than half as many seeds as our farmers generally do, we still allow more than seven seeds to the square inch, or over 1,000 seeds to the square foot, a number larger than the number of plants found in the rich and closely woven sward of an old pasture, as seen in table XV. These, it will be seen, even if we make a large allowance for bad seeds, will produce as many plants as will grow well, while we still have by far the largest number of stalks of redtop from no less than 3,600,000 seeds, though the weight of the redtop seed is but two pounds. This mixture is designed for one acre sown without grain in the fall.

A mixture like the above would answer very well, and is less expensive than the following, though it is probable that the greater original outlay for the seeds recommended in the following table will be more than returned in the additional yield.

TABLE XVII. *For Permanent Pasture.*

Meadow Foxtail,	2 pounds.
Orchard Grass,	4
Hard Fescue,	2
Tall Fescue,	2
Meadow Fescue,	2
Redtop,	2
June Grass,	2
Italian Rye Grass,	6
Perennial Rye Grass,	8
Timothy,	3
Wood Meadow Grass,	2
Rough-stalked Meadow Grass,	2
Yellow Oat Grass,	1
Perennial Clover,	2
White Clover,	5—45

If the cultivator desires to produce a close, matted sward as soon as possible, no broad-leaved clover should be used, and the above mixture will be quite sufficient without the perennial clover.

If the object be to make a permanent lawn, as is frequently desirable around or in sight of the farm house, something like the following mixture will be found to be on the whole the best.

Table XVIII. *Permanent Lawn Grasses in Mixture.*

Meadow Foxtail,	1 pound.
Sweet-scented Vernal Grass,	1
Redtop,	2
Hard Fescue,	3
Sheep's Fescue,	1
Meadow Fescue,	4
Red Fescue,	2
Italian Rye Grass,	6
Perennial Rye Grass,	8
Timothy,	1
June, or Common Spear Grass,	2
Rough-stalked Meadow Grass,	2
Yellow Oat Grass,	1
Perennial Clover,	2
Red Clover,	2
White Clover,	6—44

This mixture will resist the effects of our severe droughts better than those commonly used for lawns. If any thing is omitted from it, the red and perennial clovers, the yellow oat grass and a part of the rye grass could best be spared.

If the farmer wishes to seed down for only a year or two and then to break up again, the following is a good mixture. [Table XIX.]

If the soil be moist or peaty two or three pounds of fowl meadow, (*poa serotina,*) should be added. Some would prefer another mixture for permanent lawn pastures, as found in table XX.

If a fine lawn is wanted where extra attention will be paid to rolling and mowing, the mixture given in table XXI. will do well.

A mixture is often wanted for orchards or shaded fields similar to that recommended in table XXII.

TABLE XIX. *Mixture for Mowing in the Rotation.*

NAME OF GRASS.	For one year's hay.	For one year's hay and one year's pasture.	For one year's hay, and two year's pasture.
Redtop,	3	3	3
Italian Rye Grass,	6	6	6
Perennial Rye Grass,	3	3	3
Orchard Grass,	4	6	6
Timothy,	11	9	9
Red Clover,	8	4	2
Perennial Clover,	–	2	4
White Clover,	2	4	4
	37	37	37

TABLE XX. *Permanent Lawn Pastures.*

Meadow Foxtail,	1 pound.
Sweet-scented Vernal Grass,	1
Orchard Grass,	3
Hard Fescue,	2
Sheep's Fescue,	2
Meadow Fescue,	2
Italian Rye Grass,	6
Perennial Rye Grass,	4
Timothy,	7
Redtop,	3
Rough-stalked Meadow Grass,	3
Yellow Oat Grass,	1
Red Clover,	2
Perennial Red Clover,	2
White Clover,	4—43

TABLE XXI. *Fine Lawns frequently Mown.*

Crested Dog's-tail,	10 pounds.
Hard Fescue,	4
Slender-leaf Sheep's Fescue,	2
Perennial Rye Grass,	10
Wood Meadow Grass,	2
Rough-stalked Meadow Grass,	1
Yellow Oat Grass,	1
June Grass,	8
White Clover,	8—46

TABLE XXII. *Hay and Pasture in Orchards and Shaded Places.*

Sweet-scented Vernal Grass,	1 pound.
Orchard Grass,	6
Hard Fescue,	2
Tall Fescue,	2
Italian Rye Grass,	4
Perennial Rye Grass,	4
Timothy,	6
Wood Meadow Grass,	4
Rough-stalked Meadow Grass,	2
June Grass,	4
Perennial Red Clover,	3
White Clover,	4—42

For very sandy, dry pastures and heathy moors, the following. [Table XXIII.]

For reclaimed swamps, after draining, designed to be kept in grass for hay, the mixture stated in table XXIV. is good.

TABLE XXIII. *Mixture for Mowing on Light Sands.*

Tall Meadow Oat Grass, ...	3 pounds.
Orchard Grass, ...	4
Hard Fescue, ...	6
Meadow Soft Grass, ...	3
Italian Rye Grass, ...	4
Perennial Rye Grass, ...	10
Timothy, ...	3
Perennial Red Clover, ...	3
White Clover, ...	4—40

TABLE XXIV. *Mixture for Reclaimed Peaty Lands.*

Whitetop, variety called Fiorin, ...	2 pounds.
Redtop, ...	2
Meadow Foxtail, ...	2
Fowl Meadow, ...	4
Italian Rye Grass, ...	4
Perennial Rye Grass, ...	5
Reed Canary Grass, ...	4
Timothy, ...	10
Rough-stalked Meadow Grass, ...	3
White Clover, ...	4—40

If a reclaimed meadow is subject to occasional overflows of fresh water, the addition of two or three pounds of the manna grass, (*glyceria fluitans*,) if it can be had, will be an improvement. On such soils Fiorin, a variety of whitetop, does remarkably well, and the rough stalked meadow is indispensable. A mixture especially adapted to such situations would be something like the following :—

Table XXV. *Marshy Grounds, liable to be occasionally overflowed with fresh water.*

NAME OF GRASS.	Peaty Soils.	Alluvial Soils.
Fiorin, ...	4 pounds.	3 pounds.
Tall Fescue, ...	3	4
Manna Grass, ...	5	5
Reed Canary Grass, ...	3	4
Timothy, ...	4	4
Rough-stalked Meadow Grass, ...	4	3
Fowl Meadow Grass, ...	6	5
White Clover, ...	3—32	4—32

If it be desired to cover rocky and gravelly hills and soils of a very poor quality with grass, the mixture in the following table will be most serviceable.

Table XXVI. *Mixture for Rocky Hills.*

Redtop, ...	2 pounds.
Tall Oat, ...	2
Crested Dog's-tail, ...	3
Orchard Grass, ...	3
Red Fescue, ...	4
Meadow Soft Grass, ...	2
Perennial Rye Grass, ...	6
Timothy, ...	6
Wood Meadow Grass, ...	3
Common Spear Grass, ...	2
Rough-stalked Meadow, ...	2
White Clover, ...	8—43

If the soil be very dry, the wood meadow grass and the Timothy may be omitted from the above mixture, and a larger quantity of June grass used. The following mixture is well adapted to dry, gravelly soils, which are difficult to turf over.

TABLE XXVII. *Mixture for Dry Gravels.*

Redtop, ...	3 pounds.
Tall Oat Grass, ...	8
Red Fescue, ...	4
Meadow Soft Grass, ...	4
Soft Brome Grass, ...	4
Perennial Rye Grass, ...	5
June Grass, ...	4
White Clover, ...	4—36

For protecting banks of rivers and streams from washing and wearing away, the reed canary grass and the reed meadow grass will be found very effectual. For preventing the drifting of light sand, beach grass, (*ammophila arundinacea,*) is one of the best. It is extensively used for this purpose at Provincetown and various other places along the coast. I have sown the seeds of other species in such situations, but know of none equal to beach grass for the purpose of fixing moving sands.

As already seen, the general practice in New England is in strong contrast with the foregoing tables of mixtures, for of the two hundred towns heard from, all appear to raise the same species, but no two recommend the same quantities for mixture, and not one reports the use of more than two species of grass mixed with one or sometimes two species of clover, as at all common.

As examples of the general practice as reported to me, and with which I have been familiar for many years, the following might be stated.

I. ½ bushel (6 lbs.) redtop, 1 peck (11 lbs.) Timothy, 5 lbs. red clover.

II. 1 bushel (12 lbs.) redtop, 1 peck Timothy, 8 lbs. red clover.

III. 1½ bushels (18 lbs.) redtop, 4 qts. (5½ lbs.) Timothy, 3 lbs. red clover.

IV. 3 pecks (9 lbs.) redtop, 6 quarts Timothy, 6 lbs. clover.

V. 1 bushel (12 lbs.) redtop, 1 bushel (44 lbs.) Tim'y, 10 to 15 lbs. clover.

VI. 1 peck (3 lbs.) redtop, 1 peck (11 lbs.) Timothy, 8 lbs. clover.

VII. 4 quarts (1½ lbs.) redtop, 1 peck (11 lbs.) Timothy, 2 quarts red clover, 1 pint white clover.

VIII. 16 quarts, (6 lbs.) redtop, 12 q'ts (16½ lbs.) Timothy, 6 lbs. clover.

IX. 12 quarts (16½ lbs.) Timothy, 4 lbs. clover.

X. 1 bushel (12 lbs.) redtop, ½ bushel (22 lbs.) Timothy, 10 lbs. clover.

XI. 1 peck redtop, 3 pecks Timothy, 6 lbs. clover.

XII. 3 pecks redtop, 1 peck Timothy, 5 lbs. clover.

XIII. 1 bushel finetop, 1 peck Timothy, 8 lbs. clover.

XIV. 1 bushel redtop, 1 peck Timothy, 12 lbs. clover.

XV. 16 quarts redtop, 10 quarts Timothy, 6 lbs. clover.

XVI. 1 bushel redtop, ½ bushel Timothy, 10 lbs. clover.

XVII. 5 pecks redtop, ½ bushel Timothy, 4 lbs. clover.

XVIII. 1 bushel redtop, 1 peck Timothy, 8 lbs. clover.

XIX. 1 peck redtop, 1 peck Timothy, 10 lbs. clover.

XX. 3 pecks redtop, 8 to 10 quarts Timothy, 6 to 8 lbs. clover.

These mixtures are sufficient to show the exceeding diversity in our practice.

A little attention to the weight of the different seeds recommended in the above tables will explain why one particular quantity which may appear small at first sight, is sufficient in some cases, as it will show a vast difference in their weight; a given number of pounds of some species containing many more seeds, and therefore producing a far larger number of plants, than an equal weight of others.

There are few points in our practice, it seems to me, where greater improvements could be made than in the selection and mixture of our grass seeds. If the money which is now literally thrown away by over-seeding with one or two species were expended in procuring other species and improving our mixtures, there is but little doubt that the aggregate profit on our grass crop would be much greater than it now is.

Some maintain that one or two species are sufficient, because certain grasses are "natural," as they say, to their land, and come in of themselves. This may, in some cases, be true to some extent, for such grasses will come in, in time, but we are liable to lose sight of the fact that the loss of a full yield, in the meantime, is often very serious.

But the inference which farmers draw from this fact is not a legitimate one, for they say that it proves that the grasses that come in "naturally," that is, the wild grasses, are best adapted to the soil, and will produce more largely than others in that locality. But this, if carried out to its natural consequences, would lead to the conclusion that new species of plants should never be introduced into any soil, because those best suited to it grow there "naturally"—a principle which no man will assert. On the contrary, one great object of all intelligent farming is to improve upon nature, and to increase the natural capacities both of the soil and of the plants which grow on it; and the introduction of new species and varieties is one of the most effectual means of accomplishing this end. Particular species of plants do not always spring up in particular places because they are peculiarly adapted to the soil, but often from mere accident. Seeds are carried by the wind or by animals or birds, and being dropped, produce plants on the spot where they fall. These plants again produce seeds which fall and in their turn produce other plants. Thus a particular species of grass or any plant may be introduced into, and fixed in a locality where it has no special adaptation to the soil there, and the most common plants or varieties of plants will be most likely to spread in this way. Hence the mere fact that a certain species is very generally diffused in a certain district, does not by any means prove that it is better suited to the soil of that district than any other species, nor that it will be sure to come in if omitted in a mixture of grasses designed for such a locality.

As already said, the mixture of grass seeds in imitation of nature for the purpose of forming good permanent fields or pastures, is of comparatively modern origin. It was, for a long time after this practice commenced, thought to require a great while to form a thick and good sward or turf, by any artificial means. The use of a large and judiciously selected number of species, has been found to accomplish this object most quickly.

Though I have expressed myself with some degree of confidence on this subject, I would still refer to the importance of careful experiment. The outlay is small, when compared with the losses now sustained in over-seeding with too few species, and from small or medium crops; and the farmer can soon satisfy himself as to the profit of more attention to the mixtures of grasses.

TIME TO CUT GRASS FOR HAY.

Having carefully selected and judiciously mixed and sown his grass seed at a proper season, the farmer may confidently hope to have an abundant crop of grass the following year, when there will naturally arise one of the most important questions in the economy of the farm, and that is, when to cut grass to make into hay, or at what stage of its growth it is most valuable for that purpose. This is a point on which even experienced farmers differ, but the weight of authority will be found strongly for cutting at the time of flowering. Most practical farmers, in answer to this question say that hay is sweeter, and possesses more nutriment when cut in full blossom than at any other stage. One of the most intelligent farmers of Middlesex county says: "I prefer to cut grass when in blossom, because it will make more milk and more fat, and cattle prefer it to that standing later. It keeps them loose and healthy. I have no doubt hay of the same bulk weighs more if it stands in the field till the seed forms, and for this reason some who sell most of their hay let it stand." A farmer of Worcester county says: "When designed for milch cows, store, or fattening animals, I prefer to cut in the blossom, because it makes more milk, more growth and more beef. For working cattle and horses I cut about six days after the pollen has fallen, because it does not scour or loosen the animal so much as when cut in the blossom." A farmer of Hampshire county says: "Next to sweet, fresh grass, we think that rowen will make cows, working cattle or horses thrive better than any other feed, unless in the case of cattle hard at work. We conclude, therefore, that all hay is best cut early. Coarse hay will keep stock tolerably well, cut early, which if allowed to mature would not be eaten at all." A farmer of Hampden county says: "We cut after the blossoms begin to fall, and before they have all fallen. It has more substance and weight cut at that time than if cut sooner, more sweetness and juice than if cut later." A farmer of Berkshire county says: "Our rule is to cut hay in the blossom, as it is then in the best state for feeding, less woody and much sweeter than later, and leaves the roots in better state for a second, or another annual crop." Another very intelligent, practical farmer says: "We cut in blossom, because it is then most palatable to stock. If allowed to stand much longer there is a draft upon the soil for the growth of the seed, which is not repaid by the additional value of the hay, if, indeed, it is increased in value at all. My opinion, derived from my own experience, is, that the grasses will sooner die out if allowed to stand later." A farmer who prefers to cut all other grasses when in blossom, says: "It will not do to cut blue joint or fowl meadow till some of the seeds fall, as it will soon run them out." An intelligent farmer of Norfolk county says: "When English grass is in full blossom it has all the good qualities it can have. From that time I think it loses in value in proportion to the time which it stands. Swale hay should be cut rather green. If fully ripe it is hard and dry." Another says: "We cut about the time the blossom falls. The grass is then at its full growth. If it stands much longer the leaves begin to die at the bottom and the grass grows tough and hard, and I think the longer it stands the less it will weigh when dried. If it is cut much earlier it will shrink and dry up and does not seem to have so much nutriment in it, and I have noticed cattle will eat more in bulk than when cut at the right time." Another says: "The time of cutting depends very much upon the use you wish to make of it. If for working oxen and horses, I would let it stand till a little out of the blossom, but if to feed out to new milch cows in the winter, I would prefer to cut it very green. It is then worth for the making of milk in the winter, almost double that cut later." One other extract will suffice. A farmer of Middlesex county says: "I cut my red clover before the heads begin to turn brown. When the clover is quite heavy I cut it when only one-half the heads have blossomed, because then cattle will eat all the stems. Clover is injured more by half when it stands long after blossoming than any other kind. I find my clover hay in the barn much heavier when cut quite early."

These extracts, taken at random from a large number of letters from practical farmers all over the State, indicate very clearly the prevailing practice. The replies from about one hundred and fifty towns are, that farmers prefer to cut the principal grasses, Timothy and redtop, when in full blossom; red clover when about half the heads are in blossom, and swale grass before it is ripe, and generally before blossoming, if possible, so as to prevent it from becoming hard and wiry.

This practice is unquestionably founded on a correct principle, the object of the farmer being to secure his hay so as to make it most like grass in its perfect condition. From principles stated in another place, it has been seen that the nutritive substances of grass are those, which are, for the most part, soluble in water, such as sugar, gluten, and other compounds. Now it is evident that if this is so, the grass should be cut at the time when it contains the largest amount of these principles. In its early stages of growth it contains a very large percentage of water. From its earliest growth the sugar and other soluble substances gradually increase till they reach their maximum percentage in the blossom, or when the seed is fully formed in the cell. From this period the saccharine matter constantly diminishes, and the woody fibre, perfectly insoluble in water, and innutritious, increases till after the seeds have matured, when the plant begins to decay. Of course, if the plant is not cut in the flower, a great part of the nutriment of its stems and leaves is wasted.

There are some exceptions to this rule in the natural grasses, as already seen in considering their nutritive qualities, and in the analyses at different periods of their growth. Thus, in case of the orchard grass, Sinclair found the nutritive matter at the time the seed was ripe and at the time of flowering, as seven to five, and the stems of Timothy were found to contain more nutritive matter when the plant was ripe, than at the time of flowering, though it was found that the loss of aftermath which would have formed had the plant been cut in blossom, more than balanced the gain of nutritive matter in the ripening of the seed. Most of the grasses, too, make a greater quantity of hay when cut at the time of blossoming, though the crested dog's tail has been found to be an exception to this rule. Fowl meadow, also, contains an equal quantity of produce at the time of ripening the seed and at the time of blossoming, and the nutritive matter at both periods is about the same. It will be found in practice generally to be better to be a little too early than too late, for the gain is in two directions, in a greater nutritive substance at the time of blossoming, which is certainly a sufficient consideration of itself, and in the larger growth of the lattermath which will spring up on good land and in a good season.

We might also reason from analogy in other plants, for it is a well known fact that the best vegetable extracts for medicinal and other purposes, are procured from plants when in blossom. Prof. Kirtland, of Ohio, states that an observing, practical farmer of his neighborhood, after many careful observations on the growth of Timothy, has arrived at these propositions:—

1. That Timothy grass is a perennial plant, which renews itself by an annual formation of "bulbs," or perhaps, more correctly speaking, tubers, in which the vitality of the plant is concentrated during the winter. These form in whatever locality the plant is selected, without reference to dryness or moisture. From these proceed the stalks which support the leaves and head, and from the same source spread out the numerous fibres forming the true roots.

2. To insure a perfect development of tubers, a certain amount of nutrition must be assimilated in the leaves, and returned to the base of the plant, through the stalk.

3. As soon as the process of nutrition is completed, it becomes manifest by the appearance of a state of desiccation, or dryness, always commencing at a point directly above either the first or second joint of the stem near the crown of the tuber. From this point the desiccation gradually progresses upwards, and the last portion of the stalk that yields up its freshness is that adjoining the head. Coincident with the beginning of this process, is the full development of the seeds, and with its progress they mature. Its earliest appearance is evidence that both the tubers and seeds have received their requisite supplies of nutrition, and that neither the stalk nor the leaves are longer necessary to aid them in completing their maturity. A similar process occurs in the union just above the crown of the bulb, indicating the maturity of that organ. Fig. 97 represents the bulb fully developed and mature, from which the stalk was cut, after the nutritive process was completed, above the point where drying or desiccation had begun.

4. If the stalk be cut from the tubers before this evidence of maturity has appeared, the necessary supplies of nutrition will

be arrested, their proper growth will cease, and an effort will be made to repair the injury by sending out small, lateral tubers, from which weak and unhealthy stalks will proceed, at the expense of the original tubers. This is seen in Fig. 98. All will ultimately perish either by the droughts of autumn or the cold of winter.

Fig. 98.

Fig. 99.

Fig. 97.

5. The tubers, together with one or two of the lower joints of the stalk, remain fresh and green during the winter, if left to take their natural course, but if, by any means, this green portion be severed, at any season of the year, the result will be the death of the plant, when it will appear as in Fig. 99.

From these five propositions the following conclusions are drawn:—

1. That Timothy grass cannot, under any circumstances, be adapted for pasture; as the close nipping of horses and sheep is fatal to the tubers which are also extensively destroyed by swine if allowed to run in the pasture.

2. That the proper time for mowing Timothy is at any time after the process of desiccation has commenced on the stalk, as noted in the third proposition. It is not very essential whether it is performed a week earlier or later, provided it be postponed till that evidence of maturity has become manifest.

3. All attempts at close shaving the sward should be avoided, while using the scythe, and in gauging mowing machines, care should be taken to run them so high that they will not cut the Timothy below the second joint above the tuber.

I have frequently, during the past autumn, pulled up the bulbous roots of Timothy, from the stubble from which a heavy crop had been cut with the scythe, while in flower, for the purpose of studying the changes which were taking place in these tubers, and have found them very similar to those represented in Figs. 97 and 98, not only on moist, damp soils, but also on soils comparatively dry. Any farmer can satisfy himself of the correctness of these representations by a little observation in his own fields; and as the point is of practical importance, it is worthy of careful attention.

The facts above alluded to have fallen under the observation of a practical farmer of Middlesex county, who says: "The proper time to cut Herds-grass or Timothy, is after the seed is formed and is full in the milk. It will then give about twenty per cent. more weight than when it is just coming into the blossom, and the cattle will eat twenty per cent. less and keep on their flesh. And I prefer also to cut it at that stage of its growth on account of the roots being better able to withstand the drought. It should be cut four inches from the ground, as most of the Timothy is killed by mowing close and early before it has come to maturity. I have kept Timothy thick and strong in the land six years, by following this method. I have noticed that most of it has died out by once or twice close and early mowing before the grass has come to maturity; if it is dry weather it is sure to die when so cut. I lost a whole field of it by mowing too close and early, and I consider the four inches at the bottom of coarse Timothy of little value."

If the seed is allowed to ripen it exhausts the soil far more than if cut in the blossom.

MOWING MACHINES.

We now come to the methods of cutting grass. As this crop is one of the most important and valuable in the whole range of farming products, any practicable means offered to facilitate its harvesting in the best manner, and at the least expense, will naturally excite the interest of the progressive farmer. The ordinary method of cutting by the hand scythe is already too familiar to every one in New England to need a moment's notice in this connection, and I propose only to allude to a comparatively new method of mowing by horse or ox power, and chiefly to the success which has attended the use of machinery during the past season as indicated in the returns to the circular already given, and in reply to the second question, "Have you used a mowing machine, if so, what patent, with what power, and with what advantage?"

The inducements held out by the Massachusetts Society for the Promotion of Agriculture, by an offer of a premium of $600, in the year 1855, to the one who should make the most successful experiments in cutting grass by machinery, and of $1,000, to be awarded in 1856, to the inventor or manufacturer of the best mowing machine, very naturally led our farmers to hesitate in procuring machines till the results of these trials were known. The number of affirmative answers to the above question was, notwithstanding, very considerable, and generally wherever used, the testimony is strongly in favor of the use of machinery.

In speaking on this subject I shall state simply the facts which have been returned to me by practical farmers, without expressing any personal preferences for any particular patent. By so doing, I shall give the farmer who designs to purchase a machine the means of forming his own judgment without the necessity of any bias from mine. I will simply state that my observation of these machines and their work has been extensive during the two past seasons, and that the improvements during that time have been very great in nearly all the patents which have fallen under my notice.

A practical and experienced farmer of Hampden county, in answer to the circular says: "I use Manny's Patent Mower, manufactured in Worcester, by J. P. Adriance & Co., and have cut more than one hundred acres in the two last seasons, without breaking a tooth or the point of a knife. The whole expense of repairs has not exceeded three dollars, and it is now in fine order for years to come. The power is the same as common ploughing. If the horses are permitted to stop but a short time, and that often, in hot weather, as when ploughing, I would as soon let my horses mow a day as plough."

A farmer of Worcester county says: "I have used Ketchum's and Manny's mowing machines. I prefer Manny's to Ketchum's. It draws much easier, and is easier to manage. I worked them both with the same horses. My mowing lots are small. Farmers with large lots can use the machine to greater advantage than I can, but on my small lots it saves nearly two-thirds the cost of mowing, and all the cost of spreading." Another in the same county says: "In July, 1854, I used Ketchum's Patent Mower, with which, after many failures and repeated discouragements, I succeeded in cutting the crop of grass, and made considerable saving in the cost of getting the crop, but was of the opinion that great improvements were necessary. In 1855 I used the same patent altered, but not improved, by an iron frame and cutter bar. The present season I have used the Manny patent, manufactured in Worcester, and can say that it is a labor-saving machine for the farmer. The Manny is far superior to the Ketchum, for lightness of draught and the slowness of speed required in uneven places; the lever by which the cutter bar is raised or lowered at pleasure,—the perfect arrangement of the knives that could not be clogged or stopped in more than fifty acres,—the convenience of transporting it on its own wheels from one lot to another, and last, not least, combining, as it does, the reaper, renders it one of the most perfect machines that has come under my notice. In regard to the profit of mowing by machinery, it has cost to secure the hay on this place, on an average, about $100 a year for extra labor. This year but $34, allowing nothing for the labor of horses."

A practical farmer of Berkshire county says: "I have used

Manny's combined machine for the two past seasons, having cut all my hay and grain with two horses. The first great advantage is that I cut my hay on the day it is *fit* for cutting; second, I get more hay, as it is all cut up alike—no pointing out to be seen when the snow is a foot deep—and third, it don't make a

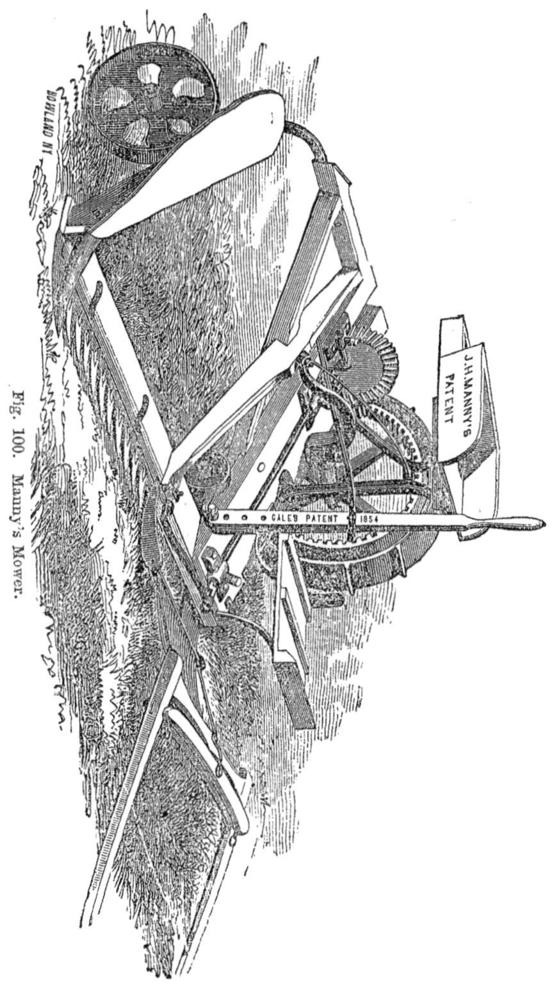

Fig. 100. Manny's Mower.

public house of my home during haying and harvesting, for day laborers. The common farm hands with a Manny machine will do the haying with all ease, and at half the expense." Another in Franklin county says: "I have used Ketchum's patent with two horses, for three seasons. Think I save from the expense of mowing and spreading by hand, together with the advantage derived from being able to cut all I wish to after the dew is off, one dollar per ton." An experienced farmer of Norfolk county says: "I have used Allen's patent, moved by horse-power, with great advantage. Horses move slowly, as in ploughing—are less fatigued than by ploughing all day. I have mowed twelve acres per day, and can mow easily and smoothly any grass, even heavy and lodged clover, and on any surface where a scythe can be used. I regard it as of great use, saving much time and hard labor. It cuts clean and smooth, spreads the grass evenly, and requires only the labor of one man in the largest field, until the grass needs to be turned or raked up." Another in Hampshire county says: "We have used a mowing machine for the four last seasons, of Ketchum's patent. There are ten others of the same patent, and three of other kinds in town, all of which are in active use. They are all worked with horses, two on each. As to the advantage gained by the use of the mowing machine, I hardly know what to say or how to reckon it. There are a number of points to be considered, some of which would be called an advantage by some, which with others might not be so considered. But, the gain in cutting the grass must be apparent to all who have land smooth enough to work a machine on; and in this connection it may be best to speak of the horse-rake with the mower, as one naturally follows the other. Our way of getting hay when the weather is good, is this: To cut and rake it into the windrow the first day. The next, open and turn it, if necessary, then rake it and cart it.

Now one man with a machine and horses, in the forenoon, and one horse and rake three hours after dinner, can put five or six acres of grass into the windrow every day if he chooses, which is as much as ordinary farmers in this vicinity wish to do, as our hay has to be carted from one to two miles, and that takes time. How many men will it take to do the same work? Any one can answer this to his own satisfaction, and as labor differs in price in almost every section of the State, the actual cost would vary somewhat. But here it would take from five to ten men to do the same work, varying as the burden of grass does per acre; for in lodged grass ten would hardly do.

"Then the advantage of having it done in good weather and cutting the grass when he chooses, whether in blossom or after it is fully ripe; I think this can be safely put down at ten per cent., and some call it as high as twenty per cent." A farmer in another town in the same county says: "Have not used any. There are a number of machines in the town. Allen's patent has done the best work this season. Ketchum's improved machine does pretty well. I think they are coming into use more and more."

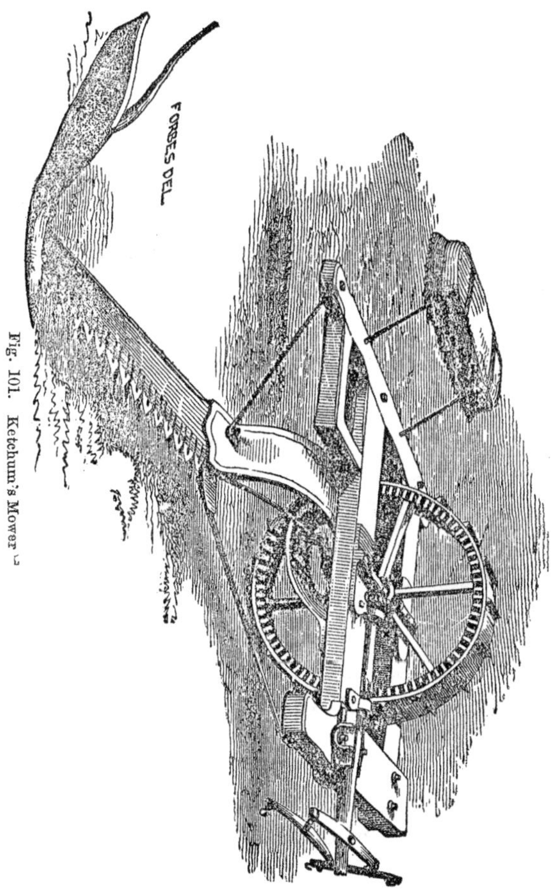

Fig. 101. Ketchum's Mower.

The following extract is from the statement of Dr. Loring, made to the Essex Society during the past season.

"The ground upon which my machine (Ketchum's) was operated, furnished a very severe test of its power. Most part of it is clayey, heavy soil, very wet in wet seasons and stiff and rough in dry ones. No special care has been taken in laying it down. And I am confident that no machine but the strongest, could endure the wear and tear to which it is subjected on such a surface.

"No difficulty has been experienced in the varieties of grass which I have cut. The heaviest and the lightest have fallen equally well, and no trouble has been met in turning the corners or in driving the machine so as to avoid clogging.

"The experience of this season has convinced me that on ordinary, rough New England farms, the Ketchum machine works almost to perfection. I do not mean to say it has no equal, for I have not experience to warrant such a statement. But in all varieties of work, light grass and heavy, lodged clover and upright Timothy, rough land and smooth, I find that I can rely on its operations, without particular effort to secure for it any advantages. Its draught is no trouble to such horses as a farmer ought to own. And it does its work without any extra and ingenious appliances.

"Of the economy of mowing machines, it seems to me there can be no question. I have found that the machine operated on the Pickman farm would cut grass enough in four or five hours in the morning to keep the laborers busy during the day, and as much as could be cured and got in with ease. The two seasons during which I have witnessed the working of the machine, I have made it, in my mind, an absolute necessity, in all economical management of the farm, to which purpose alone I have had it applied."

But the great trial in this State the past year, was in competition for the premium of $1,000 already alluded to, for the best mowing machine. Three farmers of well known good judgment were appointed to act as a committee. They gave all the machines entered a very thorough and careful examination, saw the work of each, and made a report which has been returned to me in manuscript, and will shortly be published in full. In this report, after speaking of several machines, which, after a preliminary examination or trial, were ruled out for palpable defects, they say:—

The four other machines were tried upon another lot of grass, on patches of equal dimensions, each in succession, both when the grass was wet and dry. This was a heavy crop of clover, Timothy and redtop mixed, some of which was lodged. Portions of the lot were rolling, and the surface generally quite as far from level as our ordinary grass fields, so that upon the whole, it was an excellent lot to test the machines.

They were also tried on a meadow bottom which had never been ploughed, where various wild grasses, both coarse and fine, were intermixed.

The trial, you will thus perceive, was a thorough one, and by it we were able to form a satisfactory judgment of the merits of the different machines. The remaining machines, and between which we were to judge, were patented or known as Ketchum's, Manny's, Heath's and the Allen machine, entered by R. L. Allen. The owners of the Ketchum machine allege that Mr. Allen has infringed upon their patent, and has no right to build or sell his machine except within the limits prescribed in a license procured from them, and that Massachusetts is not within those limits. However that may be, is of no consequence so far as our report is concerned, for we did not regard the consideration of that question as within our province, and it therefore had no weight with us. The Ketchum machine, entered by Nourse, Mason & Co., has probably been in use longer in this State and is more generally known than either of the others. The one which they entered for premium differs from those which have been built by them in years past, in having a driving wheel of comparatively small size, wrought iron substituted for castings wherever it was deemed practicable, and every thing about the machine so made as to reduce weight. In this they have succeeded, their machine with pole and whiffletrees attached weighing only about 460 pounds. The price of the machine has also been reduced from $100 or upwards, to $75. We think that in this, they have made no mistake, but that the reduction in weight is a great mistake. The difference in the amount of draft required to operate a machine of 400 pounds weight and another of 700 pounds weight, other things being equal, would probably be almost imperceptible, except by very accurate dynamical tests; and may it not be that the difference would then be found to be in favor of the heavier machine? Without entering into any speculation upon the matter, we think that it was a fact apparent to every careful observer that this light Ketchum machine actually required more power of draft when in operation than either of the four, and that the one which required the least power of draft was almost twice as heavy. So light, indeed, was it, that with the weight of the driver superadded, and driven at a rate of speed sufficient to cut the grass well,—which, by the way, is a little higher than that required by the other machines,—inequalities in the surface, even slight ones, caused it to bound in such a manner as to throw up the extreme end of the finger bar several inches above its true cutting level, leaving the stubble uneven and wavy.

Fig. 102. Allen's Mower.

Allen's machine required less power of draft than the Ketchum machine. Its weight with pole and whiffletrees is about 600 pounds. No machine that we have seen is so readily thrown in and out of gear as is this. It has a wooden instead of an iron finger bar. In our opinion an iron finger bar is preferable. The weather cannot affect it as of necessity it must a wooden one, and the grass which falls upon it leaves it a little more readily. Outside of the driving wheel is a light wheel which runs on a spring axle, and is claimed to be advantageous in turning and in working the machine on a side hill.

The Manny machine also requires less power of draft than did the Ketchum machine. In this respect, the difference between it and the Allen machine was almost imperceptible. It has a wheel at the end of the knife bar, which greatly assists in turning and backing, and makes it much more comfortable to transport from one field to another. We think that, other things being equal, a machine with a wheel at the end of the finger bar, has an advantage over a machine without it. Although very different in construction, we regard the Allen and the Manny machines as very nearly alike in point of merit, and if it had so happened that it was necessary for us to decide between those two machines, our judgment would have been made up cautiously and with much hesitation, for each has points of excellence which the other does not possess. Both these machines did their work generally well, but not so well as the work done by the Heath machine.

This, like the Manny machine, has a wheel at the end of the finger bar. Like that, too, it has a reel which may or may not be used, as circumstances require. But its cutting arrangement differs entirely from either of the other machines. They each have a single knife with the blades riveted to the plate and operating through cast iron fingers or guards, which, especially when the knife is dull, may be liable to get filled up and thus clog the blades. Instead of these, this machine has virtually a double set of cutters, the under set being stationary, projecting an inch beyond the upper, and thereby acting in the double capacity of guard and cutter. These, as well as the upper blades are each independent of the other, and each attached to its bar by a screw bolt. The upper set of blades is held down by a spring pressure bar, so that the operation is similar to that of shears, the grass being cut between two sharp edges, and the machine working nearly as well at one rate of speed as another. In case of accident, therefore, a blade can be removed by any body and another substituted in an instant of time. Both the upper and lower cutters are made like the best edge tools in use, of the best cast steel with wrought iron backs. The iron furnishing strength, the steel can be made as hard as desirable without so much danger of breaking by use, and being made hard do not require to be so often ground. The lower cutter or guard, as you may please to call it, is half an inch thick and one and one-fourth inches wide. The upper blades are about twice as thick as those used on any other machine. This machine very evidently required less power of draft than either of the others, and did its work the best. The Manny machine weighed about 600 pounds. This weighed about 800 pounds. In its cutting apparatus, which is perhaps the most important feature of a mowing machine, we regard it as very much superior to either of the others. In its ease of draft, perhaps the next most important feature, we regard it as

Fig. 103. Heath's Mower.

superior. We regard it also as less liable to clog than any machine with fingers or guards, like those of Ketchum, Manny and Allen. In other important features it is equal to the other machines.

We therefore unhesitatingly, confidently and unanimously express

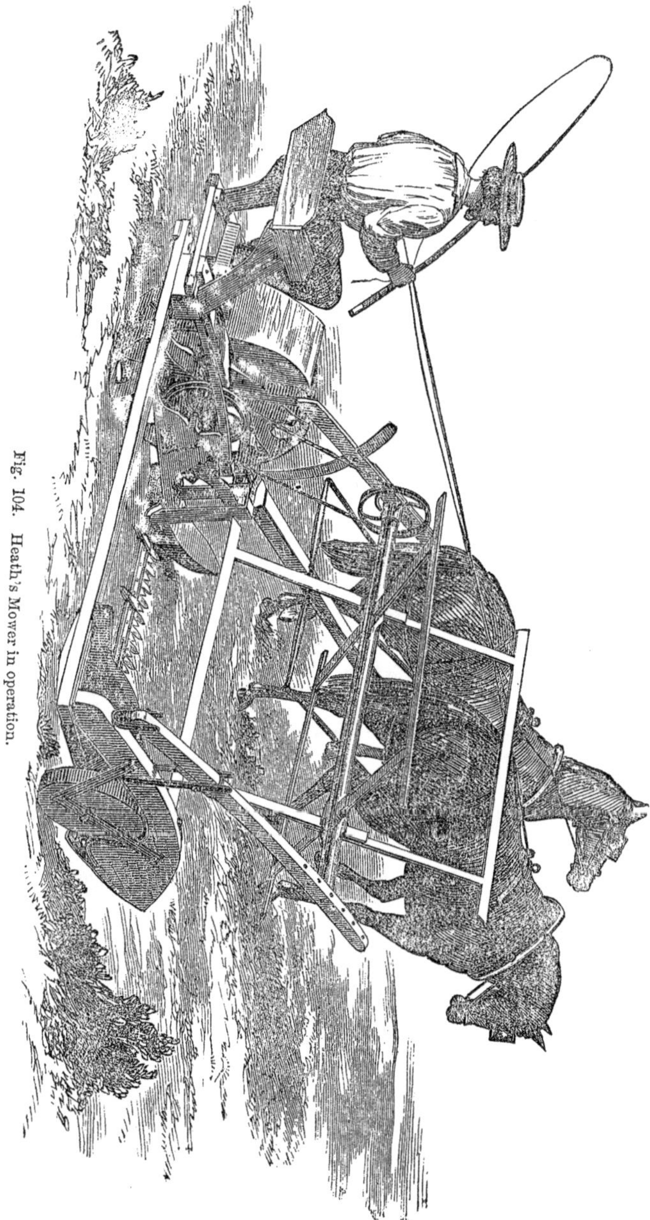

Fig. 104. Heath's Mower in operation.

the opinion, that the Heath machine, entered by D. C. Henderson, is entitled to the premium of one thousand dollars, if that premium is awarded the present year.

HEIGHT OF CUTTING GRASS.

With respect to the height from the ground at which it is best to cut grass, the practice and the opinions of farmers differ widely, for while the answers from about half of the towns say that farmers generally cut as close as possible, the replies from others vary from four inches to one-half an inch. Thus, forty-four towns return, "as close as possible;" fourteen towns, "close, or very close;" sixteen towns, "from two and a half to three inches high;" ten towns, "two inches high;" twenty-three towns, "from one to two inches;" one town, "four inches," while some say, "it might be cut too close," or "close cutting is injurious," or "most people cut too low," and many say, "close as convenient."

It would be difficult to deduce any general rule from the replies to the question, "At what height from the ground do you prefer to have your grass cut, and why?" A farmer of experience in Hampshire county says: "I should prefer to have my grass cut high enough to protect the roots from the hot sun. *I have seen Timothy grass nearly killed by cutting close in a dry, hot time.*"

An intelligent, practical farmer in Middlesex county says: "I prefer to shave pretty close, within an inch of the ground when smooth enough. I still remember some proverbial sayings of my teacher to this effect: 'An inch at the bottom is worth two at the top,' 'You are leaving your wages behind you,' &c. Possibly in very hot, dry weather, on a dry soil, some plants might be injured by a too close shaving, but I should not apprehend any harm, even then, and as a general rule I prefer to have grass cut as close as it conveniently can be." One of the most experienced, practical farmers of Plymouth county says: "Upland mowing grounds I do not like to have cut close, having an idea that the hot sun and dry weather which often follow the mowing season will have an unfavorable influence on the roots of the grass. Low and wet meadows I like to have mown close as possible. There, the heat of the sun is beneficial." A very successful, practical farmer of Worcester county says: "The height from the ground at which it is best to cut grass, depends on the season, the soil and the grass. No grass, except on moist ground, should be cut so low in a very dry season, as it will do to cut it in a wet season. The natural grasses I like to have cut within about two and a half inches of the ground. Our old fields of cultivated grasses do not afford much afterfeed after the clover is run out; what of stubble is left on them is lost, so I like to mow close."

One of the most observing, experienced and practical farmers of Hampden county says: "I prefer grass cut from an inch and a half to two inches, as it starts much quicker to grow when cut at that height, than when shaved close to the earth, as some that are called good mowers do their work. If it is true that all crops are benefited from the ammonia in the atmosphere, as I have no doubt they are, judging from grass side by side, the one cut close, the other two inches high, the grasses should have some leaves left them to receive this benefit. Grass cut two inches high will keep growing, while that closely cut will be even weeks before it will show the first signs of life."

Another experienced farmer says: "Where I top-dress immediately after, I cut as low as I can, to save all the grass I can. If I do not top-dress I cut from two to three inches high, to protect and nourish the roots. I do not feed in the fall where I do not top-dress. I intend to manure all my natural upland mowing land and never feed my old fields." And another: "I like to cut rather near the ground, for the reason that more hay is obtained. If the soil is in good condition, and not too dry, it will start again immediately. I know some say cut high, the stubble will manure the land and protect the roots, &c., but I prefer to manure with something better for protection. I top-dress my mowing land and prefer a compost made of woollen waste and meadow mud for soil not very wet; but for a cold, heavy soil, should prefer sand, or sandy loam to mix with wool waste. Apply fifteen cart loads of thirty bushels each, late in autumn."

A farmer of Franklin county says: "The farmers here cut their grass as near the ground as they can conveniently, without any particular reason for it, except to increase the quantity of hay." Another says: "I prefer to have my grass cut at two inches from the ground, where the land will admit of it. Three inches at the bottom is more valuable than six at the top; besides, it leaves the land in better shape for the next year." Another intelligent, practical farmer says: "It has been difficult to get mowers that would cut close enough, but the mowing machine gives better satisfaction in that respect." And another: "The general practice in this vicinity is, to cut as low as possible, in order to get all the fodder; unquestionably it would be better for the ground and the next crop, to cut the grass a few inches above the ground, to shield the roots, still, I consider, to cut low, followed by a top-dressing, is a better way, and leaves a smoother surface to mow over the following year."

An intelligent farmer of Berkshire county says: "Three inches. If pared too close, the hot sun kills or impairs the vigor of the roots, and stubble of some length retains the snow and gives protection from the winds of winter."

A very successful, practical farmer of Essex county says: "I prefer to cut English grass about three inches from the ground, believing that cutting it closer lets the rays of the sun to the roots of the grass, the intense heat of which, without any screen or shade, greatly impairs the growth of the plant, particularly in a dry season." Another of Middlesex, says: "Cut Timothy grass rather high; finer grasses, and especially wet meadows, should be cut as close as practicable; on upland, in fine grass, there is great loss to the crop by cutting high; in wet meadows high mowing gives the mosses and cranberries headway, which will eat out the better grasses."

Thus, the testimony on this point is somewhat conflicting; but many have noticed the injury inflicted upon Timothy by low cutting in dry weather, sufficient, perhaps, to establish the principle alluded to on a preceding page. Most concur in saying that the finer grasses can be cut lower with safety, particularly if the season be not too dry. Much, undoubtedly, depends upon the soil and the season.

CURING OF HAY.

We have seen that grasses attain their full development at the time of flowering, and then contain the highest percentage of soluble materials, such as starch, sugar and gum, and that these, with the nitrogenous compounds, then, also, most abun dant, are of greatest value as furnishing the nutriment of animals, while woody fibre and mineral matter, though important as giving bulk to the food, are insoluble and least nutritious. We have seen, also, that in the transition from the flowering to the ripening of the seed, the starch, sugar, &c., are gradually transformed into woody fibre, in which state they possess no nutritive qualities, and are, of course, of little value. This fact, which is perfectly well established by careful experiment and accurate analysis, confirmed as already seen by intelligent practice, is of great importance as indicating the condition in which most of our cultivated grasses should be cut, and our practice is pretty uniformly consistent with it.

But there is another equally instructive suggestion in these transforming processes, and it is this: If grass is cut in a condition ever so succulent, and before the transition of sugar, &c., into woody fibre has commenced, there will even then be some loss of sugar and starch from the action of heat and moisture, especially if the grass is exposed to the rain in the process of curing, and lignifaction, or change to woody fibre takes place to considerable extent, dependent, of course, on the length of time it is exposed to air and light; so that grass cured with the least exposure to the searching, sifting winds, and the scorching sunshine, is, other things being equal, more nutritious than grass cured slower and longer exposed, however fine the weather may be. In other words, grass over-cured in the process of hay making, contains more useless, woody fibre and less nutritive qualities, than grass cured more hastily and housed before being dried to a crisp. There can be no doubt which of the two would be most palatable to the animal. Some loss of nutritive elements must, therefore, take place in the process of curing, however perfect it may be, and the true art of hay-making consists in curing the grass just up to the point at which it will do to put into the barn, and no more, in order to arrest the loss at the earliest possible moment. And this fact of the loss of sugar and starch, or of their transformation into woody fibre by too long exposure to the sun and wind, I think equally well established as that any transformation at all takes place, and as equally suggestive.

But on this point, far greater difference of opinion exists

among practical farmers, some considering one good hay day sufficient, while others require two and sometimes three, as if it were not possible to dry it too much. Our practice in this respect is, I believe, better than it used to be twenty years ago. Most farmers now think that grass can be dried too much as well as too little, and that the injury and loss in the crop is equally great from over-curing as from housing green. A practical farmer of Hampshire county says: "One good hay day is sufficient to dry Timothy, redtop or wet meadow. I think farmers lose more by drying their hay too much than by not drying it enough."

An experienced farmer of Hampden county says: "As far as my experience and observation extend, I think farmers dry their hay too much as a general thing. Grass should never be dried any more than just to have it keep well in the mow. I think it is best to get in hay as green as it will possibly do, for it contains more juices, which constitute its value."

A practical and experienced farmer of Worcester county says: "Redtop is a more difficult grass to make into hay than Timothy. To make hay from any grass, it is highly important that the swaths, of the hand scythe, be well shaken; here lies the secret of making hay evenly, without having green, heavy locks. If the burden is heavy, time in making the hay, if cut in the morning, will be gained by turning it by one o'clock, P. M., and then putting it into good sized cocks while it is warm. If the weather be clear, according to my experience, this hay will do to cart the second day without giving it much attention—the sap has become candied and it is fit for the mow. The exposing the hay to the air on the second day, by pitching, is of essential benefit. When carted the same day it is mown, unless dead ripe, it will be withy, clammy, and will be likely to smoke in the mow; in which case the hay has lost much of its valuable quality.

"To keep it till the third day and expose it to the rays of the sun every day, as some practice, dries out the juices and the stem becomes hard and brittle—the life of the hay is gone to some degree. Our mothers and grand-mothers used to dry herbs in the shade—I hold to curing hay in the cock."

Another practical farmer in the same county says: "My way of making Timothy and redtop is to mow it early in the morning, and when the dew is off spread it well. I like to dry it in one day's sun if I possibly can ; if not, put it into cocks before night, then get it into the barn as green as I can and not have it hurt. I do not want my hay all dried up. It injures it. Wet meadow I put into the barn on the day it is cut, if the weather is suitable for curing it."

A farmer of Berkshire county says: "If the weather is good and the grass not too heavy, we cut in the forenoon and get into the barn in the afternoon. If the grass is heavy and the weather not good, cut in the forenoon and turn over the swaths at night, spread and get in the next day. I do not believe in drying hay as much as some do. If not quite dry, two or three quarts of salt to the load will preserve it, and it will be the better." Another in the same county says: "I prefer to cut hay in the blossom on a good hay day in the forenoon, and it is fit for the barn, if raked with the horserake and care is used to turn it over and bring the green grass to the sun, by two or three o'clock in the afternoon of the same day. Much hay is spoiled by being dried too much."

A farmer of Franklin county says: "Timothy will dry sufficient for me in one good hay day. I dry less and less every year. If there is no moisture on it there is little danger of hurting after it is wilted." He cuts his swale hay before it matures and while it is quite green, and lets his upland grasses stand till they are fully developed and commence changing their deep green color. "I think it will keep the same stock longer and better if cut at that age." Another experienced farmer of Berkshire county says: "My way of making hay is to cut when in blossom, in the morning, shake it out evenly over the ground, turn it over at eleven o'clock, and get it into the barn on the same day if the weather is good. But if the grass is very heavy, I put it into cocks over night. I consider it made as soon as dry enough not to heat in the mow. To get drier than this is an injury to the hay."

One of the most extensive and experienced stock feeders in this State, a practical farmer, says: "I prefer to cut all English or swale grass from the tenth of June to the first of July, including Timothy and clover in the same time. More than thirty years experience has convinced me that hay secured in the above time,—or just before coming into blossom,—will make cows give more and better milk and butter, will put more fat on animals for the slaughter, with four quarts of meal per day, than eight quarts of meal with hay well secured from the first of July to the first of August. That will give the second crop, if you wish, time to grow, and it may be cut the last week in August or the first week in September; there will then be a crop of fall feed, which most farmers prize very highly. If you do not wish a second crop, the feed by early mowing is very valuable. On the other hand, if the grass is cut late, the hay is not only poor but the feed is mere nothing. Every farmer of my acquaintance admits that the hay cut early is far superior to that cut late, unless it be those that are in the habit of selling hay; even that class must lose in the weight of their crop by late cutting. Many buyers have not yet learned the difference between early and late cut hay, when the real difference is, oftentimes, from four to six dollars per ton. Working horses and oxen will keep in better condition with half the grain when fed upon early cut hay; will look sleek and their eyes will be bright."

A farmer of Hampshire county says: "My method is to cut with the mowing machine, which leaves the grass perfectly spread. It is turned over between one and two o'clock in the afternoon, and while still warm and before the evening dew falls it is put into cocks. It is spread and turned the next morning, and at one o'clock is ready for the barn. I cannot tell on paper, the precise point of dryness at which hay should be housed, but with my hands, eyes and nose, I can judge when it is dry enough not to hurt in the mow, and not so dry as to crumble or to have lost any more of its virtues than necessary. The less drying the better, if it does not injure in the mow." Another practical farmer says: "I prefer two days, but want to have it lay thick together and stirred often the first day and but little the second. In this way the hay retains more of the juices, smells sweeter, looks greener and the cattle like it much better. Hay should be cured so that it will not heat in the mow and no more." Another says: "Hay may generally be dried enough in one good hay day with proper care, to be left over night in the cock and carried to the barn the next afternoon without spreading. Hay may be dried too much as well as too little." "Timothy and redtop," says a farmer of Berkshire county, "carefully spread as soon as the ground between the swaths is dry, and, if heavy, turned about noon, will dry sufficiently in one day, if a clear one, to be put into the barn before sunset. I believe many dry their hay too much. Never dry it so as to make it brittle when twisted in the hand."

These, and many other extracts of a similar import which might be given, did space permit, indicate with sufficient distinctness the prevailing practice among the best farmers, but as constantly intimated, it is very common to find hay dried far too much. Every farmer is aware of the importance of keeping his grass and hay as free from dew and water as possible. An exposure to rain washes out much of the soluble constituents of the grass, leaving a useless, brittle, woody fibre. Grass and hay are greatly injured by remaining too long under a hot sun without being turned. A somewhat different method is adopted for

CLOVER.—The natural grasses when cut for hay are generally spread and dried as rapidly as possible, in order to secure them in the best manner. Experience has proved that the same method is not applicable to the clover crops. It requires a longer time to cure it properly, and if exposed to the scorching sun it is injured even more than the natural grasses, since its succulent leaves and tender blossoms are quickly browned and lose their sweetness in a measure, and are themselves liable to be wasted in handling over. Most good farmers, therefore, prefer to cure it in the cock. A practical farmer of long experience in Worcester county says: "I prefer to mow clover when it is dry, free from dew; let it wilt, and the same day it is mown fork it into cocks which will weigh from forty to fifty weight when fit for the barn. Do not rake and roll it, that process will compress it too much.

"According to the weather and my convenience I let it stand —it will settle and turn the rain very well, and will answer to put into the mow while the heads and stalks are yet green and fresh. When fit to cart, the stalks although green, will be found to be destitute, or nearly so, of sap—the sap has candied and the clover will keep. On the day of carting turn the cocks over, expose the bottom to the sun an hour or so, and to a ton of hay add four to six quarts of salt in the mow.

"Good clover—not rank—cured in this way, I consider to

be worth nearly or quite as much as clear Timothy, to feed to a stock of cattle; and for milch cows, I consider it to be by far preferable to Timothy. Good clover hay will keep up the quantity of milk, while Timothy will diminish it."

Another practical farmer of the same county, in one of the best farming towns in the State, says: "My method of curing clover is this: what is mown in the morning I leave in the swath, to be turned over early in the afternoon. At about four o'clock, or while it is still warm, I put it into small cocks with a fork, and if the weather is favorable it may be housed on the fourth or fifth day, the cocks being turned over on the morning of the day it is to be carted. By so doing, all the heads and leaves are saved, and these are worth more than the stems. This has been my method for the last ten years. For new milch cows in the winter, I think there is nothing better. It will make them give as great a flow of milk as any hay, unless it be good rowen. For working oxen and horses its value is about one-quarter less than Timothy."

A practical farmer of Hampshire county says: "I can hardly state my own opinion of curing clover. When the weather bids fair to be good, I mow it after the dew is off, and cock it up after being wilted, using the fork instead of rolling with the rake, and let it remain several days, when it is fit to put into the barn." Another in the same county says: "I mow my clover in the forenoon, and towards night of the same day I take forks and pitch it into cocks and let it stand till it cures. The day I cart it I turn the cocks over so as to air the lower part. I then put it into the mow with all the leaves and heads on, and it is as nice and green as green tea. I think it worth for milch cows and sheep as much per ton as English hay."

A farmer of Middlesex county says: "I have found no better hay for farm stock than good clover, cut in season. For milch cows it is much better than Timothy. It keeps horses that are not worked hard better than any hay. And small clover, as the rowen crop, is better than any other kind for calves. Clover is not good market hay, as it wastes in removal from the barn. Stable keepers give much more for coarse Timothy that cannot easily be drawn through a rack." A farmer of Barnstable county says: "We mow clover in the forenoon and let it lie in the swath and put it into small cocks in the afternoon. If the weather be fair on the third day, open it to the air and sun for two or three hours and then put it into the barn. I have found clover cured in this way keep sweet and free from mould, and of equal value with other hay." Another says: "I have tried three different ways of curing clover. One was, to make it in the same manner of other grasses; another, to dry it one day in the swath till wilted and then pitch it into cocks to stand some days, according to circumstances; and the third was, to give it one good day's sun, turning it over and getting out the water, and mixing it in the barn with old hay or straw. I managed in this way a year ago, the weather being very 'catching,' cut and dried it as much as possible in one day and carted it into the barn the same afternoon. I mixed it with some old swale hay that had been left over, placing a layer of old hay then a layer of clover, building it up in a square mow. My neighbors laughed at me and said I should burn my barn down by putting in that 'green stuff.' But I must say I never had better clover hay than that. The cattle would eat all the meadow, or swale hay, as well as the clover. There was not a particle of smoke about it on feeding it out. When cured in this way or by the second method, in the cock, I think clover hay is worth two-thirds as much as good English hay to feed out to farm stock."

From what has been said in these extracts, which might be multiplied, did space permit, it appears evident that good farmers appreciate the importance of so curing clover as to preserve its tender and succulent foliage. They are careful not to overdry it, for fear of loss of the blossoms and the leaves. But it is not uncommon among thriftless farmers, to handle it in such a way that the best parts of it are shaken off and destroyed.

The method detailed in the last extract, of mixing clover with a poor quality of hay or straw, has sometimes been adopted with great success, the clover imparting its fragrant odor to the hay with which it is brought in contact, greatly improving its quality, while its own value is preserved without injury. It is not only a matter of convenience oftentimes, to have the clover so secured in catching weather, but on careful experiment may be found worthy of being more generally practiced.

The general testimony of practical farmers as to the value of clover hay as compared with that of Timothy and redtop, our prevailing natural grasses, varies exceedingly, some making it of equal value, others estimating it at one-half and from that to two-thirds and three-fourths.

Corn Fodder.—The practice of raising Indian corn to cut and feed out green by way of partial soiling, is very common in New England, as already intimated, in speaking of the natural history of the grasses. This culture has been carried still farther by many farmers, and many acres are raised in various parts of the State for the purpose of cutting and curing for winter use. And now that great hopes are entertained by many of the utility of the culture and use of the Chinese sugar cane, which, it is thought may be raised, cut and cured in the same way and for the same purpose, it is important to allude to the most approved methods of curing, though they may already be familiar to most practical farmers.

The common practice with regard to this crop, and which has been already partially stated, is to sow in drills from two and a half to three feet apart, on land well tilled and thoroughly manured, making the drills from six to ten inches wide, with the plough, manuring in the furrow, dropping the corn about two inches apart and covering with the hoe. In this mode of culture the cultivator may be used between the rows when the corn is from six to twelve inches high, and unless the ground is very weedy no other after culture is generally needed. The first sowing usually takes place about the 20th of May, and this is succeeded by other sowings at intervals of a week or ten days, till July, in order to have a succession of green fodder. But if it is designed to cut it up to cure for winter use, an early sowing is generally preferred, in order to be able to cure it in warm weather, in August or early in September. Sown in this way, about three or four bushels of corn are required for an acre, since if sown thickly, the fodder is better, the stalks smaller, and the waste less.

The chief difficulty in curing corn cultivated for this purpose and after the methods spoken of, arises mainly from the fact that it comes at a season when the weather is often colder, the days shorter, and the dews heavier than when the curing of hay takes place. Nor is the curing of corn cut up green, so easy and simple as that of drying the stalks of Indian corn cut above the ear, as in our common practice of topping, since then the plant is riper, less juicy, and cures more readily. The method sometimes adopted is to cut and tie into small bundles, after it is somewhat wilted, and stook upon the ground, where it is allowed to stand, subject to all the changes of the weather, with only the protection of the stook itself. The stooks consist of bunches of stalks first bound in small bundles, and are made sufficiently large to prevent the wind from blowing them over. The arms are thrown around the tops to bring them together as closely as possible, when the tops are broken over or twisted together, or otherwise fastened in order to make the stook "shed the rain" as well as possible. In this condition they stand out till sufficiently dried to put into the barn.

But Indian corn stooked in this way often becomes musty or covered with dust, while the rains often soak it thoroughly and wash out much of its soluble matter, and its nutritive value is in a great measure lost. Besides, every one knows that to cut up a green plant, as a willow or any other thriftily growing plant or shrub, and set it up with the cut end resting upon the ground where it can still derive moisture from the soil, will prevent its drying. There can be no doubt, also, that the exposure to the sun, wind and rain, greatly injures it by removing much of its sweetness, or changing it to woody fibre, while it takes from it its beautiful fresh green color.

To avoid the losses necessarily attending these modes of curing, some have suggested kiln drying as far preferable, and, on the whole, as economical. I have known the experiment tried in one or two instances with complete success, the fodder coming out with its fresh green color, and apparently better relished by cattle than that dried in the ordinary way. This method appears to me to be worthy of much more extended and careful experiment. The kiln need not be elaborately or expensively contrived. The process of drying would be short and the labor slight.

Another mode which has been suggested is to hang it up in sheds open to the air, precisely as tobacco is cured in the western part of the State. This process would be longer, but the nutritive qualities of the plant would probably be better preserved than if cured in the open air with the exposure to the frequent changes of the weather. It is hardly necessary to say that if it is proposed to cure in this way, it should be hung up thinly and the air should be allowed to circulate through it. After being well dried it is taken down and stowed away in the barn for use. This method avoids the trouble of stooking and the liability to injury from rains and dews, which blacken the stalks, though it requires considerable room, and is, of course, attended with some additional labor.

THE HORSERAKE.

This implement has come into universal use, and no farmer of any extent would be without one. It met with great opposition and encountered great ridicule on its first introduction, but has survived it all and become indispensable in all thrifty and economical farming. I shall do no more than give the authority of practical farmers in answer to the thirteenth question of the circular, "*Have you used a horserake, if so, what patent, and with what advantage?*"

To this, an experienced farmer of Middlesex thus replies: "I have used various horserakes for fifteen years. Much labor is saved by the use of any kind of horserake that has been introduced within that time.

"Horserakes are on a footing different from mowing machines. Grass may be cut in the morning, in the evening, or in a cloudy day. But hay must be raked at the very right time, or it may be entirely spoiled. It is, therefore, quite important to do work quick when the time for doing it comes. With a good rake a man and horse will gather more hay in half an hour than a laborer with a handrake usually gathers in a long afternoon —that is, one acre; this is considered a half day's raking by handrake.

"The independent rake operates quite well. The old revolving rake (Fig. 105) costs about the same.

"The spring-tooth rake is patented, as I am informed. One objection to this is, that the wire teeth scratch up too much earth. This is seen in Fig. 106.

"Buckminster's patent was obtained about sixteen years ago. His rake is quite simple in form and will gather more hay than either of the other kinds, in an hour. But the operator must walk, and a boy is wanted on the horse. The price is four to five dollars, as any carpenter or wheelwright can make them."

A practical farmer of Worcester county says: "I have used what is called the independent horserake, Delano's patent, I believe, and with great advantage. I have also used the revolving and the spring-tooth rake. I prefer the independent. In short, it is my opinion, that no modern invention of agricultural implements has made so great a saving over the old method of performing farm work, as the independent horserake."

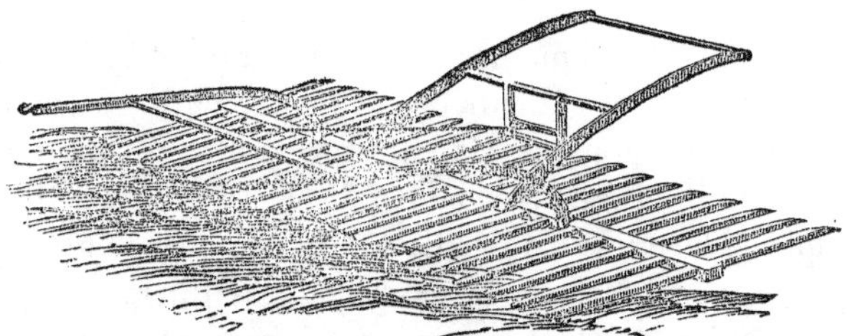

Fig. 105. Revolving Horserake.

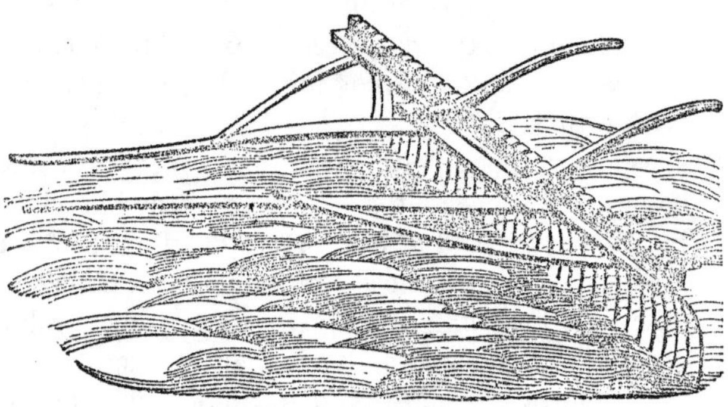

Fig. 106. Spring-tooth Horserake.

A farmer of Norfolk county says: "I have used Delano's independent rake for several years. I regard it as a valuable implement, saving thirty per cent. at least, of labor and time. This rake ought to be made of better materials and with more care, or it will be given up for some other." This rake is seen in Fig. 107. The complaint that it is very badly made and constantly liable to get out of order in consequence, is very general.

A practical farmer of Franklin county says: "I have used a revolver ever since I commenced working on a farm, and would as soon think of haying without a pitchfork as without a horse-rake."

Another experienced, practical farmer of Worcester county says: "I used an iron-toothed rake three seasons, and I thought with profit, but I bought one of Delano's independent rakes, and I think it is worth three times as much as any iron-toothed one, as it does not make the hay so dusty as the others. It is also a great saving in time and labor, as a boy twelve years

Fig. 107. Independent Horserake.

old will rake as much with Delano's patent, as a man and boy with any other kind I have ever seen, and do it better. I have used one of this kind for four seasons, and it has not cost me twenty-five cents a year for repairs, although my farm is rough and rocky."

Another says: "The horserake is a great labor-saving implement. For several successive years I used the revolving horse-rake to good advantage. There was labor in it, but it is a good rake. Delano's patent—the independent tooth horse-rake—has taken the place of the revolver with me; it is managed with much more ease, the teeth each one acting independent of all others, at all times laying on the surface, whether even or otherwise, will rake cleaner than the revolver, and will not get so much dirt on the hay as will the spring-tooth."

And another: "I use the wire-tooth. The independent, or wheel rake is used some; both are good. I cut about sixty tons of hay, and my rake I have no doubt saves me $20 every year. First in labor, and second, in quality of hay—every thing being raked at night." Another says: "We have used the revolving horserake for the last ten years or more, and my opinion is, that could I have my choice between six men or a horse and rake, after dinner, with a quantity of hay to secure, I should take the latter."

A very successful farmer of Essex county says: "We formerly used the revolver with good success; but for the last four or five years we have used Delano's independent horserake and like it better than the revolver, as it is easier for the horse, easier for the person who uses it, and rakes better on uneven land. The great difficulty with the independent rake is, that it is so wretchedly made, that our farmers cannot depend upon it, and they complain of its getting out of order at times when they most need it. They are compelled to resort to the use of other patents which are not so convenient, on account of their being better constructed." Another in Hampden county says: "I have used the independent horserake for seven years, and find it a great labor-saving machine. It has not cost me a dollar to keep in repair and it is now as *good as new*, though most farmers who use it say it is liable to get out of order from being very badly manufactured. This, if true, is enough to condemn any farm implement, because farmers are not generally so situated as to be able to afford such frequent mishaps."

Still another patent, which promises to be a great addition to our present facilities for raking hay, has been introduced under the name of "Carpenter's Improved Horserake." This rake is seen in Fig. 108. It was patented in August last, and the parties interested claim for it very important advantages over the horserakes now in common use. The driver rides upon the rake comfortably seated, and by means of a lever, which he can move at will, and without changing his position, frees the hay gathered in the teeth of the rake.

It is a double rake, made for both smooth and rough ground. On smooth ground the wheels may be used, while on rough

Fig. 108. Carpenter's Improved Horserake.

ground the driver may walk behind and manage it with ease, and adapt it without difficulty to inequalities of surface. It is simply constructed, and is manufactured by Nourse, Mason & Co., of Boston. As it is a new implement, and has never been used, to my knowledge, in this State, I cannot speak of it from personal observation or experience.

HAY CAPS.

The frequent losses to which farmers are subject in making hay, has suggested the use of hay caps, made to cover the cocks and protect them from the weather. It is but recently that their use was introduced, and like most novelties, it has met with objections from some, on the score of economy, while their use is as strongly approved by others, on the same ground. I have often seen them used, and the time taken to cover an acre of grass or hay in cock partially cured, is less than most would naturally suppose. Where they are to be used, less care is needed for "trimming down" the cock and putting it in a condition to shed the rain in the best possible manner.

An experienced, practical farmer of Worcester county says: "I have used hay caps with good results. I have one hundred made of cotton sheeting two yards square, with pins attached to the four corners with strong twine; the hundred cost me just forty dollars; I think they have saved me twenty dollars this year. I had at one time this season one hundred and thirty cocks standing out in a six days' storm. One hundred were covered, and not having caps enough, thirty were left uncovered. The uncovered was worth but little, while the covered was passable hay. I stooked some oats which I capped —they stood a two days' rain without injury." And another: "Our caps are made of heavy five-fourths cotton cloth, cut square with four little loops through which we run a slim wooden pin into the hay cock; the pins hold it better than weights in the corner. Ours cost twenty-one cents apiece—have saved the cost in one storm this season."

A practical farmer of Hampshire county says:—

"In reply to your question as to the utility of hay caps, it gives me pleasure to say, that, after using them constantly, for the last seven years, I consider them of the first importance in the most critical branch of farming.

"I can safely affirm, that my hay has been intrinsically worth, on the average, one or two dollars a ton more than my neighbors', which has been proved by the remarkable health of my animals.

"My horses have not been sick an hour, and the heaves are unknown in my stable, which may fairly be attributed to the fact that no musty hay ever enters my barn; and, it is probable, that the milk of cows may be as unhealthy, if they eat badly cured hay, as if fed on what is called swill in the cities.

"Having these covers always at hand, it has been my practice to mow my grass when it was ready, *without consulting the almanac, or waiting for a change of the moon;* and the result has been, that I have had more than my share of good luck in this important branch of business.

"They are also very useful as a protection against heavy dews; and as a cover for coarse clover and Timothy I consider them *indispensable.*

"After long experience, I have found the most approved method of making hay covers, which may be used for wheat and other grain crops with great advantage, is to take stout, unbleached cotton sheeting, of a suitable width, say from thirty-seven to forty-five inches wide—the latter is the best—cut it into squares, and attach to each corner, by a string, or otherwise, a pin made of wood, twelve or fifteen inches long, cut off smooth at one end and rounded over at the other, which completes the affair. The size of the pin should be about an inch in diameter.

"Hemming the selvages is a matter of fancy, as they would do very well without it; and if a tannery is near by, it would greatly improve them by plunging them into a vat for two or three days; this would thicken up the cloth an inch or two, and make it more durable, as well as much more effectual. A decoction of bark, with alum, or some other astringent, would probably answer equally as well, but this is not *necessary*, to make an excellent hay cover. Like a cotton umbrella, the first dash of a heavy shower would cause it to spatter through for a moment, but would do little or no harm. I doubt whether a larger size than forty-five inches square, or forty-five by fifty, would be desirable,—mine have been not much over thirty-six inches square.

"At the suggestion of several practical farmers of this State, the Messrs. Chases & Fay, of Boston, are now establishing an extensive manufactory for the purpose of furnishing the agricultural community, throughout the country, with a ready made article at the lowest possible price; but, judging from the extensive use of the covers last year, in consequence of articles published in agricultural journals in the United States, as well as Canada, it is doubtful whether they will be able to supply a quarter part of the demand. The article made by them is shown in Fig. 109."

A farmer of Norfolk says: "I have never used them myself, but they are used in the neighborhood to good advantage. A neighbor of mine who has used them for three years says they have been worth to him this year the whole cost, as with them he has been able to get all his hay in in good order, while a large quantity, where they were not used, was made nearly worthless by the long continued wet weather."

But on the other hand, a farmer of Middlesex county says: "I have never used hay caps, not having faith enough in them to give them a trial. My objections are, that they cannot be of any use as a permanent shelter, but only in a sudden shower—and then we have no time to put them on. We can save more hay by putting it in cocks and trimming well than by covering with canvas cloth. In fair weather the cap would be decidedly injurious, as it would prevent the escape of vapor or steam. Cocks of hay that are left to stand in the field over the Sabbath are often dried enough in the upper half. But in case caps were put on for Saturday night the drying would not advance on Sunday unless you should make it a business to remove them on Sunday forenoon."

A permanent structure for covering and protecting hay stacks is described by a farmer of Bristol county as follows: "I have a structure called a hay cap, which, if farmers have not sufficient barn room, I think would be economical, as hay can be more rapidly secured than in the common stack, obviates the necessity of fencing, and prevents the hay from becoming wet while the stack is open for feeding. This cap is twelve feet square and consists of two sills fourteen feet in length and eight inches square, four posts five inches square and seventeen feet long framed into the sills one foot from the end of the same. The sills are held together by two girts framed into the post just above the sill. The posts are held firmly by girts placed five feet eight inches above the sills, to which height the box part of the structure is boarded. The posts above the box

Fig. 109. Hay and Grain Protectors.

are perforated with holes one foot apart for the insertion of pins to sustain the cap or cover. This (in form of a pyramid) should be made as light as possible, so that it may be readily raised by placing the shoulder under the corner. The frame of three by four joists, must be large enough to fall outside the posts and admit of some play. The rafters are small joists nine feet in length, the feet resting upon short pieces of joist placed across the corner of the frame, thereby forming openings for the posts to pass. The tops of the rafters are nailed together over the centre of the frame. Girts should be placed half way from the eaves to the point of the roof to nail covering boards to. These should be good half-inch stuff, and run from the eaves to the rafters. The top of the post should be kept from spreading by stay lathing them. A hay cap of the dimensions given, will hold five tons of hay. The cost I do not know, as this was on the place at the time of my coming on to it."

FALL FEEDING.

This is the term applied to feeding off the aftermath of mowing lands. This practice is very prevalent, and is justified by experienced farmers rather on the plea of necessity than any other, since most farmers, of careful observation, admit that it is, on the whole, injurious. A large proportion of those who are in the habit of fall-feeding, speak like the following, from a practical farmer of Middlesex, who says: "I feed off slightly, although it would probably be better for the next crop if I did not. My cows, however, like it, and as they pay me well at the milk pail, I like to see them enjoy themselves." Another, in answer to the questions, "Do you feed off the after-growth of your mowing lands in the fall? Do you think it an injury or a benefit to the field to feed it off?" says: "I do generally, but consider it an injury to the field." Another says: "I do feed off, moderately, the after-growth of my mowing fields, and believe the grass worth much more so fed than if left on the ground to rot. A dense mass of dead grass is also much in the way of the scythe and the rake the next year." A practical farmer of Worcester county says: "I feed off the after-growth of mowing lands only when I am compelled to do so in dry seasons for want of pasture. I think it an injury to feed off, unless there is a large growth, which is better to be fed off, so that it will not fall down and heat the roots and kill them."

Another says: "I feed my mowing lands in the fall and think it is a benefit to the field in all cases where a top-dressing is used, and of no injury to an old field that is ploughed once in three or four years. Where a large growth of after-feed remains on the land it is like mulching trees, kills the grass roots and makes a grand shelter in winter for mice."

A farmer of Hampshire county says: "I feed it off and then top-dress it, and think it a benefit to the land, but should consider it an injury if I did not top-dress."

An experienced, practical farmer says: "I feed it off, but think it an injury to the field to do so, and I should much prefer not to feed mowing lands at all. The grass holds in longer and is of better quality. I feed it off because it is necessary to eke out a comfortable support for my stock." And another: "To some extent. I do not think it beneficial to the land to feed much every year, nor very injurious to feed some; but to feed close, I deem highly injurious."

A very experienced farmer of large observation, in Plymouth county, says: "To some extent, I feed it off, not from choice but convenience. The treading of the cattle is some injury, and they feed on the best kinds of grass and leave the wild grasses to extend the area of their growth. In my experience, mowing grounds are kept in the best condition by taking off the first and second crops with the scythe, and biennially dressing with compost manures."

This accords with the experience of another practical farmer who says: "My practice is to feed the after-growth or mow it. To take all from the soil without returning an equivalent, would be injurious. My custom is to top-dress my mowing grounds with good compost manure, about fifteen cart loads to the acre, once in two or three years—a portion of lots in one year and a portion the next. Where the ground is not liable to wash—carry the manure off—I prefer spreading the manure in the autumn; it is dissolved by the fall rains and winter snows, and the grass is benefited in the early spring."

An experienced farmer of Essex county says: "Farmers here are in the habit of feeding off their mowing lands in the fall, but have no doubt that the crop of grass would be better the next season, not to feed them. Some think the injury not so great as the value of the feed of the after-growth."

A practical farmer of Franklin county says: "I have had considerable experience in both ways, and do not think fall feeding is any injury if it is not fed too close; prefer feeding to mowing the second crop, and prefer feeding with sheep than cattle." And another: "The feeding of dry mowing injures it by causing it to run out, leaving the roots exposed to the winter, while moist land is injured by the cattle's feet much more than the value of the feed, in both cases taking all off and leaving nothing to renovate the land another season."

An experienced farmer in the same county, and one of the best grazing towns in the State, says: "It is now more than twenty years since I have allowed any kind of domestic animal to feed upon our mown lands, and my opinion previously has been fully confirmed by my experience. It is a decided benefit to let the after-growth remain upon the land; it is a protection from summer's drought and winter's cold. Some of my neighbor's are following my example." And another: "I sometimes feed off my after-grass. When I do feed it off, I take good care to feed it early and leave a good growth to protect the roots of the grass from frost in winter. I think it an injury to feed; mowings will last longer not to be fed at all, and the land when broken up will produce a better crop of corn or potatoes than if fed."

From these extracts it will appear that the practice of fall-feeding is very general, while the good judgment of practical farmers almost unanimously condemns it as injurious, especially to feed closely and late in the season. The reasons assigned for the practice are chiefly, the necessity generally felt for feed at that season of the year, and the importance, in some situations—particularly on interval lands—of removing all protection for the mice, which frequently prove very destructive to the roots when buried with the snow in winter. All condemn the practice of too close feeding, under all circumstances.

The fall growth collects the elements of a thrifty growth in the following spring. These are stored up in the roots over winter for the early use of the plant. If it is closely fed, the spring growth must be proportionably later and feebler.

GENERAL TREATMENT OF GRASS LANDS.

The importance of having the ground well tilled and thoroughly prepared by liberal manuring before committing the seed to it, is too apparent to need remark. When the seed is sown, it is the common practice to harrow it in, either with an iron tooth, or a bush or brush harrow, or both, and those who adopt a more careful culture follow these operations with a thorough rolling, which compresses the soil and usually causes an earlier germination of the seed. The importance of this last operation, that of rolling, is too often overlooked. By reference to table XV., the importance of covering at the proper depth is also apparent, since it will be seen that a large proportion of the seeds germinated with a very slight covering.

But if one thing more than another may be said to lie at the foundation of all real improvement of grass lands, or lands under a course of rotation, it is a proper system of drainage. Especially is this important for low, wet lands, since it not only frees them from superfluous water, thus making them more susceptible of tillage in early spring, but actually increases their temperature several degrees, in some cases as much as from eight to ten, and rarely less than from two to four, and admits the air to circulate more freely around the roots of the plants. The aquatic grasses require large and constant supplies of moisture, and when the soil is changed by drainage, the more valuable species of grass may be introduced and cultivated in it. But one of the most important questions which the farmer of New England has to meet, is the proper treatment of his pasture lands. Many of our old pastures have been stocked hard time out of mind, and the grasses in them have been literally starved out and grow thin of necessity, while, as the finer and nutritious grasses disappear, nature very kindly covers up the nakedness of the soil with moss, as an evidence of the effect, and not the cause of poverty. They are said to be "worn" or "run out." Many of them are grown over with bushes and briars and other equally worthless pests, till they carry but one animal to four or five acres, and often require twice that amount to keep an animal on foot, to say nothing of fattening him. It is a well known saying that, " Poor pastures make breachy cattle."

Undoubtedly thousands of acres in this State would be far more profitably covered with pines than with cattle, and many an observing farmer is now convinced of this fact; but still we must have pasture lands, and there are circumstances where it becomes important to improve them and increase their productiveness. Some of them are so situated that they can be ploughed and thus brought in, with other cultivated lands, to the general rotation; and where this can be done, it may be, on the whole, the best and most economical mode of improving them.

A well known farmer of Worcester county says: " I have renovated my old pasture land by pulling up the bushes by the roots, scarifying the foul or mossy places with the harrow, and sowing on grass seed and clover, both red and white." Another says: " Plough, manure and re-seed. Some have sown rye with the grass seed and then let the stock feed on the rye, as it will not produce any seed-stalks—it sometimes lasts three years. This method has been put in practice with marked success. On our hills, ground plaster or gypsum has brought in the white clover the next year after sowing." A practical farmer of Middlesex says: " The best method I have found is to plough in forty loads of good stable manure to the acre, plant, hoe, and kill the bushes and moss, then seed down with redtop and white clover, instead of taking a crop of rye without adding any thing to the soil, then seeding down with 'barn chaff' as many do." An experienced farmer of Hampden county says: " If the pasture lands can be ploughed, do it in the month of June, say seven inches deep, harrow thoroughly, sow one hundred pounds of Peruvian guano and three pecks of buckwheat, per acre, harrowing them in at the same time. Sow as much grass seed and of the kind best adapted to the soil as you please, and bush it in. I have tried twenty acres at a time with good success."

Another says: " It can be done in various ways. I have a piece of pasture land near my house that bore hardly a spear of grass, and nothing else, except five finger and other weeds that usually grow on old, worn out pine plains, and I commenced twenty-four years ago by sowing Timothy and redtop and a bushel and a half of plaster of Paris, per acre, once in two years up to this time; the grass increased from year to year so as to cover most of the land in thirteen years. Ten years ago I commenced ploughing it. I ploughed about one acre and put on fifteen loads of compost manure and planted it with corn. I sowed it down in the fall with rye, Timothy and redtop, and sowed clover in the spring, and about a bushel and a half of plaster of Paris, per acre. The next year I ploughed another part and manured it the same, except that I planted this with melons, dunged in the hill, seven feet apart, and then sowed it down in the fall the same as the other piece. The next year I took up the remainder, and all the manure I put on the piece, except in the hill, was the water carted on it from a hole in my barnyard. It was immediately ploughed under, then holed and dunged in the hill seven feet apart, planted with melons, and in the fall sowed as the other parts. Since that it has continued to bear very large grass. When I have turned my cattle into it the first of June, I have judged, and others who have seen it, that had I not pastured it I might have cut a ton to the acre. The soil of this piece consists mostly of sand resting upon a subsoil of gravel. Most of our pastures are spoiled by feeding off too early in the spring and overstocking. Cattle should not be turned in till the first of June, and then not overstocked, so that there will always be spots of grass to go to seed, which will keep the pasture well stocked with grass. Always keep your pasture stocked with grass; if you cannot keep it on any other way sow on Timothy and redtop and harrow it in, once a year. I prefer to do it in August, but any other month in which you are most at leisure, will do.

Another experienced farmer says: "Old pastures should be ploughed and planted when they are not too rough for those operations. They may then be seeded down in July among corn or beans, or grain may be sown with the grass seed in the following spring. But we have too much rough pasture unfit for the plough. It should never have been cleared for pasturing, but should have been left to run to wood. Such rough lands are often much improved by sowing plaster at the rate of two hundred pounds per acre. Plaster generally works well on clays and clayey loams which are not wet." Another says: "Where I have ploughed and planted old pastures and then seeded anew, the cattle get a much better living." One of the best farmers of Norfolk county says: "Either by ploughing, rolling and sowing down grass seed and grain in September or April, or ploughing in manure after removing the crop on old ground, and cross plough in the spring, then spread and harrow in guano, at the rate of three hundred pounds per acre, or a good dressing of compost, and sow Rhode Island bent, or redtop and white and red clover, with some variety of grain; or by scarifying mossy ground, and sowing in grass seed and harrowing it, then applying three hundred pounds of guano, or one bushel and one peck of salt, or ashes from ten to twenty bushels, per acre, harrow and bush the ground. Sow early in fall or spring."

A farmer of this State who has lived and had a large observation in England, says: "Some farmers say the plough. But in England, where old pastures are seldom broken up, I have known extraordinary results from top-dressing with crushed bones, more particularly on the large dairy farms in Cheshire. I am sorry I cannot give you the quantities. A neighbor of mine has harrowed an old, worn out pasture, dressed with a liberal coating of Barrilla ashes, from six to seven cords per acre, and sowed white clover and rolled it. It came out a beautiful pasture. The brush harrow and roller applied to all grass land in the spring will amply repay for the labor. Breaking and spreading the cattle droppings on the pasture land is well worth attending to." A farmer of Worcester county says in answer to the sixteenth question of the circular:

"This depends on the kind of land to be reclaimed. If it can be ploughed I would plough it and plant it with potatoes or something else to make it mellow and fine, and then sow it to grass. If it is too rough or stony to plough,—which is the case with a large share of the pasturing in this section,—but is good, sweet, warm land, I would feed it with sheep. I have a pasture of this description, that a few years ago was covered with briars and bushes so thick that there was but very little grass upon it; I cut off the bushes and put on sheep enough to eat every thing that grew upon it for four or five years. They have killed all the briars and most of the bushes. I have sowed some plaster of Paris, which is all I have done to it, and now one acre is worth, and will produce more feed, than three would ten years ago. I should say that my sheep have always done well on this pasture. If the land is cold and wet, and inclined to grow bushes, I let it go and never try to reclaim it, unless it is near the buildings or near the village where the land is very high. In that case it may pay to ditch and work it into good smooth land."

Another practical farmer of great experience says: "We have a variety of soil in this town; some of the best of pasture lands, stony soils, generally clay subsoil. Plaster of Paris is our renovator for pasturage. It works most admirably on almost all of our lands. Two hundred pounds to the acre, applied once in two or three years in early spring, will keep our pastures good." Another in Plymouth county says: "The best method I have ever used is to fence in small pieces and then stock hard with sheep. Feed it down till no green thing remains, then turn the sheep off days and on nights till September, then harrow the land with a sharp harrow and sow on grass seed, keeping the cattle off the remainder of the season."

An experienced farmer of Middlesex says: "It will improve an old pasture merely to plough and re-seed it without manure, but this is a slow mode and not to be recommended where it is possible to apply some sort of dressing. A better method is, without doubt, to plant for a year or two, manuring well, before sowing grass seed. The soil by being thus thoroughly stirred, and exposed to atmospheric influences, will give a sweeter grass and perhaps more of it. But it is not always convenient to plant a part of a pasture. In such cases great benefit would result from simply ploughing, manuring and seeding to grass immediately."

But perhaps the best disposition that can be made of many of our poor, thin pasture lands, and one which has incidentally been alluded to, is to take the cattle from them entirely and cultivate them with forest trees. This is frequently recommended in answer to the question proposed in the circular. A farmer of Middlesex county speaks in the following words: "Old worn out pasture lands that cannot be renovated by gypsum or ashes, had better be suffered to run up to wood. Pine lands can be seeded in the fall with a crop of winter rye, or without. Pine seed can be obtained by taking pains to collect the burs before they are open and drying them in some place where they can be threshed. This is white pine seed year."

This, I am convinced, will be found to be perfectly practicable, and a rapid growth of pine wood, intermixed, as it should always be, with some deciduous growth like the white birch, will be found to be more profitable than the use to which they are now put.

I know many pastures of good strong soil, never ploughed within the memory of the living, some of which are known not to have been ploughed for a hundred and fifty years, which require from eight to ten acres to a cow, so entirely buried are they in moss and bushes. Such lands can be planted with pines at a small cost, and would soon be covered with a growth which would pay a large percentage on the outlay. I have, during the past season, examined over five hundred acres of cultivated pines in different parts of the State, varying in age from three months to twenty years, and can testify to the surprising rapidity with which such a plantation will cover the ground, concealing the fact of their being planted by the hand of man, and assuming the appearance of a dense forest. In one instance the owner informed me that his plantation had averaged him a cord to the acre every year for twenty years during which it had been planted, while the land, a light barren sand, had apparently been improved, and a thick undergrowth of hard wood was apparently ready to succeed the pine when the opportunity offered. I have seen a growth of pitch pine, made this year, of over two feet six inches in length by measurement, and a growth of white pine, made in the same time, of two feet nine inches. The past year was an exception, for while generally the growth of wood is interrupted by the drought during the hottest months of summer, and then starts out a new growth in the autumn, it continued with extraordinary vigor all through the season, in those parts of the State which were favored by frequent rains. The average growth would not, of course, equal that stated above.

But still, there are circumstances, and they are not by any means unfrequent, where it is both practicable and desirable to take other methods of improvement for pasture and grass lands, and we come now to consider more in detail the

TOP-DRESSING OF GRASS LANDS.

The idea was formerly entertained that pasture lands were sufficiently enriched by the animals which fed them. Practical men begin to think otherwise, for it is found that a profitable return is made for the little outlay which they require. Particularly is this the case with pastures fed by milch cows. They do not return the essential elements of the plant to the ground in so large a proportion to what they take from it, as some other animals. These elements are required in great quantities to form their milk, while in other animals they are required only to form bone and muscle. The ordure of cows is, therefore, less valuable and fertilizing than that of other animals. The consequence is, that lands fed wholly by cows are exhausted sooner than those fed by other animals. For it is evident that where more is taken from the soil than is returned, exhaustion must follow.

We furnish animal and vegetable matters to the earth, to supply it with substances which the growth of plants has taken from it. It will be obvious, on a moment's reflection, that the constituent parts of the plant are taken up from the earth and the air, in much the same manner as our food and drink become our bone and flesh. The analogy is still more distinct when we reflect that all our applications for the improvement of the soil, are nothing more than the supply of food for plants. For the food of plants is found in all manures, and the value of these depends upon the quantity they contain.

The methods of renovating mowing and pasture lands by means of top-dressings, do not essentially differ. An interesting experiment, not long ago, fell under my observation. On different parts of the same field, common meadow mud, rich barn and liquid manure impregnated with lime, were used as a top-dressing. The mud was hauled out in the autumn and thrown in heaps, and there left to the action of the frosts and snows of winter. In spring it was spread about the same time the other manure was applied. Strange as it may seem, the top to which the mud was applied, appeared to far the best advantage. The grass was heavier, and after the crop had been removed, that part of the field on which the mud was applied, came in more quickly and luxuriantly than the rest. This field was a light, gravelly soil, which had not been under very high cultivation. Many of our soils are composed of gravel with a mixture of sand. These soils need the constituents of marl and meadow mud. Marl and mud contain the carbonate, or in some cases the sulphate of lime, or plaster of Paris. They contain a mixture of clay, which sandy or gravelly soils need. And on these soils clay mud has been found to do the best. Peat mud is a rich vegetable food, and if a small proportion of potash, or ashes, be added, it is valuable as a manure. Light soils are always improved by any substances which make them firmer and more compact. Stiff clay soils, on the other hand, are benefited by applications which make them lighter and more permeable. No one of the three kinds of earth, sand, clay and lime, when unmixed with the other varieties, would be capable of supporting vegetation. The mixture of them, when any one predominates, will correct and improve them, for the fertility of soils depends much on the proportion of these constituents. In some marls the clay predominates. These should be used on the light sandy soils. In others the sand predominates. These are adapted to stiffer lands. The practice of mixing soils has always been attended with success when judiciously managed.

Nor is this application of mud and clay any new fact to the practical agriculturist. The county of Norfolk, in England, is said to owe much of its great fertility to this source. The greatest European improvements in sandy soils, have been made by these means, in Belgium. As intimated in the experiment alluded to, it has always been found best to expose the mud or clay to the action of the frost. It becomes mellowed so that it may be spread evenly upon the ground. Peat mud is composed of vegetable matter which has been accumulating for ages. When taken fresh it is found to contain an amount of acid which would make it improper for immediate use. Exposure to the frost, wind and rain, entirely neutralizes the acid properties. Ashes, or potash, would have the same effect.

These substances may be said rather to ameliorate and improve the texture of soils than to furnish immediate sustenance to the plant. And in this view they cannot be too strongly recommended, for we have never known them to fail of having beneficial effects, both on pasture and mowing lands. And besides, the application of them is so simple, so much within the reach of every farmer, that it is well worth the trial. If the soils are much worn, or very barren from a great preponderance of any particular earth, a liberal allowance will be required. Ordinarily, as in the experiments which have come under my notice, some twenty-five or thirty cart loads to the acre have been found sufficient to increase very greatly the productiveness of the land. A still less quantity would be of essential service. Nor is the expense of this application so great as some imagine, for almost every farm contains a quantity of waste peat meadow, and clay is frequently near at hand. It may be removed and prepared at a season of the year when there is but little else to do. The expense, therefore, need not deter any one from its use.

But there is another substance equally accessible, which acts both as an ameliorator and a fertilizer of the soil. It is, perhaps, one of the cheapest and most profitable top-dressings. It is the rich loam which accumulates in the holes by the road side, and wherever the wash gathers from hills. Every one has observed the effect of the loam thrown out upon the grass in ploughing. The grass along the edges soon becomes greener in spring, and grows with greater luxuriance. The wash by the road side would have a far more powerful effect. For this contains, besides the putrescent animal matters, from the road, a quantity of sand, which rich soils wanting closeness and consistency, require on the surface. Spread upon such soils when covered with grass, it is very efficacious, and often makes the vegetation as vigorous as stimulating manure. Experiments have clearly shown that the effect of sand on some soils is to operate as a manure.

Among the mineral manures, lime has sometimes been used as a top-dressing. Its effect arises not so much from any direct nutriment furnished by it to the grass, but from its influence on the substances in the soil. It hastens the decomposition of vegetable and mineral matters in the earth. In this way it renews exhausted soils. It increases the temperature of cold, sour lands after being drained. It causes a rapid decay of peat substances. Hence its use in the compost heap. It destroys the mosses and coarse herbage which work in among the grasses, and indicate the want of lime in the soil. It produces from them a fine, vegetable mould, by causing the white and red clover, and some natural grasses, to come in thicker and thicker each year. Lime produces a more marked effect on the grasses than on any other crop. It seems, very frequently, to increase the nutritive quality of the grasses as well as to increase their quantity, by assisting them to elaborate the juices, the albuminous substances and the sugar, in which their value as food for stock largely consists.

But lime can never supply the place of other manures. There are properties which it cannot supply, which plaster can; others which it cannot supply, as bones can; and others which it cannot supply like ashes, and manures that contain salts. There are situations, however, in which it is invaluable. On reclaimed meadow lands, after thorough draining, and a covering of three or four inches of gravel, a top-dressing of lime has a beneficial effect. Crops of grass of two and three tons to the acre, have been taken after such a dressing of lime. In many cases the first crop will repay the expense of bringing such land into cultivation. In these situations, then, as well as on many pastures, it may be called one of the most useful applications that can be made. Such lands will bear an abundant supply of lime without exhaustion. But on poor sandy soils it should never be used. It will soon exhaust and may render them completely barren. When it meets with clay in lands to which it is applied, it forms a kind of marl, and greatly improves the texture of the soil. But when it comes in contact with sand, it forms, rather, a sort of mortar. Hence it is thought to be injurious on sandy soils. Many soils have naturally a sufficient quantity of lime, and on these a further application is not needed.

No definite rule, with respect to the amount required, can be given. It must depend upon the nature of the soil, and must be left to the judgment of those who use it. In general, on peat and clay soils, from ten to fifty bushels to the acre will be required, though less would, perhaps, be beneficial.

The addition of lime to the compost heap is often of great importance. The decay of all vegetable substances is accelerated by it; but it should not be brought in contact with decaying or fermenting animal substances unless covered by a thick coating of peat or other absorbent. Whenever lime is used in a compost—unless it be for the special purpose of hastening the fermentation of vegetable substances—it ought to be mixed with salt by dissolving the salt first in water and slacking the lime with it. A bushel of salt will thus prepare four bushels of lime. Refuse brine will answer very well.

We come now to the use of ashes as a top-dressing. Of this we may speak with more confidence. For while experiments with lime have not invariably proved successful, owing, probably, to the soils designed to be benefited, we know of no instances in which the application of ashes has not fully repaid the expense. If farmers would bear in mind that ashes contain all the elements which assist the growth of plants, they would be unwilling to part with a substance which they might turn to such profit. If the quantity is small, let it be husbanded with the greater care, instead of being sold, with the idea that so few can do no good. One substantial farmer says: "I am now, more than ever, fully persuaded of the value of ashes as a manure. Nothing in the whole catalogue of manures, compares with them on my land. The soil was a thin, clayey loam, and where the ashes were sown there was a crop of excellent clover, where for years the land had been almost unproductive."

Grasses are often more benefited by ashes than other crops, since they require a greater amount of the salts which ashes contain. For all permanent mowing lands, especially on the lighter soils, ashes are among the cheapest of manures where they can be had in sufficient quantities. In parts of Flanders and Belgium, countries in which the science of agriculture has been carried to a high perfection, the great loss of vegetable matters from the soil is constantly restored by ashes or bones, together with other manures to be mentioned hereafter. Indeed, almost all agriculturists, both in Europe and America, have attached very great importance to the use of ashes. In some parts of Germany they are held in so high esteem that they are transported to a distance of eighteen or twenty miles, to be used as a top-dressing. According to Prof. Liebig, with every one hundred and ten pounds of leached ashes of the common beech tree, spread upon the soil, we furnish as much phosphate as five hundred and seven pounds of the richest manures could yield. Phosphates are highly useful to all kinds of soil.

There can be no doubt that the process of leaching takes from the ashes a part of their fertilizing properties. For many uses this is no objection. Especially is this the case near the sea, where leached ashes are thought by some to be even more serviceable, as the salt in the atmosphere the more readily combines with them. Every practical man has heard of the amazing effects which bone dust has upon the soil. Yet this is valuable, chiefly, for the phosphate it contains. But if we may rely upon the statement of Prof. Liebig, leached ashes also contain a large amount of phosphate of lime, which would show them to be extremely valuable. But suppose we allow four bushels of leached ashes to one bushel of crushed bones, the expense of the ashes, would, in most cases, be less than the bones. But if bones can be procured, a mixture of leached ashes and bones, four bushels to one, forms a very useful application. The compound should remain a week or two before being used. Those who have tried leached ashes, have been fully satisfied of their superior qualities as a fertilizer. Careful experiments, by practical, conservative men, show that land producing one ton to the acre, has been so improved by this means as to yield three tons to the acre. Where thirty bushels were used on three-fourths of an acre, in one instance, the crop was increased more than three-fold. Nor are leached ashes subject to the objections which are raised by some against the use of lime. They do not apparently exhaust the soil. The effect of them is felt for several years. Many farmers have found by experience, that one bushel of unleached hard wood ashes is nearly equal to two bushels of plaster, as a top-dressing for the dryer grass lands. If this be true, what has been said would show that leached ashes are about equal to plaster in their effects on such lands. A peck of lime is commonly used in leaching a bushel of ashes. This, of course, adds to the value of leached ashes for grasses. They contain, also, a portion of the alkali which is decomposed by the action of the atmosphere, and the water in the soil prepares it for the food of plants.

As we have spoken of the use of peat muck, it is proper here to say that ashes may be mixed with muck in the proportion of six or eight bushels to the cord. The muck is better, as usual, dug in the autumn, though the mixture might be made in the spring, or on application to the soil. If leached ashes are used, the proportion may be about one to three. In this case, the two substances mutually assist each other, and the compound is, perhaps, better than either alone would be. So potash added to peat muck, makes a valuable compound.

In this connection we should allude to the practice of burning sea-weed as a manure. The ashes of it are spread upon grass and pasture land. They form a very useful and powerful stimulant, but the process of burning sea-weed causes the loss of its most fertilizing qualities. The most common and efficient mode of application is to carry it directly upon the grass as a top-dressing. The coarse rock-weed and kelp decay in a much shorter time than the fine sea-weed, and are, no doubt, better than this. Whenever sea-weed is used, it is best on sandy or gravelly soils. From twenty-five to thirty, or even forty cart loads to the acre, are sometimes applied. Peat ashes form, in some cases, a valuable top-dressing for grass and pasture lands. In Holland, where every fertilizer is preserved with care, peat ashes as well as wood and coal ashes, are highly esteemed. The great value of the first is well known to many, and if those who have them will spread them upon grass at the rate of fifteen or twenty bushels on the lighter, and thirty or forty on the heavier soils, they will be abundantly repaid.

If what has been said be true, and it is the result of many experiments, some of which have come directly under my own observation, farmers would do better to buy ashes on the return of every spring, than to sell them, as is often done.

Of the use of gypsum, or plaster of Paris, the most contradictory opinions have been expressed. So far as my observation goes,—and I have both seen and tried many interesting experiments on the old soils of this State, and the newer soils of Maine,—the application to moist soils has been satisfactory. It has been said that plaster does not benefit natural pastures. This, I apprehend, depends chiefly on the character of the soil. In one instance, a large pasture which had become worn and somewhat unproductive, received a generous top-dressing of plaster. The grass started sooner, and continued throughout the season to look far better than the adjoining pastures of precisely the same soil. So far as could be ascertained, the increase in grass over the adjoining pastures, was about seventy-five per cent. Nor was this all. This pasture came in the next season with the greatest luxuriance, and its load of beautiful green was the wonder of the neighborhood. Its effect on clover and Timothy is greater than on other pastures. Many have supposed that plaster would exhaust the soil. This would not seem to be the case, for as it takes four hundred and thirty parts of water to decompose one part of plaster, its decomposition is slow, and consequently its influence is felt for several years. How, then, can it have such immediate and beneficial effects? It retains the fertilizing gas which is constantly rising from fermenting vegetable matter, and gives it up at a proper time for the nourishment of the plant. It does not, like lime, cause vegetable matters to decay, but rather when they decay, holds their most important parts from escaping.

The powerful odor which rises from decaying vegetable matter, from the stable, from the manure heap, and imperceptibly from the whole surface of the earth, is one of the most important elements for the growth of the plant. Plaster fixes this, and the first shower washes it into the earth to feed the roots of plants. The relative value of manure depends, in a measure, upon the amount of this strong odor, this ammonia which it contains. This gas, commonly known as hartshorn, is an exceedingly powerful stimulant. Nor will it appear unimportant, when we bear in mind that two and one-quarter pounds of this ammonia, lost by fermentation, is equal to the loss of one hundred and fifty pounds of grass or grain. Scientific men will say that this gas is taken up in the atmosphere by the rain, and descends with the rain to fertilize the earth. This is true. This ammonia, arising from all fermenting manures, so indispensable to the earth, is not lost forever when it flies away into the air. But does not the shrewd farmer perceive that as much of this as he allows to escape from his own lands, by neglect, falls upon, and improves the fields of his neighbor as much, and perhaps more, than his own? Is it not evident that by saving all that he can, and by receiving whatever the genial rain brings with it, he gets a double benefit?

If the effect of plaster is such as we have described, no one can fail to see how important are the functions it may be made to perform. But it also adds a certain amount of lime and sulphur to the earth. It is composed of these substances for the most part, and hence called by chemists, sulphate of lime.

We shall have occasion to speak of its use in connection with other manures, when we speak of the compost heap. We now allude to its use by itself, as a top-dressing.

On some soils it is not so satisfactory as on others. But our pastures are many of them covered with the white honeysuckle. These are often called clover lands. On all clover lands, whether reserved for pasture or mowing, plaster generally has a wonderful influence. A bushel, or two bushels to the acre, have been known to double the crop, and to add more than twenty times its own weight to it. Even greater results have followed. For if we may believe one of the most distinguished chemists,* every pound of nitrogen which we add to the grass, increases the produce one hundred and ten pounds, and this increased produce of one hundred and ten pounds is effected by the aid of a little more than four pounds of gypsum, or plaster. Another accurate investigator—Sir Humphrey Davy—found by actual experiment that the ashes of an acre of red clover, contain no less than three bushels of plaster of Paris. This important fact proves that the earth already contains a large amount of this substance, and that it is essential to the growth of clover. This may, perhaps, explain the so-called clover sickness in some land. The requisite supply of plaster has been exhausted. In any case, the addition of plaster to clover lands, and especially to pastures, is of the highest importance.

The effect of charcoal is somewhat similar to plaster. Charcoal will absorb ninety times its own bulk of ammonia, which is held from escaping till it is separated by water and carried into the earth for the plant. When dry, the operation of fixing the gas is repeated till the next shower sends the gas into the earth, and the particles of water take its place in the charcoal. In this way, as a top-dressing, charcoal as well as plaster, performs the most important functions. If we take any decaying animal matter, which has begun to give off its offensive and noxious odor, its ammonia, and cover it with charcoal or plaster of Paris this escaping gas is immediately stopped. No disagreeable odor arises from it. The decay of the substance has suddenly ceased. This simple fact will show the intelligent farmer to what purposes these substances may be applied. His choice of these should depend somewhat on the expense of pro-

* Boussingault.

curing them. The relative expense depends so much upon circumstances, that we need not make the estimate. As an absorbent and retainer of the valuable properties of manure, peat mud and loam will also be found of essential service. If used on a high and dry soil, the effect of plaster will not be very apparent the first season, unless like the past, there are frequent rains.

There is an impression among many that plaster does not produce so good results in the immediate vicinity of the sea shore. If this is so, it does not arise, probably, from the proximity to the sea, but from other causes. Many of our lands do not need the application of plaster. I have seen it used, to the best advantage, within two miles of the sea. If there were any thing in the sea air to prevent plaster from performing its usual functions as an absorbent, the effect would be perceived to a far greater distance inland. If any failures have occurred in its use in the vicinity of the sea, they were probably owing to the soil rather than to the atmosphere. There is one other remark in this connection. When plaster has been applied without immediate effect, we should not at once conclude that it is useless on the particular soil to which it is applied. The first season may be dry, and ill adapted to its decomposition. In such cases, good results have ordinarily followed the second year.

The great utility of bones as a manure, arises from the large amount of phosphates which they contain. On all pastures which have been long fed, the phosphate of lime is exhausted. It is constantly taken from the earth in the grass, to form the bone, the muscle, and the milk of animals. Of the earthy matter in bones, nearly five-sixths consist of phosphate of lime and magnesia. Nitrogen is also abundant, and, of course, ammonia, for nitrogen is an element of ammonia. A few bushels of bone dust will often quite restore old, "worn-out" pastures. Indeed, almost every part, of which bones are composed, goes directly to the nourishment of vegetable life. The ashes of all grains are very rich in phosphate of lime. This shows the importance of furnishing this element for their use.

A mixture of crushed bones and ashes, or leached ashes, forms a valuable top-dressing. Nor will this application, in small quantities, be thought expensive, if what is said be true, that the animal part of bones, which amounts to about one-third, contains eight or ten times as much ammonia as the manure of the cow, and that the fertilizing salts in bones are sixty-six times the amount of a like quantity of the manure of the cow. So that a smaller quantity of bone dust will answer the purpose of a much larger quantity of manure from the stable. We can but hope that every farmer will try the experiment. It may be done on a small scale, at first, though in the vicinity of every butcher's establishment, bones can commonly be procured in any quantity.

Thus far I have spoken of manures which belong more peculiarly on the surface, as a top-dressing for grass. For though they are sometimes used, especially plaster, on ploughed land, with potatoes and other crops, yet their influence on the surface is thought to be far more effective. Indeed, the benefit of lime, plaster and charcoal, would, in a great measure, be lost were they to be buried to any depth in the earth. But there are other manures which are often used as top-dressings.

One of the best practical farmers of Hampden county, says: "I top-dress almost all of my mowing in the fall, cut two crops on all of them, and on some a third. I make a compost of earth and manure—make in the lot where it is used, by ploughing off a thin turf on the lower side of a small hill or knoll, taking the turfs to the hog-yard, and then cart from the stable three, five, or ten loads, or more, as I have the manure. Drop the manure upon the ground that the turf was removed from, then plough on the upper side of the hill and shovel two loads of earth upon each load of manure, beginning in the spring, so on through the season. As the manure of the barn increases, cart to the meadow, placing it upon the upper side of the first heap and plough and shovel as before. From one hundred loads of good stable manure it makes three hundred loads of good compost, and will make as much grass as so many loads of stable manure. For grass, put ten cart loads, per acre. Spread in the fall upon mowing, this compost makes more grass than green manure carted and spread upon mowing in the spring. In almost all cases the knoll or hill carted until it is level with the adjoining ground, produces more crop than before."

Another, in Berkshire county, says: "Top-dressing for mowing lands is very beneficial, but too expensive, if barnyard manure alone is used, so much passes off by evaporation. A compost of one-half or two-thirds turf or swamp muck, and one-third good manure, is quite as beneficial to the land, and probably better or more enduring than all manure. If ashes are mixed in this compost it is all the better. But if stable manure alone or in compost is to be applied, it should be in autumn, so that the frosts of winter may incorporate it with the soil."

Another farmer, of great experience and observation, in Plymouth county, says: "I top-dress generally late in the fall, but should prefer early spring dressing, if we could cart on the fields without injury, and the time could be spared from other business. My land is chiefly of a cold, tenacious soil, and a compost is made of one-fourth stable manure and three-fourths light loam. For warm land peat mud would be used instead of the loam. Twenty common ox-cart loads, from thirty-three to thirty-five bushels each to the acre, is as small a dressing as can be judiciously applied. Double that quantity would not be excessive." A practical farmer, of Norfolk county, says: "With respect to top-dressing for mowing lands, I would state, that for several years we have been in the habit of raising from one to three acres of early potatoes for market. We have usually dug them early in August, and before the tops were dead. The tops are taken directly from the field, and spread on the mowing lands, to very great advantage. We think the tops from an acre of potatoes sufficient to top-dress an acre of mowing land, and the effect is equal to three or four cords of good manure."

The practice alluded to in this extract is worthy of a careful trial by those who are so situated as to adopt it. It is known that the tops of potatoes contain a large percentage of the organic elements of plants.

Fromberg found in 100 lbs. of the leaves in a natural state, from .82 to .92 per cent. of nitrogen, and that 100 lbs. of leaves dried contain from 5.12 to 5.76 per cent. of nitrogen. If his results are correct, and there is no reason to distrust them, we add to the land 50 lbs. of inorganic salts, besides nearly 20 lbs. of nitrogen among the organic constituents of every ton of potato tops. This would make a ton of them equal in value more than two tons of the best Ichaboe guano.

In a case which I have in mind, a very poor, worn out grass lot, was top-dressed with fourteen ordinary cart loads of good stable manure to the acre. The quantity of grass was increased fourfold. Clover and Timothy came in as luxuriantly as on any new laid piece. If the top-dressing were repeated once in five or six years, there would be no danger of exhaustion, though there would be an advantage in loosening the earth with the plough. But the use of stable manure should be confined mostly to mowing land. On closely fed pastures it would be injudicious, from its exposure to the sun. On these, ashes or plaster would be better.

An Essex county farmer says: "Peruvian guano, mixed with loam, is unquestionably the best manure for top-dressing that can be found. Ashes are very good for lands that are liable to be washed by the fall and early spring rains. I should think that the spring would be the best time to spread it, but on lands not so situated the fall would be more proper. In the latter case the manure would be entirely mixed in around the roots of the grass, and all the strength of the manure would remain in the ground."

An experienced and intelligent practical farmer, of Bristol county, says: "I top-dress moist mowing lands in winter or early spring, with eight or ten loads of fine manure, or with about 300 lbs. of guano, mixing the guano with twice its bulk of dry sand moistened with water containing about two ounces of sulphuric acid in solution to the gallon of water."

No farm should be managed without a compost heap, since it may be so made as to form an extremely valuable article for top-dressing. A quantity of meadow mud should be dug out in the autumn for this special purpose. Two cords of peat mud, added to one cord of good stable manure, will make, in the estimation of many practical farmers, a compost of three cords of valuable manure. This has been tried repeatedly, and is constantly done by those ambitious to excel in farming. To this compost heap should be added, from time to time, all the animal and vegetable matter adapted to ferment and enrich the soil. Woollen rags, the remains of fish, the blood and flesh of animals, the hair of animals, all these make an exceedingly rich manure. A most intelligent gentleman connected with a wool factory, informs me that a cord of matter collected at the establishment, is worth at least five or six cords of the best stable manure, for a top-dressing. This we cannot doubt, for here are the blood, the wool, pieces of the skin of the animal, a little lime, and many other substances, all collected together. A fermentation takes place, by which the richest gases are formed. Such a compost heap, with an addition of loam and mud, would be invaluable for a top-dressing. But though in most cases all these substances cannot be procured, many of them can, and should be saved by every one who is desirous of improving his land. Those who are near the sea, or near the market, can procure an abundance of fish to add to the compost. Nothing is better for soils than this. A little lime added to the heap, causes its rapid and thorough decomposition. Ashes should also be added. When additions of manure are made, they should be covered with mud or loam, to prevent waste.

We need not enter more minutely into the details of forming the compost heap. It is sufficient to say, in a word, that every thing capable of fermentation should be added to it. The lower layer should be of loam or mud. Nothing is more common among farmers, on the death of a horse or any other animal, than to throw the body away. It is estimated by some, that the body of a single horse, when divided and mixed with peat mud and loam, will make a compost worth fifteen or twenty loads of the best and richest manure. This is, perhaps, too high an estimate, but animal substances ferment rapidly, or rather they may be said to putrefy without fermenting, so quick is their decomposition. If leaves, grasses, moss, straw and other substances of like nature, are used, lime will be useful in causing their rapid decay. When these are well fermented, the heap should be thrown over, and if made long and narrow, so as to expose the greater surface to the air, it will be the better.

The value of a compost, properly made, is greater than the aggregate value of the several ingredients applied separately, no matter what or how rich they may be. Besides, some divisor is needed for concentrated or other powerful manures, by means of which they may be more evenly and judiciously applied. Peat, or dry meadow muck, is one of the best and most available of these divisors, if properly prepared by exposure to the influence of air and frost. No good farmer would ever use lime in compost with barnyard manure or animal substances, unless peat muck, gypsum or charcoal were largely used in the same mixture.

Animals fed on rich food make far the most valuable manure. This will serve, in part, to show why the manure from the sty is so fertilizing. Swine are fed on a great variety of rich food. The actual profit of raising them, arises mainly from the amount of substances they will mix together and make into good manure. If the sty be supplied, at intervals, with mud, loam, and other vegetable matter, the farmer will not complain of the cost of these animals.

Liquid manures are highly useful to grasses. Care should be taken to apply them, also, to the compost heap. The richness of manure from the sty is due to the quantity of liquid matter it contains. Hence the importance of adding a great variety of vegetable substances, loam, and mud. In a word, it may be said, that all liquid manures contain a large amount of nitrogen, which is one principal ingredient of ammonia, to which we have alluded. The importance of saving the liquid of the stable, either with the compost, or to be applied by itself, may be seen, also, in the fact that the exceeding richness of guano, and the manure of all fowls and birds, is due to the union of the liquids and solids.

After fermentation has taken place in animal manures, in the compost or elsewhere, they may be spread without much loss by evaporation, and hence it matters not whether the top-dressing is applied in the autumn or in the spring. Plaster is better spread in the spring, when the moisture of the earth makes it immediately available. Some prefer the autumn for spreading compost manures, while others prefer the spring, just before the thick grass surrounds and protects them from the sun and wind. The soil, in autumn, is not injured by the loaded cart, as is liable to be the case in spring. Others still, apply them after the first mowing, and before the summer rains. The new crop preserves the manure from drying up and wasting. This, however, is ordinarily too busy a season to attend to it with convenience.

We have then, these several methods of improving our pasture lands. First. To allow some of them to run to wood, or which is far better, to plant them with forest trees, which should never have been entirely cut from them. This applies to poor, thin soils at a distance from the homestead.

Second. To plough and cultivate where this can be done on strong, good soils, which are not too stubborn and rocky. This applies to many lands which have been used as pastures time out of mind, the soils of which are naturally good, but have run out from neglect. Put soil into a good state of culture and rich and nutritive grasses will flourish as naturally as weeds. The former are nearly as spontaneous on good soils, as the latter are on poor ones. The success will depend chiefly on good culture if this mode is adopted.

Third. To scarify the surface thoroughly with a sharp tooth harrow, sowing on a suitable mixture of grass seeds spoken of above, and then harrow and brush over again, the work to be done in September or very early in spring, if the surface is hard enough to go over with cattle without too much poaching. This applies to old pastures covered with moss, where the sweet grasses are run out, but which from their particular location may not be desirable for woodland, nor pay for a more complete and careful improvement.

Fourth. To mix the grass seeds as evenly as possible with a finely divided compost and use it as a top-dressing, first harrowing the surface to loosen it, and after spreading the compost, brushing it over with a brush harrow to break up the lumps. This will cost a little more than the preceding method, but the grass seed will start sooner, make a larger and finer growth the first season and give greater satisfaction. This applies to very much the same class of lands as the preceding. In both cases, if the pasture, or any part of it is covered with bushes, they should of course be cut or grubbed up; if it is wet or covered with stagnant waters they should of course be drained off so as at least to leave a dry and healthy surface. It is unnecessary to say that the top-dressing should be free from weed seed, and be in a finely divided state. This method of improvement is perfectly practicable on thousands of acres which are now in a state both discreditable and unprofitable to their owners.

Fifth. To pasture sheep, turning in as many as the pasture will carry, stocking, in other words, pretty closely, for a few years. The first objection that many farmers raise to this method is, that the cost of fences is great, and that it is a branch of husbandry with which they are not acquainted. This may be so, but the testimony of those who have tried this method is uniformly in its favor. I have had some experience and considerable observation in sheep husbandry, and my attention has been called to the changes wrought by sheep upon rough pastures covered with bushes and briars in part, and it appears to be a practicable method of improvement, while the raising of sheep and lambs for the shambles, is destined to be a profitable branch of farming.

IRRIGATION.—Another practicable means of improving our grass lands is by irrigation. Every casual observer, even, is familiar with the fact that lands are fertilized by irrigation, and especially that the grass by running streams shoots earlier in spring and makes a far more thrifty growth than lands on the same kind of soil which have not the advantage of running water. The introduction of the hydraulic ram among the implements of the farm, offers facilities for irrigating grass lands, not hitherto known, and it will unquestionably become hereafter an important means of guarding against our severe summer droughts, and of increasing vastly the production of our lands.

It would be impossible to state with any detail the different methods adopted to effect the objects of irrigation, since it would require a distinct treatise upon the subject, and it is sufficient to allude to the simplest mode employed with success, and the advantages offered.

Superficial irrigation, which is, perhaps, the oldest and the most common form in which water is artificially applied for the purpose of increasing the growth of grass, was undoubtedly suggested by observing the wonderful effects arising from the overflow of rivers. Remarkable examples of this are familiar to many, as the annual or periodical overflowing of the Nile, where the water without being left to stagnate upon the surface, is moving gently over it, depositing whatever alluvial matter it may hold in suspension. The extraordinary richness of the Valley of the Mississippi, and on a smaller scale, of the Valley of the Connecticut and other rivers, is mainly due, also, to this kind of irrigation; and this is imitated in our attempts to conduct the water over grass land by a system of shallow, open drains, which take the water from its natural channel, keeping a constant flow without allowing it to accumulate in any part.

The process of surface irrigation is not so simple as many would suppose. It requires considerable skill and practice, and many failures have followed experiments of this kind, made without due care and attention. Sir John Sinclair, however, in speaking of this operation calls it one of the "easiest, cheapest and most certain modes of improving poor land in particular, if it is of a dry and gravelly nature. Land when once improved by irrigation is put into a state of perpetual fertility, without any occasion for manure or trouble of weeding, or any other material expense; it becomes so productive as to yield the largest bulk of hay, besides abundance of the very best support for ewes and lambs in the spring, and for cows and other cattle in the autumn of every year. In favorable situations it produces very early grass in the spring, when it is doubly valuable; and not only is the land thus rendered fertile without any occasion for manure, but it produces food for animals, which is converted into manure to be used on other lands, thus augmenting that great source of fertility."

The effect and value of irrigation does not depend altogether upon the artificial supply of moisture which it furnishes to the plant. "The mechanical action of the irrigatory current of water, in exercising the plants, strengthening their organisms, keeping their stems and root crowns clear of obstruction, promoting the equable circulation of water and oxygen around them, and causing an equable distribution of the soluble materials of their food, probably plays a considerable part in irrigatory fertilization. The differences of effect, from the mere circumstance of flowing or stagnation of the water, are prodigious; for while flowing water coaxes up the finest indigenous grasses of the climate, and renders them sweet and wholesome, and nutritious, and luxuriant, stagnant water starves, deteriorates, or kills all the good grasses."

The effect which surface irrigation produces on the nutritive qualities of the grasses may be seen by reference to the tables of analyses found in a preceding section.

This subject ought to receive the careful attention of the enterprising farmer. Even a farmer of very limited means may do something each year towards improving his pasture lands. He may lessen the area of the bushes, he may plough up a small piece at least, and seed down at once with grass seed and winter rye, either in the spring or in the fall, and in either case his stock will fare enough better to pay for it, and the next year he may take another piece in the same pasture till the whole is finished, when it will carry more stock, and more stock will give him more manure, and more manure will increase the fertility of other lands, and increased fertility will add to his means of further improvement. The difficulty with most small farmers is to begin. Well begun is half well done, for the moment any real improvement is begun in earnest, the interest is excited, the mental activity is increased, the desire for improvement partakes the nature of a passion, and hence, though the beginning may be small, the ending may be the renovation of the owner as well as the land.

In conclusion, I have one farther suggestion to make, and that is, as to the propriety of encouraging the collection of grasses for exhibition at the anniversary festivals of our agricultural societies. It would be an easy thing, I think, to engage many in this fascinating pursuit. Some, undoubtedly, would be interested by the simple suggestion, but the offer of small premiums for the largest and best arranged collection would induce others to attempt it who now want something to stimulate them to the work. The premium, however small, might afford the necessary stimulus, and if an interest were once excited, the subject would be still farther pursued, till many others were interested, while the collections, if properly named, would do much to disseminate a higher knowledge of the exhaustless riches of this class of plants.

> " The royal rose—the tulip's glow—
> The jasmine's gold are fair to see;
> But while the graceful grasses grow,
> O, gather them for me!
>
> The pansy's gold and purple wing,
> The snowdrop's smile may light the lea;
> But while the fragrant grasses spring,
> My wreath of them shall be!"

INDEX OF SYSTEMATIC NAMES.

GENERAL INDEX.

ERRATUM.—On p. 102, sixth line from the bottom, for p. 49, Fig. 30, read p. 41, Fig. 30. The same occurs in the last line on the same page.

www.ingramcontent.com/pod-product-compliance
Lightning Source LLC
LaVergne TN
LVHW050515100826
845148LV00002B/342